Dialogues on Opera and the African-American Experience

Edited by
Wallace McClain Cheatham

The Scarecrow Press, Inc.
Lanham, Md., & London
1997

SCARECROW PRESS, INC.

Published in the United States of America
by Scarescrow Press, Inc.
4720 Boston Way
Lanham, Maryland 20706

4 Pleydell Gardens, Folkestone
Kent CT20 2DN, England

We gratefully acknowledge permission to reprint the following chapters: Chapter 4, "Sylvia Olden Lee: Lady Sylvia Speaks," originally appeared as "Lady Sylvia Speaks" in *Black Music Research Journal* (Spring 1996). Reprinted by permission of the author and the Center for Black Music Research, Columbia College, Chicago.
Chapter 7, "George Shirley: A Renowned Divo Speaks," originally appeared as "A Renowned Divo Speaks" in *The Black Perspective in Music,* © 1990 The Black Perspective in Music.

British Cataloguing-in-Publication Information Available

Library of Congress Cataloging-in-Publication Data

Cheatham, Wallace.
Dialogues on opera and the African-American experience / compiled and edited by Wallace McClain Cheatham.
p.   cm.
Includes bibliographical references and index.
1. Opera—United States—Interviews. 2. Afro-American musicians—Interviews. I. Title.
ML1711.9.C5   1997   782.1'089'96073—dc20   96-7914   CIP   MN

ISBN 0-8108-3147-3 (cloth : alk. paper)

♾ ™ The paper used in this publication meets the minimum requirements of American National Standard for Information Sciences—Permanence of Paper for Printed Library Materials, ANSI Z39.48—1984.
Manufactured in the United States of America.

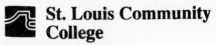

TO POSTERITY

CONTENTS

PREFACE

Enthusiasm for this project grew more intense with the writing of each word, the interactions with each artist, and the ever-increasing awareness of the broad-based genius in the African-American community of classical artists.

The African-American experience as it relates to the classical arts has been left largely untouched by the schools of systematic research. Most African-American classical artists remain unknown to minority and majority populations. When African-American heroes and heroines are identified in the media, there is very often a conspicuous absence of African-Americans identified with opera.

This anthology provides a forum for ten African-American artistic giants—all of whom in some way have been or are involved with opera—to freely articulate their success within a profession that has historically treated members of their race with disdain, hostility, and skepticism.

Each of the artistic giants in this book could be the subject of a major biographical and analytical study. Their statements and revelations call to mind countless ideas for research. The content of these dialogues transcends anything that is purely ethnic, nationalistic, or racial. Their substance speaks to the greatness of the human spirit.

I wish to thank many people who have helped: the artists for their interest in and time given to the project; an anonymous donor for supporting preparation of the manuscript; Dr. Patrick Bellegarde-Smith, professor of African-American studies at the University of Wisconsin-Milwaukee, who supervised my first research in African-American studies and told me that I could make a contribution to historical research and oral history; Dr. Eileen Southern, eminent musicologist and professor emeritus at Harvard University, who, in addition to providing sage counsel for this anthology, published my first study dealing with opera and the African-American experience in *The Black Perspective in Music* and encouraged me to continue researching this area; the Milwaukee music community for helping me to keep a sense of urgency about keeping this work alive; and Mrs. Precious Baldwin, a colleague and friend who, in addition to typing this manuscript, has for several years typed my papers.

I am particularly indebted to Robert McFerrin, the first African-American singer to be trained at the Kathryn Turney Long Opera School, and the first African-American singer to become a regular member of the Metropolitan Opera. Working with Mr. McFerrin as a private voice student some years ago provided the initial catalyst for my wanting to know more about the involvement of African-Americans in opera.

For this collection of dialogues, I am honored to have Camilla

Williams write the foreword — a dramatic essay detailing the events surrounding her historic American operatic debut — and Willis Patterson, the introduction.

As this anthology was nearing completion, death took from our ranks an individual who played a pivotal role in the development and opening of professional doors for two of the personalities with whom the compiler dialogued. Maestro Max Rudolf passed away on March 1, 1995, at age ninety-two. Maestro Rudolf remained an important figure in the lives of both Maestro Everett Lee and Madame Sylvia Olden Lee until his death. Maestro Rudolf, still alive when I talked with both Maestro Lee and Madame Lee, is spoken about very candidly in both of their conversations.

The death of Gilbert Moses, an eminent director in film, television and theater, on April 14, 1995, at age fifty-two, has made me realize more deeply the urgency of doing research into opera and the African-American experience. As a part of this anthology, I wanted to have a conversation with Mr. Moses, who in 1971 staged Verdi's *Rigoletto* at the San Francisco Opera and was a pioneering figure in the founding of many theatrical opportunities for Black Americans. Mr. Moses was interested and very much wanted to become involved, but finally confessed to me that he was too ill to participate. Consequently, what would surely have been a rich document in the literature will be forever beyond our reach.

Undergirding it all is the support of a wonderful family: my wife, Faye, an excellent musician and singer in her own right; and our daughters, Tosca Carme and Kimberly Ann, graduates of Wilberforce University and Carroll College, majoring in clinical psychology and music, respectively.

Camilla Williams. *Courtesy of Camilla Williams.*

FOREWORD

Camilla Williams

Hungarians have played a great part in my life: Marian Szekely Freschl, Eugene Ormandy, Laszlo Halasz. When Ada Cooper of Columbia Artist Management took me to Halasz, head of New York City Opera, to sing, Maestro informed them after hearing me that I had the perfect voice for Puccini's *Madame Butterfly*. World War II was going on and *Butterfly* was banned since its plot concerned an American soldier involved with a Japanese girl. However, Maestro Halasz said when the war was over, the opera would be returned to the repertoire. When the war ended, Maestro Halasz called me in and I was given the role of Cio Cio San. There were many pitfalls to encounter. A formidable concern was my being a Negro. Halasz wanted everything right.

Eugene Bryden was brought in from Hollywood as the stage director and Eddie Sens for makeup. Sens's father, a famous wig maker at the Metropolitan Opera, made my Japanese wig. John White was there to check on my Italian, which I had studied at the University of Pennsylvania.

Costumes were at a minimum. Maestro got the best silk kimono available, as silk was hard to come by. Nora Holt, the only recognized Negro music critic, was invited to my rehearsals. I was always being auditioned.

There was a dear, powerful lady, the head of New York Stadium Concerts, in great control at this time in New York music circles. She was pushing her singer for *Butterfly*.

Just before the premier, I was auditioned on stage. The house was darkened so I could not tell that a very critical audience was assembled. Later, Halasz said I did so well and saved him.

The new *Butterfly* staging by Bryden had Pinkerton carry me over the threshold into the house after the "Love Duet". Halasz was told that if this happened, he would be shot in the back. The tenor resented me as a Negro woman, but during the love duet, when he touched me things happened and all could see his torso. His face turned beet red. A year later he came around and became a fine, compassionate colleague. Maestro always remarked how he changed.

The Great Geraldine Farrar was invited to my debut. Farrar's close friend, Mrs. Gilmour, was the niece of Lady Astor from Danville, Virginia, my hometown. Mrs. Gilmour, Farrar, and the white lady my father worked for, were all dear friends.

Danville, Virginia was in an uproar upon learning that a great singer was coming out of retirement to hear this young unknown singer. *Newsweek* asked her opinion of me: "She is already a great Butterfly." I was voted the Page One Award along with (conductor Serge) Koussevitzky and Sir Laurence Olivier for bringing democracy to opera in America and, for the first time, a Negro received a steady contract with a major opera company.

As I look back on my career and the goodness of God, I am so grateful for all my wonderful blessings. I have sung on all the continents of the world and have met many of the world's great musicians and have also performed with them. This gives me a great deal of experience to give to my students at Indiana University School of Music, where I am honored to be the first black professor of voice.

Willis Patterson. *Courtesy of Willis Patterson.*

INTRODUCTION

Willis Patterson

The subject of opera in America conjures up images of European music with indistinguishable words, large ladies and men singing with pained expressions on their faces, big orchestras conducted by very seriously expressioned white males, expensively clad audiences—all of this taking place within the confines of formidable, seemingly inaccessible, high-ceilinged buildings, totally remote from my real world. These were the visions of opera from the perspective of most African-American youngsters of the 1930–1945 depression days. They were images that remained quite vivid until one significant, unexpected event penetrated and gave us the reason to take a somewhat closer look at this world of opera.

During my early childhood years, certain tunes lingered around the house as a result of the Saturday afternoon broadcasts of the Metropolitan Opera Company. My mother listened to them on the radio, not because she had an understanding of any of the elements listed above, but because she liked the vocal sounds. There were lovely, lilting, catchy melodies, some of which she frequently found herself humming while doing her household chores, in spite of the annoying interruption of words that made no sense and were impossible to pronounce. It was strange how some of those tunes found their way into the sounds she made while scrubbing clothes on the washboard and moving from room to room with dustcloth in hand. Breaking the usual sequence of hymns and spirituals that were so automatic to her sweeping and dusting was an occasional theme from "La donna e mobile" or "Pres des ramparts de Seville". To a non-African-American, sounds like this may have seemed an unusual presence in the Saturday afternoon musical fare of our ghetto home in the 1930s and forties. It would have seemed strange even to some blacks not accustomed to being in our neighborhood, but they were not uncommon occurrences to those of us who lived there.

It was, therefore, not entirely unexpected when in 1955, contralto Marian Anderson finally became the first African-American to be signed to a regular Metropolitan (the Met) Opera Contract. Baritone Robert McFerrin became the first African-American male to receive such a contract, and Mattiwilda Dobbs, the first soprano of the race with that company. To us, the wonder and shame was that it had taken so many years. There had long been, among us, an impressive number of singers who were sufficiently talented and well-enough prepared to perform as effectively as Anderson, McFerrin, Dobbs, and many others on the roster of the Met. Just a few of those who had achieved such prominence were: baritones William Powell, Harry Williams, Fred Thomas, and Paul Robeson; tenors Sidney Woodford, Thomas Bowers, "The Colored Mario", Roland Hayes and Charles Holland; contraltos Marian Anderson and Louise Burge, sopranos Marie Selika "The Queen of Staccato", Rachel Walker "The Creole Nightingale", Abbie Mitchell, Elizabeth Taylor Greenfield, "The Black Swan", and Sisseretta Jones "The Black Patti". Though several had begun to have some impact on the stages of European opera houses, it was not until Marian Anderson and Robert McFerrin made their debuts that African-American singers began to experience some rightfully deserved recognition and opportunity to perform opera in this country. Since then (though the ranks of black male opera singers have remained small), African-American opera singers have witnessed steady increase in prominence and opera performance opportunities in the United States.

The Wallace Cheatham book *Dialogues On Opera* is, therefore, of some considerable relevance, timeliness, and interest. It contains a series of very interesting interviews of African-Americans who are performing (or have performed) opera, not only with the Metropolitan Opera Company, but in most of the important opera houses throughout the western world. The form of these interviews is modeled upon Cheatham's article in the 1990 issue of *The Black Perspective in Music,* volume 18, which is entitled *"A Renowned Divo Speaks: Conversation with George Shirley"*. The professional careers of a select number of singers is examined in this book. The issues covered include: their preparation; the obstacles that had to be overcome before they were allowed to portray opera characters of races different from their own; the quality of association with their colleagues; the quality of treatment from the media in reporting on their artistry; the response of the traditional opera audiences to their efforts; and the impact of their operatic experiences upon their careers and upon the careers of other African-Americans. These are topics of significance to other African-American singers and to the world of opera in general, but particularly to American opera performance. The responses to these questions confirm to the reader that, in spite of the reputation of music being the " international language", and the profession that looks past race, ethnic and social differences, in America, opera performance remains a microcosm of many of the race and class difficulties that continue to plague our society. The historically important presence of African-American singers in the professional world of concert and opera music did not begin with their inclusion in the ranks of opera singers. It was with the careers of such magnificent performers as are listed above, who began to make their presence felt in the professional world as early as the middle and late 1800s, that a recognition of the special uniqueness of the African-American singing voice began to be recognized. But it was left to the musical objectivity of European and Asian music lovers to give honor to this special talent and ability. Though these performers displayed their talents with great regularity in this country before African-American audiences, and were heralded in the Negro press, they were given scant notice and little opportunity to practice their artistry in the great concert and opera halls of this country. The tradition of ignoring these magnificent vocalists (as if in so doing, they and their lush, richly produced sounds might somehow eventually disappear from the face of the earth) basically remained intact until the middle of the twentieth century.

Fortunately, the appetites of late twentieth-century opera impresarios and their audiences for the African-American sound and presence has experienced a gratifying growth. The resistance to the African-American male presence on the American opera stage still remains, though even that taboo is showing signs of weakening, thanks to the effectiveness of Robert McFerrin, George Shirley, Simon Estes, and many other younger performers in the long tradition of African-American vocal prowess. Of course, the international recognition of the extraordinary talents of such current divas as Leontyne Price, Shirley Verrett, Martina Arroyo, Kathleen Battle, and the incomparable Jessye Norman has made their appearances on all the prominent stages of America, and the world, events of major importance. The insights into the private memories, experiences, and travails of these performers as reflected in the pages of Cheatham's *Dialogues on Opera* will provide compelling and important information on the world of professional vocal music for the reader. It will also be highly instructive to the sense of history for the twenty-first-century counterparts of those inhabitants of the African-American communities of the early 1930s. I recommend it highly.

Carmen de Lavallade. *Courtesy of Carmen de Lavallade.*

1

Carmen de Lavallade:
Involvement in Opera from the Perspective
of a Dancer and Choreographer

Born on March 6, 1931 in Los Angeles, California, Carmen De Lavallade has long been recognized as one of the greatest dancers in the world.
Well known and highly respected for her artistry, Miss De Lavallade has
performed in concerts, theater, television, films, and clubs. The recipient
of an honorary degree from Boston Conservatory, Miss De Lavallade is
currently a professor and director of the dance department at Adelphi
University in Garden City, Long Island. In this very candid conversation,
she talks about, not only her participation in opera as a dancer and choreographer, but also her beliefs concerning the perception, role, and treatment of dance, through the years, in the most grandiose of art forms. My
conversation with Miss De Lavallade made me begin to think more
deeply about the very powerful part that dance and choreography could
play in story-line conception, development, and completion—within the
framework of an opera.

Wallace Cheatham: What were the stimuli that motivated your interest
in classical dance?
Carmen De Lavallade: I would have to say that Janet Collins, my first
cousin, influenced my desire for classical dance. I never saw Janet perform until I was in high school, but my family spoke about her all of
the time, of her work with Katherine Dunham, and her duets danced
with Talley Beaty. My family had wonderful photographs of her and
Talley. Janet was this magical being that I wanted to emulate. Well,
of course, no one could ever dance like Janet. She was absolutely
unique in the way that she moved. Never have I seen anyone move so
quickly across the stage. Janet could change directions as quickly as a
dragonfly. She was like a spark on the stage. It is a pity that there were
no videos then to catch her performances. Unfortunately there is very
little film on Janet. What a dance artist she was. She is also a very fine
painter.
WC: What is the sibling bloodline that makes you and Janet Collins first
cousins?
CDL: My father and Janet's mother were brother and sister.
WC: How has the super nigger syndrome been reflected in opportunities
for the black dancer in opera?

1

CDL: I really don't know what that means.

WC: Super nigger refers to a belief that was, once upon a time in the segregated south, firmly, sometimes silently, but surely taught to all blacks, Negroes, or colored people, as we were then calling ourselves. The meaning: you can't be just as good, you must be better, if you want to make it in a white man's world.

CDL: It's very hard to answer that question. I've never heard that term before. I grew up in a multicultural neighborhood. I was competing with blacks, Mexicans, Asians, and whites. That was the makeup of my neighborhood. It was out in Vernon City, East L.A. Yes, I was aware that I wouldn't be able, for example, to be in a movie, except in some bit part or in the background, but I think children at that time always had some hope they would have the possibility of being on stage in film, and radio. But I don't think it would have made any difference if you were better than your white counterparts, you would never have gotten the job. It just wasn't done.

WC: Your response is well taken. Even today, being better than your white counterparts may make no difference in getting the job, for the same reason. It hasn't been, and it's not going to be done—just now. The black classical artist in all areas is being, and is yet to be, fully liberated. Would you speak to what it means to dance in opera—from the initial encounter with the score to the curtain call?

CDL: Well, you have about four weeks rehearsal, you work only with piano and the choreographer. Then, about the last week, you go on stage and have a piano dress. Sometimes dancers can get a little extra time by themselves, but not very much. Then, you have your orchestra rehearsal without costume. Then, orchestra dress, all the way through, no stops and usually with an invited audience. At last, opening night. With hope, by the time you bow, the audience will be pleased with what you did.

WC: Is the development and presentation of a dance or a dance scene in opera pretty much left up to the choreographer, or the choreographer and the dancers? How much influence does the opera's story-line have in all of this? Is there ever any input from the conductor?

CDL: The choreography is usually left up to the choreographer. The director will have his or her say if the choreography is in keeping with the idea of the scene. If not, the choreography is reworked until it's approved. The dancers and the conductor have no input in the production, unless, maybe, you're James Levine at the Met. I've noticed he may sometimes have a say-so on some things, but I am not sure.

WC: You did thirty-six performances in three operas, *Aida, Faust,* and *Samson et Dalila,* with the Metropolitan, performed in both the old house, the current house, and on tour. Which one of these operas did you find the most difficult? Why? The easiest? Why?

CDL: There was no one ballet that was easiest. They all have their level of difficulty. You must have all of your concentration during the performance, making sure the audience understands and feels what you're doing. I must say the adagio section in *Samson and Delilah* was frightening. There was a platform in the middle of the stage; and I had to climb from the stage level onto the platform, up the legs of two men who were standing on the platform to stand on their shoulders, facing the audience; then twist and fall backward into the arms of two other men on the stage level.

WC: Wow! That must have brought quite an ovation from the audience!

CDL: The chorus used to gasp. So you see dancing is not always a safe profession. Each ballet has little difficult things like that in them. So to answer your question: there is no easiest.

WC: What were your experiences like at the Metropolitan with management, singers, and other personnel?

CDL: My experience with the Met Opera has always been enjoyable. In 1955 I was hired by the choreographer, Zachary Solov—who, by the way, with great courage was responsible for hiring my cousin, Janet Collins. Rudolf Bing, the artistic director at the time, was absolutely charming. He was another very courageous person because it was his final word that made the hiring of Janet possible. In 1990, when Arvin Brown, the director of Long Wharf Theater in New Haven, Connecticut, was asked to redirect *Porgy and Bess,* he asked for my services and Mr. Joseph Volpe, currently the artistic director of the Met, rehired me for three other operas: *Lucia di Lammermoor,* directed by Francesca Zambello; *Die Meistersinger and Russalka,* directed by Otto Shenk. I also choreographed a small opera by Carly Simon, called *Romulus Hunt,* for the Metropolitan Opera Guild, directed by Francesca Zambello. The wonderful dancers in *Porgy* were hired outside the opera because the ballet company itself has no black dancers. Practically the whole company of *Porgy and Bess* was hired outside of the Met Opera. I was told the Gershwin estate states that only blacks can perform *Porgy.*

WC: That's true, for full-scale productions in this country.

CDL: The ballet company itself was a pleasure. They are very, very nice people, particularly the ballet mistress Diana Levy. When I was a soloist and did *Samson and Delilah,* and *Faust,* I was treated royally. I never had any complaints; and as a choreographer, it has been nothing but a happy experience. I remember being in *Aida* with Renata Tebaldi. I dressed where all of the lead singers dressed. So I had the privilege of listening to Miss Tebaldi rehearse and warm up before the performance. Even at intermission she kept warming up. She always kept her voice agile. Her mother, a very sweet woman, was always sitting outside her dressing room with a little cup of tea. Blanche Thebom was dressing in the same area. The dressing rooms were on one side of the stage. That was terribly exciting, and they treated me in a very special way. They were wonderful people to be around. Janet, being the incredibly generous person that she is, introduced me to everyone there, and if it had not been for her, I would not have been there. In fact, I would not have come to New York City because my coming to New York City was to join the show *House of Flowers*. Janet was the one who encouraged me to leave Los Angeles and come to New York. One thing led to another, and I ended up at the Metropolitan Opera.

WC: Are you now on the Metropolitan staff?

CDL: I am not on the Metropolitan staff at this time. With my teaching duties, I don't think that I could do a production; but I hope in the future I will be able to choreograph another opera for the company.

WC: Have you been a member of other opera companies and performed in operas other than those done at the Metropolitan?

CDL: Yes. I was at the New York City Center Opera. That's when it was on Fifty-fifth Street in the opera *Carmina Burana,* choreographed by John Butler. I was one of the solo dancers along with Veronica Mlakar; (Mary Hinkson later went in for Veronica); and the gentlemen were Glen Tectly and Scott Douglass. The original singers I believe were John Reardon, Sherrill Milnes, and Margaret Tynes. The other opera at City Center Opera was *Bomarzo,* choreographed by Jack Cole, in which I was principal dancer.

WC: You are also an actress and a singer. How has your training in these art forms impacted your approach to dancing in general, and to dancing in opera in particular?

CDL: I am not a singer per se. I can sing in a cabaret, but I did study voice to help strengthen my speaking and singing. The wonderful part of studying voice is that it helps a dancer's breathing. Dancers have a tendency to shallow breathe: that means they breathe up in the chest. The voice work makes you breathe lower in the back, and allows more oxygen to the body, and therefore more energy. Acting, on the other hand, helps to clarify and bring understanding to what the choreographer would like in his work. My teachers, Lester Horton and Carmelita Maracci, taught very much like directors. They gave meaning to the movements given us. It was not just technique, but the meaning behind your technique that turned dance steps into performing. Then your art became more exciting and vital. Therefore, I found the study of voice and acting to be of great help for dancers. In *Carmina Burana* my solos were sung by the soprano. Knowing her breathing helped me with my phrasing and tempo because dancers cannot follow the conductor. Most singers when they're singing look at the conductor. The volume of their voices, I believe, makes it difficult to hear the orchestra. By breathing with the soprano, I became one with her and the music.

WC: Are there operas in which you would particularly like to dance?

CDL: Even if I were dancing today, there are still no operas in which I would particularly like to dance. Other than *Aida, Samson and Delilah,* and *Faust* there are no operas that really give a soloist an exciting ballet to perform. So as you see, it's a very limited field.

WC: After that, I'm somewhat embarrassed to ask this next question, but it does refer, I think, to ensemble dancing in opera, rather than to soloists. What wing of the repertoire offers the most opportunity for dancers?

CDL: Opera is all about singing. If you're a member of the ballet company, you will hope that the season will bring in operas where you will be needed. Many times if there is no dance in the season, or very little, the dancers will be used as part of the people in the village, things like that, almost like spear carriers. There was a time when soloists were hired from outside the Met, but not anymore. So if there are big ballet scenes with solos, they will be taken by one of the dancers in the company. If you're one of those persons, you hope that it will be your good fortune to be chosen. Opera dance is a very small part of the production. You are light entertainment in the form of festivals, *Aida* with its triumphal marches, and solemn ceremonies of some kind. I think it is much nicer to be a soloist. You're hired to do one big piece in the opera, and then you leave to do other things outside the opera. Otherwise you're waiting for the next time *Aida* comes along, or *Faust,* or whatever. To have a profession and a career as a dancer in opera is very difficult.

WC: It has been said that in opera the African-American singing voice, in terms of timbre and resonance, is in a class unto itself. Are there special qualities that the African-American brings to classical dance?

CDL: Either you come here blessed with the ability or you don't, and it doesn't have anything to do with who you are. For many years I have been around dancers of all races, and no one is really better or more talented than the other. Since I'm not an authority on the voice, I don't know whether that applies to the African-American singers, and quality in voice. I don't know.

WC: To what extent does typecasting exist for the black dancer in opera?

CDL: Mr. Cheatham, you know there are only two operas that I know of where black dancers are always used: *Porgy and Bess* and *Aida.* I think typecasting is built in to begin with. Very few opera companies have a ballet company; so it's rather a dead end. On the other hand, black singers fare much better. The Met has blacks as principal singers and members of the chorus as well. There are no black dancers in the Met ballet. I don't know about other houses like La Scala Opera, etc.; all I know is that at this time the Met does not have black dancers.

WC: Is there a relationship between support from the black community and opportunities for the black classically trained dancer?

CDL: Arthur Mitchell could probably answer this much better than I. Not having had a company, I haven't had to deal with raising money. My understanding is that there is more monetary support from the white community and corporations than from black. I think support is growing because when I go to the theater, I see more people of color. After all, blacks were kept away from classical dancing, or classical anything. It's just now that you're beginning to see more black musicians in orchestras. Years ago, Janet Collins was not allowed to dance with the Ballet Russe unless she made herself lighter which she was not about to do. I think blacks are beginning to feel more comfortable going to the theater and participating in classical dance, classical music, thanks to Arthur Mitchell. He is the one who started, at least, to let people know that blacks could perform, and that they have the bodies for, classical work.

WC: What steps can be taken to make the system work more effectively for the black classically trained dancer?

CDL: I suppose the formation of more companies would help, except that classical companies are now having a hard time because there is a lack of work. Seasons are much shorter than they used to be. It's not like popular dance. Hip-hoppers make better livelihoods than dancers who have spent many, many years training. It has to do with the public. If classical dance were as popular as baseball, hip-hop, or MTV, many companies could be formed. Popularity in dance comes in waves like anything else. In the sixties and seventies it was terribly popular. Then, it dropped down. Until we hit another high, there will be difficulty joining, or even starting companies. So I don't think there is a system per se; what can one say, what can be done? It's very hard to know where you're going if times are not good.

WC: Black dancers have been a part of Metropolitan Opera productions since 1933 when Hemsley Winfield danced in *Emperor Jones;* and then of course, the major breakthrough for dancers came in 1951 when Janet Collins became the first black dance soloist with the Metropolitan. What can be expected for involvement of the black dancer at the Metropolitan and other houses in the world as we approach the year 2000? Also, what other issues concerning classical dance and classical dancers would you care to raise?

CDL: I don't know. I actually don't think very much is going to happen. As I've said before, there's very little in opera for dancers. You must always remember that opera is for singers. The only way we're going to get more dance into opera is for someone to write operas that employ the dance. Until then, dance will be that little part of the opera that is entertainment. But I don't see that the opera will ever change its format. I think opera is what it is. I love the opera. If a dancer loves that kind of atmosphere, being around the wonderful music and the singing, if they want to be in a secure position, why not? As of now, the hiring of black dancers in opera has not had a very good record, and I don't know that it will ever change. It may. The Metropolitan company itself is very small to begin with, and they are doing operas that are European, that were written quite awhile ago; and of course they, the Europeans, wrote about themselves. So in the minds of most people, it doesn't make any sense to their eyes to see blacks dancing in the background. I believe that's where they get that idea. Yet I see that there are blacks in the chorus, aside from your soloists. So maybe the next step will be that black dancers will be a part of the ballet company. It is a wonderful job if that's the kind of job you want to do. I, on the other hand, wanted other things. I wanted to be freer in my activity. I wanted to experience many choreographers and many kinds of dances. Fortunately, I was a guest, so I was not married to the Met or the opera.

WC: Thank you for these very precious moments. More importantly, thank you for your artistry, depth, and insight.

New York City
July 1994

Andrew Frierson. *Courtesy of Andrew Frierson.*

2

Andrew Frierson: A Singer Speaks Out on Racism and Other Issues

Andrew Frierson was unknown to me when I began this project. Upon the suggestion of Dr. Eileen Southern, I asked Mr. Frierson for his participation. The crossing of our professional paths has been, for me, a most rewarding experience. Born on March 29, 1929, in Columbia, Tennessee and reared in Louisville, Kentucky, Andrew Frierson is a graduate of the Juilliard School and the Manhattan School of Music. Coming out of a rich background as singer, studio teacher, college professor, composer, and administrator, Mr. Frierson's responses suggest that he has thought about many things as they relate to opera and the African-American experience with the mind of a musicologist.

Wallace Cheatham: Why has there not been a black male to become a "real" operatic superstar, a parallel to Leontyne Price?

Andrew Frierson: Well, let me give you a quick and simple answer, if I can. There has not been a "real" black male operatic superstar because of racist and sexist attitudes in America. Now, in opera we often find love and romance favorite themes; in eighteenth- and nineteenth-century opera, and in twentieth-century operas also. Audiences, particularly white audiences, may tolerate a black woman being wooed and pursued by a white male, but to have a black male wooing and pursuing a white female is totally unacceptable by the powers that be. Such a scenario wouldn't sell tickets, would not fill opera houses, would cause cancellations of subscriptions, and more than likely, would trigger resignations by opera boards and financial supporters of the opera. The roles for the black male in opera are indeed very, very carefully chosen. He might perform the role of a good spirit, a good guy, without romantic ties; or he may perform the role of an evil spirit, a bad guy, without romantic ties. He might even perform a comic role, which we call buffo in opera, that is a funny guy, without romantic ties. Such restrictions limit the black male opera singer, limit his growth, development, and mobility. I think that in the minds of all too many, the black male is still perceived as a superstud; and to have a superstud, a King Kong, if you will, wooing a white female is out of the question. And then there's another part of the answer to this question. The opera world is dominated by white males. They are in the seats of power and control. Just take a look at the various opera companies throughout the nation. For the most part the general directors are white males. The chairman of the board, indeed the boards of the opera companies themselves: white males. The primo conductor: white males. Those in the position to hire and fire: all white males. Perhaps the situation would be a little different if white females were in power. So then, if any overtures to blacks are made at all, it is to the black female. Perhaps your question would have to be rephrased if it were the opposite; and then you would ask: Why has there not been a black female to become a "real" operatic superstar? But my answer would still be the same: because of racism and sexism.

WC: How has the "super nigger syndrome" been reflected in opportunities for the black male and the black female in opera?

AF: I view the opera world no differently than I view the corporate business world, the sports world, or any other industry in the country. There are, to my way of thinking, three general categories for workers, and we might substitute the word performer in the case of opera: (a) the extremely gifted and well-trained performer or worker; (b) the competent or average worker or performer; (c) the incompetent worker or performer—that is, a worker or performer who is very bad, who may have connections. Black males and females are not afforded the luxury of being simply competent or average, and certainly not incompetent. So that leaves only one category: the extremely gifted, or well trained, or overqualified. As I see it, blacks move up the corporate ladder at just about the same rate as blacks move up the ladder in the world of opera. Now this holds true whether he's performing as a solo artist, the corps de ballet, the chorus, or the orchestra. I assume this interview is concerned with the solo artist. One might, however, take a look at the chorus, the ballet, the orchestra: all a part of the opera. There you will find tokenism. One or two blacks in the chorus, or perhaps none. One or two blacks in the ballet, or perhaps none; and one or two blacks in the orchestra, or perhaps none. In the case of ensembles, one might be just competent, or average, and do a satisfactory job. In the case of blacks in ensembles, in opera, they, too, must perform well above the level of their white counterparts. All the way around, blacks are expected to perform above the level of the job required. Whether in the corporate world or in the world of opera. Whether he or she is performing a leading role or in one of the ensembles.

WC: As a college professor and singer, your thoughts on the operatic instrument: criteria for identification; training; technique; qualities of a good teacher; a good coach; vocal perseverence; role preparation.

AF: Wow! First of all, let me say, this is a loaded question! Books, even volumes, have been written on either and all parts. But I'll try to deal with each part of the question, and I might add, only in part. To successfully perform in opera, one needs a voice of ample power, range, and beauty. The voice is God given. Those of us who have been blessed with such voices can only be grateful. I would like at this point to say that there is a difference in the black voice and the voice, or voices, of white Americans or white Europeans. According to the late Hall Johnson, "Our voices have been developed from centuries of singing and speaking out of doors, as opposed to singing and speaking in doors." I think, as a result of this practice, the black voice is strong, agile, often dark in timbre, most expressive, and abounding in beauty. Gunther Schuller, musicologist, who is not an African-American, writes in his book *The History of Jazz,* Volume I, "African speech, singing, and playing are all marked by an open tone and natural quality." Now, opera is a European art form. So we might say, so far as the African-American opera singer is concerned, Africa meets Europe in America. The results are stunning. For an example, Leontyne Price's *Butterfly* is fabulously different; and I think it is because of her Africanness. Now, so far as the training and preparation for any opera role is concerned, I say prepare and train as thoroughly as possible. Try to be prepared well beyond the task that is to be done. This calls for many lonely hours of study, practice, and research, and translating from foreign languages—Italian, French, German, and so forth—into English. Know your score. Know your score well. On the issue of vocal technique, I have always felt that the African-American singer must be extremely careful. Here again, Africa meeting Europe in vocal study, the wrong teacher could just train out of him or her those qualities that make his singing unique.

WC: The African-American studying voice: how would he or she know when those unique qualities are being trained out of his or her voice?

AF: Unfortunately, many, or I should say, most young African-American students of voice do not know when these unique qualities are being trained out of their voice. Even some adults do not know. Now, the teaching of voice is usually done on a one-to-one basis. Some small classes in voice are offered, say, for example, where singing is a secondary subject or an elective. Whether in an institution or private studio, the study of voice is on an individual basis. So the student, particularly if he or she is young, becomes close to that teacher and puts absolute trust in that teacher. Some singers, young and old, follow their instincts and sense that something is not right. They realize that songs and arias they used to sing quite easily have become difficult. Pitches they use to make handily, be it a high B-flat or low-G, they can no longer make. Their voices change in timbre, and tensions abound. The singer becomes inhibited and frustrated. Now, the sad situation that I have just described could happen to any singer or student of singing, black or white. It is particularly tragic when it happens to

African-American singers whose voices are generally capable of so very much and are fairly well equalized when they begin their study. It is sad to see a singer give up and seek another field because of this. In the case of African-American students studying at institutions where changing a major teacher is discouraged, that student must endure such instruction as described, usually for four years; or, he or she might transfer to another school, which could well be a case of jumping from a frying pan into a skillet.

WC: The uniqueness of the black voice period is a subject that has been explored so little, if at all, in the literature. I would appreciate your speaking to this phenomenon. Also, is there a nationality or ethnic group that comes close to the African-American in vocal uniqueness?

AF: The black American voice is distinctly different from the white American or European voice. You asked in the latter part of your question, "Is there a nationality or ethnic group that comes close to the African-American in vocal uniqueness?" I do not think so. The other ethnic groups also have individual qualities: the Asians; the Hispanics; the Native Americans; and so forth. Qualities different from each other and certainly, the African-American. One might listen on the telephone to a person he or she cannot see and does not know, and yet be able to identify the voice. And I do not mean the speech or the accent, I mean the voice. In such a case, one might say, that was an Oriental woman on the telephone, or that was a Hispanic man, or that was a black man, or that was a white woman, and so forth. Vocal qualities are identifiable. So then, what makes a black voice so outstanding in its identification, and so adapted to singing and the making of music? I agree with the musicologists who believe that all African-American music is based upon speech; indeed all African music is based upon speech. In turn, our very speech is musical. I often think of the early black preachers who in the heat or height of their sermons would lapse into a singsong style of delivery. These men were great storytellers and singers. Yes, I said "and singers!" We might hear this kind of delivery in some of the more humble churches today where this kind of delivery is not looked down upon; where this kind of delivery has not been educated out of the preacher. This kind of delivery is most electrifying to hear, whether you believe in what is being said or not. Those of us, and there are many, who come from this background slip easily into singing and music making for there is music making in our speech. The black voice is capable of so many, many different colors. It can paint pictures so vividly and turn a phrase so colorfully. Now, some white American teachers and singers say this coloring is not good. One should use a straight, pure tone always. That is good, they say. A student of such a teacher will lose what he has naturally. Also, there is the African practice of sliding pitches in which one intentionally does not try to make the pitch accurately and squarely. He or she will slide into the pitch. When this practice is employed, it makes for exciting vocalism. The American white community definitely frowns upon this practice. The pitch must always be exact and true, they say. The student of such a teacher will begin to sing like a mechanical machine. These examples are some of what I mean by having certain qualities trained out of one's voice.

WC: Would you speak more to the Africanness in Leontyne Price's *Butterfly?*

AF: Well, I have already pointed out some of the African practices in singing that Miss Price certainly employed in her singing of Madam Butterfly and other roles as well. As you know, the opera *Butterfly* in three acts is based upon the American short story *Madam Butterfly* by John Luther Long. The music is by Puccini. The opera concerns itself with an American naval lieutenant B. F. Pinkerton, captivated by a beautiful Japanese girl, Butterfly, or Cio-cio-san. Although he will be on duty in Japan for a short while, a self-important marriage agent, Goro, arranges for Pinkerton to marry Butterfly, who is helplessly in love with Pinkerton. They marry. Pinkerton soon leaves. Butterfly has his child and waits and prays for his return. He does return, years later with his American wife, Kate, to adopt the child had by him and Butterfly. Upon learning of all this, Butterfly, at the end, kills herself with a dagger. This story reminds one of so many black women who bore children by white men during slavery. These men had no intention of loving that woman or caring for that woman. So Miss Price not only brings her magnificent voice to the role of Butterfly, but she also brings her history, the history of her people, and the African musical practices of coloring, intonation, and a deep, deep level of understanding to the role of Madam Butterfly.

WC: There are singers whose voices and temperaments are best suited for opera, not recital or concert. The opposite is also true: singers whose voices are best suited for recital or concert, not opera; or singers whose voices and temperaments are best suited for just one of these genre. How does a singer find his identity?

AF: My advice to all singers is to forget about temperament. Somehow temperament suggests to many people a certain ranting and raving, or histrionics. A good singer should be able to cope with both opera and recitals, and concerts. I believe a singer might, however, show a preference based upon the capability of his or her voice and personality. No singer is able to sing every song or role that has been written for his or her voice category. Instead of the word temperament, I would like to substitute the phrase diligent study and preparation.

WC: In our time, it borders on being impossible for a singer to have a major career without an identity with opera. Would you speak to this phenomenon?

AF: Yes, it seems that opera is the most popular today of all classical vocal music. I use the word classical for lack of a better known term. You must realize that opera is theater, and all the elements of theater are enjoyed in opera. Singing, acting, costumes, dancing, orchestra and lights, you name it. So then, it is no wonder that a singer today must establish himself or herself in the field of opera or Broadway shows, which I view as American opera, or America's version of opera. Recitals and concerts are no longer as popular as they used to be, as they were say twenty-five, thirty years ago. In fact, only opera stars are able to present recitals and concerts these days. The reason for this, I believe, is due to the national and global economy. The cost for presenting a recital or concert is astronomical. The producers want to make sure the tickets will be sold and a profit gained. Many, I might even say most, opera singers, still find it necessary to go to Europe for a while to establish themselves in opera, and there's a reason for this. And the reason is: there are many more houses and greater opportunities in Europe. Many European houses are supported by the state, and it is a little easier to gain experience in them, although Europe seems to be catering to its own singers these days. American singers are not quite as welcome as they used to be. This, of course, is very bad news, especially for the African-American singer. Once established in Europe, however, reentry into the United States is made a little easier. So with the concert, recital field dead, or dying, only opera is left.

WC: This business of American singers not being as welcome in Europe as they once were: Is it because of a change in the political environment; a change in available talent within their own ranks; or a combination of the two?

AF: A nationalistic spirit has always existed throughout countries of Western Europe. Many of these countries lost so many people during World War II, especially in England, France, and Germany. Many of their great singers and singing teachers and other musicians as well were lost or misplaced. Others took refuge in this country. There was a great shortage of professional musicians in Europe after World War II. So American singers were quite welcome to fill those vacancies. Now that Europe has rebuilt to a great extent, Europeans have reared a crop of singers of their own. So there is not so great a need for outsiders.

WC: I know there has been some crossover: opera singers doing leads in Broadway musicals. Do you see more of this happening?

AF: It is very difficult for me to answer this question at this point in time. As I see it, the national economy will determine whether we see more crossover, as you say, of opera singers to Broadway musicals. If the economy continues to improve and fully recover, I don't think we will see much crossover; however, if the economy slips further back, we may well see more of this. Americans are completely hung up on the star system. So when an opera star does a Broadway musical, management knows that he or she will attract not one, but two different audiences: the opera goer and the Broadway musical goer. This could be very good for a slow business.

WC: Is there a character in a Broadway musical that is as difficult as any character in opera; and if I might take this a step further, is there a Broadway musical as difficult as any opera?

AF: The older product, the opera, was made in Europe and, of course, concerns itself with life in Europe. While usually opera makes greater demands upon the voice, I do not see it as being more difficult. The difficulty lies mainly, for Americans, in dealing with the languages. Each country in Europe will want to hear the opera, understandably, in its language. If an American singer is invited to sing, say, Amonasro in *Aida* in Italy, he is expected to sing that role in Italian. If the same singer is invited to sing the same role in Germany he is expected to sing that role in German. This makes it difficult for the American singer. The other product, the Broadway musical, is a newer product and was made in America. It is American. Always performed in English. Always concerning itself with aspects of life in America, including American racism. Therefore, we have a black show, or we have a white show. If a European singer came to America to do a Broadway show in English, he or she would find the same difficulty. The language would be the most difficult part for him. All theater, opera and American musicals alike, is very hard work, but so rewarding for those of us who love it. Performers rarely think in terms of the difficulty of a work, or the difficulty of a character in that work. If the performer finds a scene, or an act, or an opera difficult in any way, he enjoys the challenge as much as an athlete. I do not see opera being more difficult than a musical. One might relax a bit more in the American musical role because he is thoroughly familiar with the language and the lifestyle of America.

WC: Is there a "Broadway character" that you would particularly like to do?

AF: I can think of no character from Broadway musicals that I would like to play at this time. I would like very much to do a role that was written for me, however. A role written especially with me in mind. I would like that very much.

WC: What are the preparational steps that one must take to become an effective college professor, and what were the stimuli that triggered your interest in performance and college teaching?

AF: I'll begin by saying first and foremost: a proper education is absolutely necessary to become an effective college professor. All advanced degrees and study are not only important to one as professor, but to the accredited institution at which he or she will serve. Most institutions are rated in part by the academic achievements of its faculty. And next in importance, I would say, would be the life experiences in the particular discipline of one's interest. In my case, music or singing. Often, universities, colleges, and conservatories will give an outstanding candidate for a position extra credit for his life experiences. Some institutions have hired professors who do not have advanced degrees simply because they have accomplished spectacular work in their field of concentration. Most African-American professors are almost always required to be accomplished both in academic achievement as well as professional life experiences. In my case, knowing this, I made sure that I had paid my dues. Even before I applied for a position, I came to my professorship with several years of performance experience in opera and in recitals, served as director of a community music school in New York (the Henry Street Settlement Music School in New York), and had composed several works, some of which are published. I felt more than qualified. Now, as to the stimuli that triggered my interest in performance, I can only say that was always there. I knew that I had the gift of music, singing. And with a gift of any kind comes the urge, the need to use it. The gift could be singing, building ships, spanning bridges, painting, drawing, dancing, whatever. And I think people with gifts come to a feeling in their consciousness that they were divinely authorized, divinely authorized to fulfill its work. I was always comfortable on the stage, as though I belonged there. I enjoy performances, and I enjoy passing on to others what I have learned. For, as they say, to teach is but to learn again.

WC: How has the role of the college professor in music, particularly the African-American college professor in music, changed through the years?

AF: Frankly, I don't think the role of the African-American college professor has changed that much. I have found little difference in teaching at an all-black college (I taught at Southern University in Baton Rouge, Louisiana); and a predominately all-white college (I taught at Oberlin Conservatory of Music in Oberlin, Ohio). In both instances, I found that aside from teaching subject matter, I nurtured, scolded, praised, criticized, and served as mentor and role model. I'm really a little bit ashamed to say this, but say I must. At the all-black college, many of the students were lacking in academic background. Some had graduated from rural schools, rural high schools, which permitted them to graduate after the eleventh grade. We were successful in remedial work with those students. I found the students motivated, and many moved on to more celebrated colleges and universities. In the predominantly white college, I found the black students quite keen academically and talent wise. But I found them a bit confused, lacking in direction, and with a false sense of pride. Since most of the teaching in a conservatory is on a one-to-one basis, I found myself also acting and serving as surrogate parent. The black college professor is indeed in the minority, a token, in the white college. He, or she, remains outside the mainstream. In other words, they are a guest. Most African-American professors are not on a tenured track in the white — predominantly white — institutions. At the African-American college, the black college, I found that most of the professors there, also black, were welcomed and appreciated. So many African-American professors and professional performers alike are in denial so far as racism in America is concerned. I have often heard many, especially black, divas say, "I have never experienced racism in America." Now, how can that be?

WC: Are black male professors and black male professional performers more likely than black female professional performers to admit the existence of racism in America?

AF: No, I don't think so. There are some black male and female professional performers and professors who admit to the existence of racism; then there are some black males and females who are in denial about racism, or they admit it to one another only behind closed doors. I mentioned earlier the denial of some black divas only because of their high visibility. We have already established that there are no black male opera superstars in America.

WC: Your observations about personality traits of black students in black colleges and black students in predominantly white colleges — are there any reasons for these very sharp differences?

AF: Yes, I think there are. In a black college, a black student once admitted feels free, wanted, and accepted. If he or she, say, does not make the college choir, it is only because he or she does not sing well enough or has no interest in it, not because we have never had a black in the college choir here. Furthermore, he or she may choose any sorority or fraternity on that campus, and may develop lifelong friendships. Not so on a predominantly white campus. You see, at a predominantly white college, when a young black student is eighteen years of age and has met all of the requirements for admission to that college and has been told that he or she has been accepted with all the rights and privileges of that college as a fully matriculating student, he or she arrives to find cool attitudes toward him, resentment. The young student becomes confused at this double message. He feels powerless. It is like inviting a guest into your home, and when the guest arrives, your attitude is one of hostility. The guest becomes confused. But back to the student. He is caught between a rock and a hard place. He has no place to turn. If he goes to the black college professor for comfort and direction, who I might add, is in the same position as the student, the professor might even be afraid to direct the student, lest he get out of the good graces of the administration. The student is lacking in direction with no place to turn. So the student decides, "Since I'm treated indifferently here, I will see how different I can be." He has seen his A paper graded as B, and his B paper graded as C. He may decide, to his detriment, not to attend classes regularly. He will begin to spout black pride rhetoric. The rhetoric is merely to show resentment for his predicament. It is not true pride, but a false sense of pride. The young student becomes confused, lacking in direction, with a false sense of pride. He may eventually drop out of school. What a tragedy. What an American tragedy. I see academia as a macrocosm of the American government.

WC: Did you teach voice at Southern and Oberlin?

AF: Yes. I taught voice at both schools. At Southern, I taught private voice to voice majors, and in addition, I taught a small voice class to music education majors. I also directed the university choir. At Oberlin, I taught only voice, and I directed the Oberlin black ensemble, which specialized in works by African-American composers.

WC: From the perspective of a college professor and singer, what operatic role would you identify as being the most complex. Why? The least complex. Why?

AF: Oh, there are so many roles for my voice category. I am a baritone; and of course I have not performed them all. As for the most difficult and complex, I would certainly list Porgy in Gershwin's *Porgy and Bess*. This role is sung usually on the knees, since Porgy has no use of his legs and feet. The very position causes great discomfort in the lower back and in the knees. Not only is one in this position for two or three hours, he must produce some powerful singing, covering all human emotions. When I first performed the role of Porgy, I was told that if I didn't have trouble with my legs and knees, I would eventually. That certainly turned out to be the case. So far as a simple, less complex role: I would name Don Alfonso in Mozart's *Cosi fan tutte*. A one-dimensional, delightful role with no complexities for the performer. The music is straightforward, charming, beautiful, and there are no extra demands made upon him physically in any way.

WC: Is there a role that you would particularly like to do?

AF: At this point in my life, I can't say there is a role that I would particularly like to do. When I was younger, there were many of course.

WC: Is there a concert work and song that you would say is as difficult as the role of Porgy?

AF: Yes, there are, but works are difficult in different ways. Now, let me give you a few examples. Porgy is difficult physically, while it is vocally satisfying. The singing position makes it difficult. I always find

Beethoven's Ninth Symphony difficult because it is vocally awkward. We know Beethoven primarily as a composer of instrumental music: symphonies, piano music, chamber music, and so forth. His vocal music, including his opera *Fidelio,* has this problem. The melodies seem to be written for an instrument, rather than the human voice. Also, the African-American composer, Wendall Logan, wrote a song cycle, *Ice and Fire,* especially for me and my wife. Two songs from this cycle are published in the *Anthology of Art Songs by Black American Composers.* This short cycle is difficult musically and interpretively, although vocally rewarding. So we have vocal works that are difficult physically, vocal works that are difficult vocally, vocal works that are difficult musically and interpretively. I know of no piece that is difficult in every way.

WC: Is there a concert work and song that you would say is as easily approachable as the role of Don Alfonso?

AF: Oh, yes, indeed. There are so many of these works, that is, easy works, that I would not dare attempt to mention even the ones that I know, to say the least of the ones I do not know. Such beautiful, simple pieces are usually crowd pleasers, and, moreover, they have the greatest power to touch the human heart, the human soul. Such pieces move the human spirit easier to tears, rather than the complex and more difficult pieces. Nearly all of the early Italian songs, so beautiful and simple, have this power. I think also of John Work's arrangement of the spiritual, "This Little Light O'Mine," simple and elegant; and I am especially fond of the vocal works of the composer Stefano Vanaldo, whose songs are unpretentious and extremely well written for the voice. His "O del mio amato ben" will always be one of my favorites. We must remember that beauty lives in simplicity. Who can deny the effectiveness, the simple beauty and dramatic descriptiveness of *The Seven Last Words of Christ* by Dubois? This piece is simple; but who can look down his nose at it?

WC: Is there a relationship between support from the black community and opportunities for the black "classical" artist?

AF: I do not believe, as many people do, that the African-American artist is not afforded more opportunities because of the African-American community's lack of support for the arts. I think that more African-Americans would, for example, patronize opera if there were more works about their culture, if they were able to see more people on stage who looked like themselves, more people who looked like them in leading roles, in the chorus, in the corps de ballet, and in the orchestra pit. This, I believe, is the main reason more African-Americans do not support this European art form. Now, I know that some say this noticeable absence is due to the lack of exposure. I say that African-Americans would read and study libretti like everyone else, and would

eventually come to understand the works like everyone else. Unfortunately, there is still an elitism attached to opera and other classical music forms. When you stop to think about it, the relationship between
the support from the black community and the opportunities for the
black artist is just about even: that is, few opportunities for the black
artist, and few from the black community support classical productions. As work for the black artist and works about blacks are increased, support from the black community will increase; and this has
been proved many times.

WC: What steps can be taken to make the system work more effectively
for the black singer and black college professor?

AF: We African-American singers and professors struggle within a system that was not designed for us. It was not designed with us in mind.
Every single accomplishment is an uphill battle. This cross we bear,
this burden we share, makes life more difficult than it should be. Perhaps we might stop worrying about a system that grudgingly tolerates
us and start to think about what we can do to establish our own companies, what we can do to strengthen our own schools and colleges
where we would be in the seat of power and not always in the position
of head bowed and body bent and hands stretched forth asking for
help. So I say we blacks must change our consciousness. Rid ourselves
of our dependency complex and start thinking about what we can do
for ourselves. Then, and only then, will we have a system that works
for us.

WC: Many operas have been written by black composers. Yet, to my
knowledge there isn't a single opera of a black composer in the active
repertoire. Why? Is it just racism?

AF: Well, I sort of feel that I have already answered this question. But
let me say there are some opera works by black composers, not many,
as you point out.

WC: Perhaps I should qualify my use of the statement, "Many operas
have been written by black composers." I'm thinking of the somewhat
extensive involvement of black composers with composing operas
from the time of Saint Georges—in spite of this genre being a European art form with limited performance opportunity—and our coming
out of, historically, an oral, not a written tradition of composition.

AF: It is extremely difficult for anyone, black or white, to get a new work
mounted unless he or she has been especially commissioned. Cost being a major factor, and the unwillingness on the part of impresarios to
take a chance on a new work—they seem to prefer the tried and the
tested. That is why we see listed year after year the same operas: *La
Boheme, Carmen, Figaro, Faust, La Traviata, Aida,* and so forth. I notice that even along Broadway, America's answer to opera, we are
now witnessing revivals of old shows. Word just came to my ears that

they are now reviving the show *Showboat,* which expects to reappear sometime in 1994. On occasion, certain individuals or private enterprises have commissioned and/or underwritten new works. Need I mention the last to be considered for such an opportunity? If a black composer writes a work about black life or culture using the Afro-American idiom, his chances are quite slim for his work to be done. If a black composer writes a work using the European tradition, his chances of having his work produced are also quite slim, but he might, just might possibly have a slight edge. That's the story.

WC: What can be expected for involvement of the black college professor in music as we near the twenty-first century?

AF: Without sounding flippant, I think we can expect more of the same practices in the twenty-first century as we experienced in the twentieth century, unless there are some dramatic changes in the system itself and in the hearts and minds of all Americans, black and white.

WC: What can be expected for the involvement of blacks—singers, conductors, stage directors, designers—at leading opera houses around the world as we near the twenty-first century?

AF: Here again these token men and women will strive solely to maintain their positions as long as they possibly can. This will be their primary concern during the twenty-first century. A performer, it is said, is no better than his last performance. This is especially true for the black performer. The position of black singers, conductors, etc., is a very insecure one. The black performer in Europe and around the world today is almost in the same fragile position that he is in the United States. He or she may be replaced at any time since he or she is usually a guest at these houses. Most singers, conductors, directors, and so forth, are invited by leading opera houses to perform, say, an Aida, or a Carmen. They perform and they leave as any guest would. Most of these performers are not on the regular roster at such houses. Few, if any, black performers are a regular part of the company.

WC: I have asked a lot, and you have certainly said a lot. Is there a concern or are there concerns about opera and the black experience that you would particularly like to address?

AF: Yes, there are a number of things I would like to say, but I will try to be as brief as possible. But first allow me to apologize if I have appeared to be pessimistic, jaded, or negative in my response to your questions. The truth is that I consider myself an extremely positive person. That is why I believe I have survived in a most difficult profession, or professions. The problems that we face, that is, we African-Americans, are real. We must not deny these problems. We must look them squarely in the eye, decide what action is to be taken, and roll up our sleeves and go to work, moving as swiftly as possible. I always say that if you don't know what the problem is, you surely will not know how to deal with it. And we must be extremely careful in the teaching of our young. Yes, we should make them aware of what they will face, and at the same time, in the words of Reverend Jesse Jackson, "Keep hope alive. Now, this is very difficult to accomplish. It's all so easy to discourage, kill dreams, and hopes. So, while pointing out negatives on one hand, it is very important to point out solutions on the other, and point out those who have overcome and solved problems. Young people, and old people alike, need hopes and dreams. This is the glue that holds individuals together. This is the stuff that propels us forward and upward. Unfortunately, we do not have a minister of culture in this country as they have in many western European countries. Since America is a country of many races and cultures, I personally think it would be a good idea to have such a minister, who could fairly assist with the cultural needs of each group. We do not have such an office. The arts are left on their own more or less. The black classical artist, representing in the United States a subculture, or the underclass, is indeed alone. African-Americans have had other cultures forced upon them while they have systematically been taught that their own culture is worthless; and therefore, they are worthless, or we are worthless. African-Americans remain for the most part excluded. It is for this reason that I believe that the answer to this unique situation in which we find ourselves lies in the formation of our very own companies. The task is monumental, but I believe this is the quickest way to open more doors for more of us. There is a national organization of African-Americans in this country—I will not mention the organization by name—but it has chapters in most American cities across the nation. This organization meets yearly for a national convention; and it has been successful in awarding some scholarships to a few black, young music students. Also, it honors each year some outstanding African-American performers. This is all very well and good, and I think this work should continue. But such an organization should have as its main thrust that of creating performance opportunities for black Americans. It should consider creating its very own company. And the reason being, we have so many excellent, excellent, black performing artists. I'm referring in this case to singers. Beautiful talents, well-trained talents, and nowhere to go with it. We have in New York Opera Ebony an all-black company that has produced many opera performances; and these productions have all been on a very high level. Every large city or state, or at least areas like the northeast, the northwest, southeast, southwest, might consider such a move. Would it be a lot of work? You bet! Yes, indeed, it would be a tremendous amount of work. But it is better than waiting and waiting and waiting and waiting. Such a young company might have to begin on a small scale. Perhaps without costumes, orchestra, and so forth.

But begin nevertheless. If standards are high, the lack of certain things would not matter that much. It wouldn't make that much difference. When opera is performed on a full scale, as I pointed out before, it is very, very costly. Such a company with African-Americans in control would not have to limit its presentation to European opera. Programming, like performers, would be at their discretion. We must begin to think in terms of self help instead of "please help" to gain entry, to gain independence, to gain mobility in the marketplace of music. Africa could indeed meet Europe—in fact, the world—in America with much more grace, ease, and, above all, pride if this were so.

New York, New York
1994

Everett Lee. *Courtesy of Everett Lee.*

3

Everett Lee:
Counsel from the Podium

The career of Everett Lee stands as a brilliant example of talent in triumph over racism. Born in 1916 in Wheeling, West Virginia, Maestro Lee grew up in Cleveland, Ohio, where in 1941 he graduated from the Cleveland Institute of Music.

The Maestro, an accomplished violinist, was a student of the renowned Joseph Fuchs. Early on, he performed as a soloist, chamber musician, and first violinist of the CBS orchestra. The success of his performance as a substitute conductor became a career turning point.

While continuing to study, Maestro Lee organized the Cosmopolitan Little Symphony, conducted on Broadway, and was active as a guest conductor. Since settling in Europe in 1956, Maestro Lee has been music director of the Munchener Opernbuhne, Chief of the Norrköpking (Sweden) Symphony Orchestra, Conductor for the Symphony of The New World, Titular for the Bogota (Columbia) Philharmonic, and Conductor for Opera North in Philadelphia. Additionally, Maestro Lee has been guest conductor for many of the leading orchestras in the world.

An artist of uncompromising standards, Maestro Lee is conductor of the Nordic Youth Orchestra in Sweden and Opera Ebony based in New York. Maestro Lee is without doubt the dean of living African-American conductors.

Wallace Cheatham: Why has there not been a black male to become a "real" operatic superstar: a parallel to Leontyne Price?

Everett Lee: This question has been asked many times over, and seemingly the only patent and/or usual answer is that it is the tenor who usually wins the soprano's heart; or the mezzo-soprano, as the case may be; or there is some sort of a romantic situation with them. It seems that baritones and basses somehow fare better. I really cannot give an otherwise good account as to why males have not reached superstar status. Among the ladies there are quite a few in the upper bracket: coloraturas, sopranos, mezzo-sopranos. But as we know, the choice of voice in all categories is a highly personal opinion. And as far as I know, there are but few males who are permanent members of major American theaters. There are some over here in Europe, in Germany especially, who are permanent members. Vinson Cole, the tenor, George Shirley, the tenor, and Simon Estes, bass baritone, are three, right off the top of my head, who have made or are making big careers and enjoying big-star status. Robert McFerrin, too, was a star to be reckoned with in his days at the Met. The late Lawrence Winters,—Whisonant, was his real name, he used Winters professionally—was far better known over here in Europe than he was in the States, but a huge star he surely was. Larry was a member of the Hamburg State Opera, as you may know.

WC: How has the "super nigger syndrome" been reflected in opportunities for the black conductor?

EL: I have to say, don't laugh at me, but I am not aware, or have not been aware, of the "super nigger syndrome," as you put it. But perhaps there is that thought in back of some people as to judging and/or the engaging of a conductor of color. That epitaph has not been leveled at me; perhaps because more than half of my life I've lived in Italy, Germany, South America, and here in Sweden. It has been said of me that my approach to music is European. My answer: That is quite possible as I was trained for the concert hall and the theater by Europeans, and it is mostly in Europe that the greater part of my career has taken place. Something would be wrong with me if the things that I have learned, lived among and with had not rubbed off. I am still, though, as American as barbecue and apple pie. Each time that I am at home in the States, I'm always asked, "Oh, when are you coming back home?" "Oh, when are you coming home to make music?" Yes, I will be back there yesterday, when I have a fine engagement to come home to. I am not at all bitter. Dean Dixon was bitter, I'm sorry to say. I was at a big party a few years ago after a concert in New York. Many people were there talking to me, and among those was Jimmy [James] Baldwin. I said, yes, I would be coming back to America to take over an orchestra. Jimmy said, "Everett, if you want to keep your sanity, stay in Europe." Well, as I said, I'm not bitter, not at all. I have enjoyed some fine successes in my own country; however, it is still blooming here. So whenever something pops up and I'm invited home, I will be there.

WC: How have you avoided becoming bitter?

EL: Perhaps there are several reasons why I'm not bitter, though I have been terribly disappointed and very disenchanted a few times. After a so-called upset or setback, I've just gritted my teeth and pushed on. Studied all the more and cast off the negative picture or pictures projected at me. I do not think that there is any gain in being bitter, as that triggers negative signals, shows sorrow, pain, even enmity; and none of this works in a positive or productive way; we must be positive in recreating and expressing music. Competition is keen, to say the least, and it takes courage and inner strength, not only to attain, maintain, and sustain a high standard, but to outlive and overcome whatever hindrances one may be confronted with or may be put in one's way. The fellow music students I grew up with worked very hard—all of us aimed at being another (violinist Jascha) Heifetz or (Conductor Arturo) Toscanini or whatever. You know, many of these same fellows are principal players in major orchestras and/or prominent chamber music players. Some have even become quite successful as soloists; and I, being right along with these fellows, worked hard just as they did. We inspired one another, helped one another, and worked to be established in our respective careers. So, as I said, I made my pitch just as they did. One of my close friends now, and member of a famous string quartet, told me, "Well, Everett, you have to be at least as good as we or even better to make it and get ahead." This was said to me after I was denied even an audition with two major American orchestras. I then made up my mind that if I can't join you, then I will lead you. I did make good on that promise to myself. Those two orchestras that denied me even an audition, I have conducted. I just had to. I just had to show them that I was there. Besides, it is my religious outlook that rejects my accepting anything that surfaces as race, color, or nationality. This outlook supports me, to close my thought firmly against the false human beliefs of race, color, or nationality.

WC: Did Dean Dixon do anything in opera?

EL: If I remember correctly, he did *Fidelio* in Bonn, Germany. Dean may have done other opera performances, but that I cannot answer accurately. I know that he did many symphony concerts. Symphony concerts were Dean's main activity. But opera, I'm not so sure. [I have not been able to document whether or not Maestro Dixon (1915–1976) conducted *Fidelio* in Bonn. There is an indication in the literature that he had an association with The Frankfurt Opera. I have not, however, been able to unearth the level of this association. Yet it is not difficult to unequivocally believe that Mr. Dixon, the first African-American conductor to achieve international stature, had opportunities to work in the lyric theatre. Also, a reality that cannot be overlooked is that if Maestro Dixon conducted any operas, it was not done in the major houses. Accordingly, those performances received little or no real attention in the press.]

WC: You are an important conductor with many historical firsts. Would you speak to the art form of conducting?

EL: This is a big one. I could expound for hours in answering this question. Yet, to be as coherent as possible, a modern conductor must be highly trained with all that that means. He must know theory, counterpoint, solfeggio, compositions, etc., etc., and have the ability to play at least one instrument well. Preferably an orchestral instrument, such as one of the strings, a wind instrument, and something of the percussion. It is not expected that a conductor be a virtuoso in any one, or all; but he or she should have a good working knowledge, though, of everything in the orchestra. And very important, a conductor should be able to play the piano, at least decently, especially if he is to do opera. There are, and have been, notable conductors who do not, or did not, play the piano, and they have made good careers. We modern conductors are in an awesome position. Just think of the music we have inherited. And just for the sake of argument: from way back to the Renaissance, the Baroque; the Romantic; the Impressionistic; the atonal; polytonal; neoclassic; twelve tonal; all the rest. Well, that is formidable. Then comes the opera literature, which is in itself staggering. And a good opera conductor should know something about the human voice. It is amusing to add that very few of us who do opera have decent singing voices. Usually we sound pretty horrible. Right off the top of my head, I can think of only three or four conductors I know who do opera, that have rather decent singing voices. We're not many. I remember once doing an opera and one of my singers came down from the stage and came around to the pit where I was standing conducting. She said, "Please, darling, don't sing with us." It is obvious that the modern conductor cannot embrace completely all of the apexes that I have just mentioned. Nor is it likely for him to have in his repertoire everything for the opera. I must say, however, it is admirable just how many opera conductors here in Europe do have such an enormous repertoire, those who are working continually in the theater. I have done a great deal of opera—in Germany when I was there, I was with a traveling opera company and we performed throughout Germany, in France, in Sweden, in South America. But in the States, it's been a little bit less. My repertoire, however, has circled around the fifty some-odd operas that I have conducted, for the most part, in the Italian repertoire. That is the most popular, of course. And I have even had the opportunity or the challenge of having to do some of these operas in four different languages. You can see how that would make me know them pretty well. In Germany, for the most part, all operas are done in German. And in Italy, you know everything is done in Italian; and when they do want to have something from the German repertoire, they import a German cast and conductor. And here in Sweden, just about everything is done in Swedish. So I have been obliged in German theaters to do in German; in Swedish theaters in Swedish; in France, in French.

WC: What about technique?

EL: Yes. A conductor can learn a great deal about how to conduct an orchestra in opera or oratorio from an experienced conductor. This can be learned by private instruction, in class, and in close observation of an experienced, excellent, conductor. But I think and this is the most important, it is the actual doing, in front of an ensemble, that is the best teacher. What is and can be learned privately, or in class, just may not work for the conductor. He must learn and be able to adjust, or readjust, right on the spot, within a split second, whatever the case may be. If I may, a personal note, if you wish to have it.

WC: Absolutely.

EL: I am a product of the magnificent Max Rudolf from whom I learned a great deal of the so-called classic orchestral repertoire, also the opera literature. I also learned from him how to lead these ensembles, and these techniques that I learned from him are still with me today. Through my experience in conducting both opera and symphony, certain of my gestures and expressions have changed a great deal, and for two laughable, or amusing, or even unfortunate happenings. Let me back up a bit to say that I was once advised that the more excited the music gets, the calmer I should become. When I was told that, I thought my maestro crazy indeed. I thought, "What about all those thrilling moments in Tchaikovsky, Wagner, Rachmaninoff, Verdi, and Puccini?" It was in that gorgeous love duet at the end of the first act of Puccini's *Butterfly* that I forgot all about staying calm and not getting excited. I should have stayed calm, and not gotten excited but I should have made everyone else get...! You know, Richard Strauss said that we conductors should not sweat, but make them sweat. He meant making the audience sweat. Well, anyway, I came down on that resolving chord with such force in my right arm that I pulled sinews that took several years to heal. I had to teach myself how to bring about big climaxes without any injury. And now I'm even more effective in bringing about these climaxes without injury to myself. The other thing that happened to me was in South America as I was conducting Chabrier's *España*. When the full orchestra came in with great exaltation, I stupidly enough threw an enormous cue with my left arm, which again stretched my shoulder, the sinews in my shoulder, and that took a bit of time to heal, too. So I've learned to give cues at exciting moments, but now with less force and with hope, with more effectiveness. Less is more, even though my basic baton technique is still there more or less; there is quite another style in my conducting. And again, this I learned during rehearsals and in performances, all of which demand immediate changes and/or corrections.

WC: There are singers whose voices and personalities are best suited for opera, not recital or concert. The opposite is also true: singers whose voices and personalities are best suited for recital or concert, not opera; or singers whose voices and personalities are best suited for just one of these genre. There are singers who comfortably interact with all of these genre. How does this work from the vantage point of the podium? What makes a conductor more palatable for the concert hall, the opera house?

EL: Your question is a difficult one to give a definitive answer. What makes a conductor more suited for concerts or opera perhaps has to do more with personal preference, or taste, and/or personality, or from his or her natural bent. The majority of conductors, there are a few exceptions of course, all have come out of opera houses. Even there, in the theater, conductors do a great amount of concert work. And so, of course, for them it is more or less natural to grow up with both repertoires. This is not to say that these conductors do all or both equally well. No, not at all. As with singers in opera, a conductor may do a Verdi very well, but a lousy Puccini; or in turn a good Wagner, or a bad Strauss; or vice versa. Conductors are often, and should be, cast in opera just as carefully as are the singers. A very fine critic once said to me, he didn't think that I would make a good *Rosenkavalier* conductor, but he thought I would make a fine *Arabella* conductor. So you see, there we have it. Judging a conductor's merits are just as unpredictable, unstable, and undependable as just about anything else. Again, in my own case, one reviewer wrote that I was not a Verdi conductor. Another critic wrote that Lee is a Verdi specialist. A so-called colleague friend of mine, who incidentally had never been to one of my concerts but surely he had heard some of my recordings, told an orchestra manager that Lee is no Mahler conductor. Yet, when I did conduct said Mahler, with said orchestra manager, the concert and the notices turned out to be one of the best I ever did. The reviews were wonderful and I felt good about the performance. So there.

WC: In our time, it borders on being impossible for a singer to have a "real" career without an identity with opera. Is this also true for the conductor?

EL: No. There are many conductors today making good careers and not doing opera.

WC: What are the preparational steps that you take to conduct an opera?

EL: I think what I've said about conducting as an art form and conductors and repertoire just about covers what you now ask. However, to go on, to prepare an opera well, the conductor ought to know everything about the history of whichever opera he's doing, the libretto, the time of the work, the composer's state of mind at the time he was writing, the composer's own thoughts of the work that he was writing and of each character, the roles that he has written. A good example of what I'm saying would be for the conductor to look into the writings of Verdi. Then besides that, the conductor should have a thorough knowledge of the orchestra score, which may be quite complicated indeed, and he must know each of the roles to be interpreted, why and how, and this should be taken up in consultation or walk-throughs with the singers before the rehearsals and with the chorus master and rehearsals with the chorus, as well as rehearsals or a rehearsal with the ballet, if such is in that opera. It is not necessary for a conductor to know another language, other than his or her mother tongue; however, it does facilitate overcoming many problems and questions that can and do pop up during conferences, rehearsals, and private discussions. The legendary Toscanini spoke a minimum of English and a minimum of German, and most of his rehearsals, or all of them, were done in Italian. But he must have known a lot more than he let on. Because of his terrible nearsightedness, he had to learn everything from memory. And so during rehearsals at Bayreuth, he knew the German text completely, and this I know firsthand from older singers who performed with him there. Our own wonderful Dean Dixon spoke only English in his rehearsals, though he did understand a good bit of other languages. Remember that Dean did work a long time here in Sweden and in Germany. It is good for the conductor to have a decent knowledge of German, French, and Italian. It can be helpful and useful.

Now, I remember in my own case down in Colombia, at the opera, at the Teatro de Colon in Bogota, Colombia, we had a Bogotaian basso who was active in Germany and spoke only German and his mother tongue. Here this man was in a Spanish-speaking country and I was the only one the poor fellow could talk to in German. Again in my own case, my learning of languages came about as I was preparing *Trovatore*. Max Rudolf was helping me prepare. I went to him one Sunday morning for a lesson. I came prepared pratically note perfect with the chorus, orchestra, solo parts, etc. I had it very well in mind. But going along, Maestro Rudolf stopped; he stopped me and said, "What is this person saying?" I don't remember which one at this moment. It was in Italian, of course. Oh, I stuttered and stammered, and I was grasping desperately for an answer. But to save me further embarrassment, he translated the passage for me. Now, here was a German translating Italian into English. I was so humiliated, mortified, that I was no good for the rest of that lesson. Afterward I went home, laid across the bed, and cried like a baby. I made up my mind right then and there that I would never again be caught not knowing everything, including the text, no matter whether in Italian, French, or German. So the next morning I went to the Berlitz school and signed up for Italian lessons. My time in Germany made me learn all of the operas we did in the extensive repertoire in German. And then on being engaged and living in Sweden, all of the operas here, for the most part, done in Swedish.

WC: You spoke about the need for a conductor to know the composer's state of mind when he or she was composing the score currently being prepared. If one is working on a living composer's score, direct interaction may be possible, but if nothing has been documented through the channels of research and recorded in the literature on a composer who is no longer alive how does this happen?

EL: Well, I think in contemporary music, whenever possible, I try to get the composer's thoughts about what he or she has written and put my

questions to him or her—as to tempi, dynamics, and whatever things
did not work well at some earlier rehearsal before our conversation—
and when it is possible, I try to get the composer to sit in on my rehearsals and make comments to the orchestra and to me, which can be
of help to all of us. When a composer is not present, I usually try to
have a long phone conversation before or after a cleanup rehearsal.
This usually gives good results, especially if the composer really
knows what he's put down on paper. I have had the unfortunate experience of discussing scores with composers who really were of no help
whatsoever, sorry to say; but generally I've had good assistance from
today's writers. Now, as to music of former generations, there are
reams of literature about all of these composers that give idea of the
character and personality of said composer; and it is useful in performing a so-called masterpiece to know the composer's state of mind
at the time or at the period of writing this work; and it is also good to
know some other works that he has composed around the same time
of this work that the conductor is preparing for performance. It is well
to know other compositions of this composer that is being prepared
for performance. This helps to give insight as to how the composer
thinks and works, and perhaps why the music is written in a certain
way. Not just what he has written, but why this music is written in this
way.

WC: Once upon a time, a conductor was king in the opera house. How
has the conductor's role in operatic production changed?

EL: The conductor is still king in the opera house. After all, he is the
one responsible for the production, even when the curtain goes up. He
is the one setting the pace, the musical standard; inspiring, leading,
and accompanying as the situation requires. Now, that does not mean
at all that the conductor is to be a nasty dictator. He should be able to
understand the peculiarities of his soloists. What a soloist can and cannot do, and he should be able to readjust and cooperate, and his job really is to be helpful. All details should be worked out in rehearsals—
piano rehearsals. Yes, he is to inspire, to lead. He should be able to
lead his singers when the singers are not aware of it and follow them
when need be. The conductor's job is very complex in the theater. A
conductor's job is to be helpful if something goes wrong and not dogmatic, which does sometimes happen. I have seen performances
where the conductor just did not care about his soloists. A good conductor, if he has only mediocre singers, can raise the standard, and
make a fine performance. But with a good cast, a mediocre or bad conductor, can ruin a performance. The man who was my principal second violinist with my opera orchestra in Germany once came to me
and said, "Maestro, you know, there's no such thing as a bad orchestra, only bad conductors." There could be something in that because a

good conductor can make a bad orchestra sound good, but a bad conductor can make a good orchestra sound not so good. Many of the musicans in great orchestras have said, "It doesn't matter to us who's up there, we're going to play beautifully anyway."

WC: Of the operas that you have conducted, which one was the most difficult? Why? The flip side of that question is what opera has been the easiest to conduct? Why?

EL: All operas are difficult. Even the simplest in construction or in technical difficulty. I don't think that there is any easy opera. Even the simplest passages can present enormous problems for clarity or expression. Just take any one of the Mozart operas. There are certain arias that are in construction, as simple as anything.

WC: "Dalla sua pace," one of Don Ottavio's arias in Mozart's *Don Giovanni,* is an example.

EL: Simple, but to make something out of them, that's another ballgame.

WC: What about concert works, the most difficult and the easiest, why?

EL: Perhaps what I said about operas applies here, too. Such concert works as Stravinsky's *Rite of Spring,* the Mahler Fifth, Ninth Symphonies are difficult. Any of the Mahler symphonies could be difficult: the first, the fifth, ninth, the eighth is the monumental, that is difficult. It takes an enormous amount of preparation, and thought, and delving into Mahler's mind. With Stravinsky, knowing how he thought and worked, and how he put things down on paper, those are quite difficult. You look at any of the Beethoven Symphonies, which is the bible for conductors, and there's not one of them that is not difficult for the conductor. One very well-known conductor who does *The Rite of Spring* like . . . oh, he can shake it out of his sleeve . . . but with the first Beethoven Symphony, he said that offered him more problems than *The Rite of Spring.* So, perhaps it's the individual.

WC: Is there a particular opera or concert work that you have an overwhelming desire to conduct? Why?

EL: Of my modest list of some fifty-five or sixty operas that I have conducted or know—I say modest because some of my European colleagues who work continually in the theater have almost double that amount in their repertoire. I should add that my repertoire is heavily accented in the Italian, with some French and German thrown in. The Italian operas in my repertoire are those that are the most popular. As I stated earlier, in Italian theaters works are done in Italian, in French theaters, French, in Swedish theaters, Swedish, in German theaters, German. I have conducted some of the very same operas in four different languages: German, Swedish, Italian, and English. Twice I had one singer singing in Italian, the others in Swedish; and on another occasion, one singer was singing in German and the others in Swedish.

You asked what I'd like to do. Of all the many Verdi things that I have performed, I have conducted many of them, but I have never conducted *Otello* or *Falstaff.* The dramatic situations in *Otello,* from beginning to end, inspire and intrigue me greatly, as much or even more so, than *Tosca.* Of course, *Tosca* I've done quite a few times. I did it with soloists from the Royal Opera of Stockholm. I am sure that whenever I do *Falstaff,* all of us, my soloists, the orchestra, chorus, and I, will be bursting at the seams, both in rehearsals and performances. I am just that keyed up about the opera.

WC: You talked about conducting operas that were being simultaneously sung in more than one language. When I was studying voice with Robert McFerrin, he talked to me about it not being unusual to hear, in some countries, operas performed this way. To say that I was very shocked is indeed putting it mildly. I asked no questions, probably because of it sounding so unbelievable. How difficult is this for an audience? Does it present any difficulty for the singers? The sound must be somewhat strange, and quite silly, at best.

EL: Yes, it is crazy, but this opera business is a crazy one. I remember Boris Goldovsky, from whom I learned a great deal of opera, saying you have to be a little bit crazy to love opera. There's something in that. You asked, does this present any difficulty for the singers. Yes, in a way, it can be difficult. Singers have come to me saying they were hearing one text and thinking in another language, the language they were singing in. They became quite confused. A last minute change in the cast could create a situation to make this happen. Management might have no choice but to engage a singer for a role who only knows that role in a language that is unknown to the other singers in the cast. It doesn't happen too often, but it does happen, where two or three languages, different languages, are sung in the same opera. I said earlier that I've had the experience (is that the right expression) where I've had German and Italian, Swedish and German, Swedish and Italian, whatever. I think one time I even had three languages at once. You can imagine what that was like. It's confusing, but we all become rather amused by it all. Yes, the sound can be, as you said, somewhat strange, and quite silly at best. You're quite right. The question pops up too, should operas be sung in the original language, or what? Some operas should not be translated. It is very difficult to translate into other languages the Rossini, middle period Verdi, and a few others. I remember once doing *Un Ballo in Maschera* at the Royal Opera in Stockholm, and Birgit Nilsson was in the audience. She thought it was terrible that the opera was sung in Swedish. She felt that the whole bit was lost. There was a bit of truth in that. I remember doing operas in Philadelphia with Opera Ebony and Opera North. We were doing them in English. I, of course, had the Italian style in my ears, in my head; and in trying to work with coaching the singers, I would be trying to get an expression that was very difficult for the singers to give. Verdi had composed an Italian opera, in Italian, and translated over into English, it left a lot to be desired, especially style and line. It poses a big problem for the singers and for the conductor, too. I understand the idea behind it all. In Germany it was demanded in the traveling opera company that I was with—we had to do everything in German. The audience rather much demanded it. They wanted to know what was being said, and one can understand that. But, one loses a great deal of the real inside, the meat of the opera, when it is done in another language. Getting back to two or three languages sung in the same opera: that can and does happen, not with monotonous regularity, but on occasion. It's a good idea—again I go back to the conductor being able to be flexible—it would be a good idea for the conductor to know what his singers are singing when they are singing it.

WC: Why is it difficult to translate into other languages the Rossini and middle period Verdi operas?

EL: The best answer I can give is that Italian is a "living" language, as is ours, and thereby undergoes changes. I remember talking with Dr. [Riccardo] Picozzi in Rome about such, especially in *Traviata* and *Trovatore,* for example, and even he, this well-read, learned man had some difficulty in putting into modern parlance meanings of several passages. As you know poetic expressions often are a problem to give a day-to-day meaning.

WC: The first black to conduct opera in full performance in a reputedly established house; the first black to conduct an established symphony orchestra below the Mason-Dixon line; the first black to conduct a hit Broadway show on Broadway that was not black; guest conductor all over the world; you are certainly one of the most acclaimed conductors of our time, race withstanding. What were the stimuli that triggered your interest in conducting?

EL: Italian and German musicians with whom I played and later conducted were the ones who encouraged me to become a conductor, saying that I had a natural conducting talent. They, too, encouraged me to learn opera, as that would really teach me the art of conducting. They said in opera there is not only an orchestra to conduct, but there are solo singers, secondary singers, a chorus, plus ballet, all thrown together with the orchestra. It is quite an apparatus to conduct, and it is not just directing traffic or time beating. Then, of course, the work with Maestro Rudolf was very inspiring, and he was very encouraging. Even today as experienced as I am, when I run across something that I'm not too happy about, or I wish to know something more about, I give him a call. I remember two occasions. I did *The Marriage Of Figaro,* and there were a few places that I just was not happy about. I called him at his summer place at Mount Desert, Maine, and I told him where I was, not necessarily confused, but would like to have more clarity of thought. I got it. Another time, in New York, I was doing the *Paris Symphony,* again Mozart. I was not happy about certain things that I was thinking about doing; again, I called him up. He told me, you have the wrong score. He told me which one to buy. Then I called again. We discussed it again, thoroughly, over the phone. Then, I restudied the Paris Symphony; and the orchestra, during the rehearsals and afterward, complimented me on the fine Mozart that I was doing. So you see, one never stops learning. And I think it is very important to do a great deal of reading and to do a great bit of research. This gives the conductor far more security and assurance in performing.

WC: Your years as a performer playing the violin; how has that part of your life influenced your approach to conducting?

EL: As a string player, yes, of course. My being a violinist has played, and is playing, an important part in my training an orchestra in rehearsals. I am very pleased and quite flattered when musicians say to me that they see immediately and feel that I am a string player. In the recent few years, I've been working with two young people's orchestras. One is the Nordic Youth Orchestra, young people from all over Scandinavia, and the beautiful string playing has been noticed and remarked upon, and I am very grateful for that, and I attribute it to my experience as a string player.

WC: Does typecasting for black singers in opera on both sides of the Atlantic still exist? If so, what are the similarities and differences?

EL: Typecasting is subsiding greatly, as is obvious when Jessye Norman is singing Wagnerian and Strauss roles. Barbara Hendricks, Kathleen Battle, Harolyn Blackwell, Leona Mitchell, and others are all performing German, Italian, and French characters.

WC: Is support from the black community for the black "classical" artist growing?

EL: Yes, from my experiences in New York with the Symphony of the New World and in Philadelphia, not only with the opera company of Philadelphia but with Opera Ebony and Opera North, the black community is giving more support for the black classical performers.

WC: What steps can be taken to make "the system" work more effectively for the black conductor?

EL: It would be desirable to be accepted for what the conductor can do as an artist and as a person, and not from the color of his or her skin. It is true that different organizations have different requirements from the board of directors, and they put these stipulations into engaging a music director and chief conductor. I think, however, that it is enough that the conductor's efforts be confined just to music, working with and developing the orchestra, and composing imaginative programs that are interesting and intriguing for the orchestra and for the public.

Some organizations require that the conductors be very active in the community corralling musicians from different places, making speeches, attending meetings of different groups connected with the orchestra. All of this is time-consuming and takes away time that the orchestra conductor should be devoting in preparing his programs. The conductor should be confined just to his music making, and that is a great deal of doing.

WC: I am a composer. Many operas have been done by black composers. Yet, to my knowledge there isn't a single opera of a black composer in the active repertoire. Also, there are not many concert works of black composers performed; yet many have been written. Why? Is it just racism?

EL: This is a very difficult question for me to answer definitively. I and all of my other active colleagues are urged to the utmost by composers to perform their works. I remember being at the rehearsal of a well-known conductor when three composers descended on him with their respective scores during the intermission. The poor man almost lost his temper complaining that he was already swamped with contemporary scores. It has happened to me. My studio is filled with scores that perhaps I will never be able to conduct. I just have that many. I could fill up a whole season with contemporary music; and of course that would never do. A lot depends, too, on locality. Here in Sweden, I have done an enormous amount of music by Swedish composers, both older and contemporary. The same was true for me down in Colombia where I was chief for a long time. I remember there during one season, the administration wanted a festival of Colombian composers. So on each one of my concerts I had at least a contemporary piece on the program: compositions of only Colombian composers. I've had precious little opportunity to do American music abroad, and when such was proposed, only the known composers were to be accepted. In Europe and in South America, I've done Ives, Barber, Copland, Bernstein, and Gershwin. In the States and among the black composers, I have performed or introduced works by David Baker, Ulysses Kay, Mark Fax, Hale Smith, T. J. Anderson, Hall Johnson, William Grant Still, and William Dawson. These I speak of right from the top of my head. There are perhaps a few more. If I have left out some, please do excuse me. Leslie Adams will be coming up sometime next year. Speaking of Bill Dawson. Leopold Stokowski performed in concert and recorded Dawson's *Negro Folk Symphony* with both the Philadelphia and the American Symphony. When I conducted the Detroit orchestra a few years back—I don't remember at this moment the date exactly—Maestro Dawson called me up; and so we met at the hotel where he was stopping in New York. There he went through that symphony with me with a fine-tooth comb, with such enthusiasm that it was infectious. I really knew his work very well, and he was very happy about the way that it was performed. The work was very well received. Later I proposed to record this symphony with a major European radio station. I submitted the score, but it was returned to me several months later with no comment. When I called to find out what was to be, the response was that they had no spot in the programming, nor the budget. I got the feeling, however, that they were not impressed with the work. As for operas of American black composers, William Grant Still's *The Troubled Island* is the only one that I am aware of that has been performed by a major American company, the New York City Opera, and that was quite a few years ago. I do hope to stand corrected. Again, may I speak for myself?

WC: Certainly.

EL: I've never done a complete opera performance of an American black composer. Opera Ebony premiered Dorothy Rudd Moore's *Frederick Douglass* a few years ago; and with Opera Ebony, I did excerpts of her *Frederick Douglass* in Göteborg, Sweden, in 1993, at the opera house. I have also done excerpts of operas by Mark Fax and Lena McLin. In the eyes of backers mounting an opera, a new opera is risky business; plus, it is enormously expensive. It seems that I've not yet answered your question. It could be some racism, but I hesitate to condemn organizations for such. Composers should make contact with performing organizations and conductors who are possibly in a position of influence, or other persons who could be of help. Composers should make contact with chamber music groups, etc., etc., etc. I'm aware that it is most uncomfortable to promote oneself and to promote one's own music; but I'm afraid that it must be done, in face of so many difficulties: resistance to much new music; finances; cliques; contexts. One can easily see what an unknown or relatively unknown composer is up against.

WC: I didn't know that Lena McLin had composed operas. I also did not know that Hall Johnson composed for the orchestra. You said that you had conducted works by Hall Johnson. Would you share the names of these works?

EL: Lend McLin's work is called *Oh Freedom*. It is written for soprano, chorus, and orchestra. I did this work once in New York in Carnegie Hall; and I've done parts of it, also in New York, with Opera Ebony. We did it last year in Merkin Theater, which is right around the corner from Lincoln Center, and we did it once here in Sweden. I did it once in Goteborg, Sweden. The Hall Johnson things were spirituals that Hall wrote for voice and orchestra. I did these with the Atlanta Symphony with William Warfield as soloist. Sorry to say, I don't remember the names of these things that I did. One text said, "Just like John." But the whole title, I don't remember. That was quite an exciting performance that Bill and I did down there. It was at a NANM [National Association of Negro Musicians] conference a few years back. They got the Atlanta Symphony to come in to play. As I remember, it was only for string orchestra that we did this. It got to be quite an exciting performance. Bill got really inspired. He liked the music, the text, and he hopped in and did something a little bit sooner than I expected. We had quite a wonderful time. He gave me a lift, and I gave the orchestra a lift, and the audience went wild! [Conversations with Mr. Warfield and Sylvia Olden Lee revealed that this convention was in 1979. The Hall Johnson spirituals were "City Called Heaven" and "Ride On King Jesus." The complete title of the "Just Like John" text is "I Want To Be Ready." The setting performed was by Harry Thacker Burleigh. The program also included two Thomas Kerr arrangements: "Gospel Train" and "Oh, What A Beautiful City." "Oh, What A Beautiful City" was a duet performed with Joyce Mathis. Ms. Mathis is now deceased.] McLin's *Oh Freedom* had another title before, which I don't remember. It was inspired by a Martin Luther King speech; and then she changed it to *Oh Freedom*. I'll be doing it again for two performances in Reykjavik, Iceland, in November with Opera Ebony. The complete program has not yet been finalized, but among other things will be Lena McLin's cantata. [Lena McLin gave Wayne Sanders, music director of Opera Ebony, permission to do an adaptation of her cantata, *Free At Last,* for the stage. Sanders entitled the adaptation: *Oh Freedom. Free At Last* was inspired by the life of Martin Luther King and composed by McLin immediately after the assassination of King in 1968. The first words of *Free At Last* are "Oh Freedom." It has been performed to great acclaim around the world.]

WC: How have conducting opportunities changed through the years in America and other parts of the world for African-Americans? How have they remained the same?

EL: I think things have changed and are changing. There are black Americans associated with orchestras in the States, and big ones, too. James De Priest is chief of the Portland Orchestra, which is one of America's major organizations. Isaiah Jackson was head of the Dayton Philharmonic, but he told me he's leaving there for Australia. I've lost track somewhat of Paul Freeman, who at one time headed an orchestra in Canada. You surely know that Freeman made a lot of recordings for Columbia Records dedicated only to black composers.

WC: Yes. I am familiar with those recordings. I wish that someone would do something similar with the choral orchestral works of black composers. What about your recordings?

EL: Yes, I've done a lot; mostly radio recordings with orchestras here in Scandinavia, in the States, and down in South America. As a matter of fact, I'm thinking of cataloging my recordings whenever I can find the time. The idea is from my maestro Max Rudolph who cataloged all of his recordings from the Cincinnati Symphony, his days at the Metropolitan Opera, and other guest performances. He cataloged all of his; and that gave me the idea to do the same with my own. There are quite a few.

WC: You have been involved with productions of Gershwin's *Porgy and Bess* outside America. How do these productions differ? What makes them unique?

EL: I've done stage productions of *Porgy* in France and in Sweden. Though in France we had an all-American black cast, the chorus was French, and the orchestra, of course, was French. Very good, too. In Sweden, now get this, I did *Porgy* with an all-Swedish cast, done in Swedish with an excellent translation, no dialect of course, as no dialect in Swedish could correlate to the dialect in *Porgy*. But the translation was very well made over into modern Swedish. The chorus had an awfully difficult time with the rhythm, but managed decently after much work. The soloists, too, were very good indeed, and approximated very well the feeling for their respective roles. We did, though, work and work hard, and the result was wonderful indeed. Actually, those performances are still being talked about. The orchestra at the opera was truly wonderful.

WC: Was there anything done with makeup and wigs to create a black or ethnic look? I know that in the States, *Porgy* can be done only with African-American casts.

EL: Yes, of course in the States it can only be done with an all-black cast. When I did *Porgy and Bess* here in Sweden, in Malmo, at the opera with a Swedish cast, they had makeup and wigs to look like the ethnic folks. When I did it in France on tour, in Toulouse—I think we started off in Toulouse—even the French choruses were made up with wigs.

WC: Maestro, we are now ready to hear your final words of counsel.

EL: I would say to keep a positive mentality and outlook. Close no doors, and remember that no doors can be, or are, permanently kept shut. Work! Work! Work! Watch and be prepared and ready whenever an opportunity presents itself. One never knows when or how an opportunity will come. It's just like the wind. It comes from any direction. When an engagement of some kind does pop up, plunge into it with full energy, and interest, and love for the art and love that is in the heart, your heart. Then you can't miss, as one has the power and the force of Providence with and behind you. You know, today there are no secrets anywhere in the world, thanks to the media. Through television, radio, we get the news, everywhere, just about at the same moment it happens. Just about everywhere in the world, all know of the race problems in America and the attitudes. Some say the race problem in America is better. Some say it's worse. Some say there is no change. But in any case, something of the race attitudes does still exist. Now, we know—everyone knows—that all Americans come from everywhere. We have ancestors from Scandinavia, from Russia, from Germany, England, Switzerland, Hungary, Italy, just about everywhere. I've been asked, "What are you, Maestro?" When I say that I am an American of color, they say, well, you can't be. Then I have to go on and explain that if there is one drop of Negro blood in one, that makes you a black man. Well, that caught the devil himself in Germany, in France. They said that I was cashing in on cheap publicity. They asked me, "What is your ancestry?" I went on back to my great grandmother. She was Indian, and her husband was Negro. My paternal grandfather was Greek and maternal grandfather was Spanish, Mexican, Negro. They said, how can you call yourself a black man with all of this European blood running through you. I could only say, that is the way it is in my country. However, it is no shame at all that I have the same blood running through me that ran through Homer, Socrates, Pocahontas, Sitting Bull, George Washington Carver, Sojourner Truth, [Haitian emperor Jean-Jaques] Dessalines, Serapis [a deity of Egyptian origin whose worship was introduced into Greece and Rome], Ralph Bunche, Martin Luther King. That's not a bad group of people to be related to, is it? Heavens! When will we people learn to see one another as human beings, related to one another, all of us descendents of the same one and only God. I pray to be seen, known, and desired as a man created in the image and likeness of God just as is stated in the first chapter of Genesis. I hardly think that one can do any better than that.

Easter Eve 1994
Löddeköpinge, Sweden

Sylvia Olden Lee. *Courtesy of Sylvia Olden Lee.*

4

Sylvia Olden Lee:
Lady Sylvia Speaks

For nearly six decades, Sylvia Lee's accomplishments have been extraordinary, trailblazing, and unique. As an accompanist, she appeared at the White House for the inauguration of the National Council of Negro Women; she performed with the students of Todd Duncan in the early thirties, and toured with Carol Brice in the late thirties and Paul Robeson in the forties. In the early fifties she accompanied recitals in Perugia and at the Castel Sant' Angelo in Rome, and in the late fifties and early sixties she served as the official accompanist for the annual International Voice Competition in Munich. She has performed in more than five hundred lieder recitals in Munich, Stuttgart, and Berlin. Her professional appointments include Talladega College, Dillard University, the University of Cincinnati, the Curtis Institute of Music, Howard University, and the Philadelphia College of the Performing Arts. A vocal coach from 1943 to 1952, she worked with students of Elisabeth Schumann, Eva Gautier, Konraad Bos, Rosalie Miller, and Fritz Lehmann. She also prepared singers for the New York City Center Opera and the Metropolitan Opera. Lee served as a technical adviser for the world premier of Britten's *Peter Grimes* and worked with Boris Goldovsky as an opera coach at Tanglewood. With her former husband, the eminent conductor Everett Lee, she prepared concert versions of many operas with the Cosmopolitan Symphony. She also appeared with the Cosmopolitan Symphony as a piano soloist and toured with Thomas Kerr as part of a piano duo. In 1953 she was appointed as the first black vocal coach of the Metropolitan Opera. She served as a consultant to James Levine for the 1985 Metropolitan Opera premier of *Porgy and Bess.* Lee was one of the two music consultants for the 1990 CAMI video *Spirituals In Concert,* produced for television in association with Deutsche Grammophon, and starring Kathleen Battle and Jessye Norman. Lee was involved with two of the songs that were programmed: as arranger and piano accompanist in "Scandalize My Name," and as arranger for "Lord, How Come Me Here?"[1] The following conversation took place during the 1991 National Association of Negro Musicians Convention, Chicago, Illinois.

---

1. Additional biographical information can be found in Southern (1982, 242) and Borland (1983, 254).

Wallace Cheatham: Why has there not been a black male to become a real operatic superstar, a parallel to Leontyne Price?

Sylvia Olden Lee: [Black male vocalists] are imagining in some instances that they need not try for it—superstar status. They are busy trying to make a living. The fact that some of them actually don't work at the craft—and of course the main reason, if they're really hot, and would really make a wonderful, stellar person on the Metropolitan stage, they get the feeling that they're black and will not have a chance to shine, so they don't really knock on the door. Seth McCoy has been there, at the Metropolitan, since Mr. George Shirley.

WC: Simon Estes has also been at the Metropolitan with star status since George Shirley.

SOL: Yes, but Seth McCoy was dragged there, because they actually insisted that he try out for Tamino in Mozart's *Die Zauberflöte*. And he did perform. But he did not stay. [His] voice is a small one, and he really did not feel that he would carry; but he at least had the welcome mat there.

WC: Mr. McCoy told me that there was no desire to audition for the Met, that he was approached through his manager, and he finally said, "Well . . . why not?" He also said that he did not think of himself as having been a member of the Metropolitan. "I was a guest," he said. "I did not give my blood there like George Shirley." [McCoy did four performances of Mozart and five performances of the singer in Strauss's *Der Rosenkavalier* during his tenure.]

SOL: Now Vinson Cole is of a recent vintage. The last two or three years, he has been a lead. He is a good, serviceable, wonderful singer; but he does not go about the making of himself as a star in other, outside things like television. Today, if you're really trying to command stardom, you almost have to do something like that. It wasn't obligatory in Leontyne's day. But the people really commanding leads, and the respect of the Metropolitan, have come by way of Europe to soar all over . . . Chicago and other big houses here. So, I don't really know. There is some justification for the thinking of what Mr. George Shirley published in *Time* magazine about twenty-five years ago[2]: They are not ready for black *heroes;* whether they look very black and African or not, [the establishment is] not ready to have them embrace the flower of the world—the female white. Of course this doesn't quite go through all of the time. It is not consistent. But that would be one reason to have [a lack of black male stardom in the arts], not being ready for seeing black heroes; but it's happening in Europe so much, so I just don't see why not here. Mr. Paul Cravath, who died about fifteen years or so ago, was for a long time head of the board of the Metropolitan.

---

2. *Time* August 13, 1965:54.

He tried to bring (it was in his obituary) at the height of her career, in the thirties, Caterina Jarboro as Aida, because she was drawing so many people's attention away from the Aida at the Met. It piqued everybody's curiosity. She was a sensation. I never heard her, but Mr. Cravath said, "Why don't we take advantage of this woman's stardom and bring her in as Aida? We could play down the visual for a while. Just grab her while we can get her at the height of her fame." But sadly he said the Met was not ready. And Paul Robeson, Mr. Cravath wanted to bring. He felt sure that there was some opportunity at the Met for him. Paul Robeson was beginning to rise as a singer, and Mr. Cravath felt that he should have been at the Met. Why not in the premier of *Emperor Jones,* since he had starred in the O'Neill play?

WC: Yes, and also in the film. If Mr. Robeson had starred in the opera, he would have come full circle, artistically, with that character—something that would have established a unique historical precedent. They used Lawrence Tibbett in blackface.

SOL: They would not let Jarboro or Robeson in there. That was in the thirties. I guess they had to wait twenty years. In the forties when my husband was studying conducting with Max Rudolf[3], who at the time was the artistic administrator at the Met, right next to Mr. Bing, Mr. Rudolf once a year would invite us to his home on Riverside Drive for dinner. So I just broke into the subject, right at first. I said, bluntly, "What are the chances for a Negro" (that's the term we were then using) "to get into the Met? We have so many marvelous people." "Oh, it will come," he said. "But I want to tell you right off the bat: they've got to have the greatest of talent with the best of training . . . the greatest voice in the first place . . . and a good knowledge of all the languages. There must be dramatic ability *and* the first appearance must be in a character visually believable." So I let it drop. We, my husband and I, went to Italy on Fulbrights. We came back. At a friend's home, who was not musical—but it was Sunday afternoon, Toscanini was broadcasting, and that was the one time when people, whether they were musical or not, did listen. So this man put it on—the broadcast—for us. We talked all through dinner and suddenly it dawned upon me that the opera being broadcast was Verdi's *Un Ballo in Maschera.* So I thought, "We're going to the Rudolf's within the next week or so." At that dinner I said, "Do you remember what you said to me?" He said, "What?" "About the first Negro at the Met?" "Yes" "It had to be as a character visually believable." "Yes." "Every year I notice, no matter what you've planned in the repertory, you manage to squeeze in two or three performances of whatever Toscanini has put on because it has created some kind of furor; and so

---

3. Specifically, Everett Lee's study with Max Rudolf took place from 1948 through 1950.

you know what this year's opera was?" "No." *"Un Ballo in Maschera."* "Yes." "Do you remember about the believable, visual person, Ulrica?" "Uh huh." "What about Carol Brice?"

WC: Carol Brice did have an operatic voice! She would have been a marvelous Ulrica!

SOL: Miss [Marian] Anderson never occurred to me. If there had been any aspirations, she could have burned the globe—everywhere but here. Miss Anderson was so popular, and so fanatically . . . just plain hailed in Europe and all over; and had she wanted to do opera, she could have, and they would not have confined her to the believable complexion and all. So Miss Anderson didn't occur to me. I thought of Carol Brice because I had played an audition there for her to do [Wagner's] Erda. At the time of the audition, Carol had not recovered from a cold and vocal trouble that had developed during a tour of Alaska; consequently, the audition did not go well. "You know," Mr. Rudolf said, "when you don't have a good performance at a Met audition it's hard to get back, but *this* would interest us. Does she know it . . . not the whole role, just the aria? . . . I've played it for her so often. Certainly she does. Tell her to get it together," Mr. Rudolf said, "and bring it to me, and if it works we'll call in Mr. Bing." I went and worked with Carol for three weeks, four weeks. She dragged her feet because she still had this vocal difficulty. I told her she had a chance to make history, and that kind of set her back. But this girl was the greatest musician and the most beautiful artist. Then came July . . . August . . . and the Old Vic came and used the Metropolitan. There are so many different stories about how Miss Anderson was approached. You know, they claim that Miss Anderson was in the box, just a spectator at the Old Vic performance, and Mr. Bing looked at her, and it—the idea— hit him. Other people say that Mr. Bing had made contact with her on a different occasion. Miss Anderson put in that she was at the Old Vic performance and someone talked to her. And someone had it that Mr. Bing reached right over the banister in the box and asked, and then she was called in. So nobody got it straight; but they did ask her; and she said, "Well, maybe, if I could do the part well."

WC: This is truly intriguing, because the accounts published in Miss Anderson's autobiography *My Lord What A Morning,* and Mr. Bing's memoirs *5000 Nights at The Opera,* don't completely jibe. Your declaration, "Nobody got it straight," has great merit.

SOL: I thought about the dramatic role that Mr. Rudolf had said was essential. I knew that Miss Anderson wasn't going to do too much drama; but it, the role of Ulrica, doesn't call for a lot. She's a sorceress.

WC: Yes, two of the reasons that Mr. Bing gives in his memoirs about why Ulrica was chosen for Miss Anderson's debut are that the role doesn't require much acting and the role can be managed by a voice past its prime.

SOL: But she ended up doing more acting than anybody on the stage! Miss [Zinka] Milanov, Mr. [Richard] Tucker, all of those people up there. She didn't stand out vocally, but her dignity was there. With that I knew that it had finally come through, black singers at the Met. Bob McFerrin was brought in within a month.

WC: I studied with McFerrin, and working with him made me want to systemically research the black experience in opera; he made his debut as Amonasro in *Aida,* and went on to do Valentin in Gounod's *Faust,* and the title role in *Rigoletto.*

SOL: Mattiwilda Dobbs,[4] the next season, did Gilda in *Rigoletto.* Then Mattiwilda did Olympia in Offenbach's *Les Contes d' Hoffmann,* and then she did Zerbinetta in Strauss's *Ariadne auf Naxos.* I think because she had done both of those roles in Europe.

So things began to roll. I have kept a log. Twenty or twenty-five blacks were brought in before Jimmy Levine's era. Jimmy Levine has brought in about forty-eight or fifty blacks during his administration. Soloists. I'm not talking about supporting singers or chorus members.

The thing about the black soloists that have come into the Metropolitan, many of them have not had dramatic ability; but that does not make them stand out in a negative way from the white members at all. It's unusual for singers to come into opera with great skills in acting. We're doing better with opera now, even though they're messing with the staging in terms of time and place — all of the production concepts. But if the traditional approach is used, we have not had people to fall down below the standards of what is expected on the operatic stage.

WC: Yes. I agree. The black singers that I have heard on the Saturday broadcasts, heard and seen on the telecasts, and listened to on the recordings have been right up there with their white colleagues.

SOL: And thank goodness, they have all fulfilled what he, Mr. Rudolf, established as criteria to me in my conversation with him years ago. They've had unusual voices, very well trained, and in most instances lots and lots of experience before coming to the Met, and they've been young and fresh. They do not take any singers into the company for the first Met appearance if they are Americans, black or white — they don't take them if they are in vocal trouble. They have been known to take them from Europe in vocal trouble because they sign them up two or three years ahead and if they didn't have a wobble before that, they've worked themselves up and the voice has gone down. So many times you hear in broadcasts that the voice is beginning to go; but it's not among us. We haven't had anybody with bad vocal health, and they're all good musicians, every one of them. There has been one disappointment out of eighty or ninety soloists.

---

4. See Southern (1982, 109-110).

WC: Would you speak to the operatic instrument, things like the criteria for identification, the kind of training needed, technique, vocal perseverance, role preparation?

SOL: First, you are supposed to have the most unusual voice in the world. Many a star, though, many an immortal has had, not quite what has been an unusual instrument, but then they batted a thousand in everything else. Such people as Mary Garden, [John] Brownlee—these people had nice, what we call choir voices. Nobody would perk up his ears to hear their sound; but they have batted a thousand on being the best actor, on being really into the part, on being authentic, and having honed their instruments the best that they could, and keeping those instruments in good shape. And they were not such wilting flowers. Today we must address ourselves to vocal health in every way, because we have the influence of all media. But I'm speaking particularly about television, not just recordings and movies. Television has made it possible for everyone to tune in for whatever he wants to hear . . . and see. The majority of people are not going to tune in on an opera; but now that we have subtitles and translations, people will tolerate it a bit more. They are beginning to pay more attention to realism as far as the visual side goes. More attention is being paid to the action, so you don't have quite so many people standing and holding a spear forever, and acting like they don't know who is on stage with them. That doesn't go anymore. Subtitles and translations have made it necessary to be more concerned about matching what is there with what you are singing. And to keep vocal health. We are having to fight the fact that our youth, white and black, are becoming involved with country and western, going to Sunday school and taking part in gospel, and possibly going over into rock gospel. By the time they're nine, ten, or eleven, they have a voice that shows it has been used in church praising God. . . . They go to rehearsals and they mutilate those voices before they get them, so that by the time they are ready to start training technically, if they feel that they like the classics and would like to pursue them, chances are, in many instances, the instrument has already been disrepaired, and sometimes permanently. A whole lot of kids are enrolling in conservatories, majoring in voice, whose voices already have a wobble, something that is very desirable for rock and pop music. If you have that kind of tremolo, it can be, I am told, gotten rid of. But it takes, sometimes, silence for a year and the greatest of therapy to get it back.

WC: The situation is getting worse. It's not uncommon to now see rock gospel choirs in many urban elementary schools. We no longer have a lot of balance in the black community with musical offerings and musical interests. We are on the verge of losing, if we haven't already done so, an entire generation of voices in the black community that could have made contributions to the classics.

SOL: So it only behooves us to pass some kind of law that a child show-ing a voice, even before puberty, and loving to sing, should be kept psychologically happy, and active enough to fulfill what he wants to do, without having heavy material and ruining the voice. If you can keep them interested until they get out of school, some people can with certain teachers go in at eighteen, major in voice, and come out un-scathed. The biggest barrier [is that] too many of them are given "Pace, pace" in the first year because they have a big voice; but they don't have the big voice that they should have. I don't care how many decibels it makes and how deep the bass goes, you haven't got your voice in college. You should sing, and do—not everything so light—but you don't do the passionate nineteenth-century, early-twentieth-century, heavily orchestrated accompaniments. Because if you do, and keep doing them—"Oh, but she can; this is an unusual voice"—Yes, she may do it very well, but by the time she graduates, nobody wants to hear her. Now the people at church will still want to hear her sing "His Eye Is on the Sparrow," but don't come and try to sell *Aida* or *Traviata,* because the minute they hear a quaver that is not a natural vibrato, you are just plain out. That is here and Europe. That's one cat-egory where they have a solid front.

WC: How does one go about preparing a role? What is the best way to study and prepare?

SOL: In the first place, if you find that you are vocally endowed, you love it and want to learn. You should get musicianship together, and that doesn't mean use your throat to do it. You ought to play a flute, a clar-inet, or something, and piano. Not with the idea of being a fine pianist, but as a tool to enable you to look at the soprano clef and know how to prepare yourself. You should not need a coach, a *repetiteur,* to play the accompaniment and feed you the lines and all. You should be able to read the line. If a pianist can read five fingers worth on each hand, cer-tainly a singer should be able to sing intervals. So you should have sight singing and ear training done; but you do not work at preparing a whole role of anything. I don't care how crazy you are about it. You see, it's hard to keep that fine line, to keep a singer from being frustrated and yet not being suicidal. That's up to these voice technicians—to keep them satisfied, singing things that will give them an outlet, but leave them with a throat. Because the minute you hear someone say, "Oh, her voice is as big as mine was when I was twenty-five and she's only eigh-teen," well then, work with that voice, and don't push it. Push your foot to the floor on it! Give technique. Learn history. Do not learn whole roles. . . . Arias, however, should be further down the line. Coming to college and starting right out with [Madame Butterfly's] "Un bel di" is kind of suicidal. You should learn the songs of the different languages with the idea of getting the voice settled. Technique, getting the breath controlled to support your tone so that you're not singing on the throat. And this business of roles. When I played in Europe for the biggest agents—I didn't apply for it, they heard me accompany some people and they asked me if I would be an accompanist—I was in on many an audition. Agents who were in Munich handled most of Germany, Austria, Holland, and Switzerland. They really had people trooping in. I would sit there and hear what they would tell them. I learned in no time at all what they would say to these singers, and I knew what they required of them. It doesn't mean that it's right, but that's what prevailed over there. [These singers would say] "Well, I'm coming next year"—I could hear very easily, and anybody who was from Wales, New Zealand, or America, I could understand; with Spanish and French I could glean a little—"what roles should I . . . " "No roles. Do not wear your throat out learning a whole opera. You can learn a dozen operas and we'll give you the thirteenth. But don't learn whole roles. Study those operas you feel that you could do if you were hired, but learn only the arias." I said to James Levine, "What do you think when you see a great long list of eight or ten roles?" "You know, when I see it, I automatically decide they're not worth listening to because they haven't got any throat left. If they are of any young age, up to thirty, and they've got all of these lead roles that they've digested, it only means they're not worth hearing; because they've used all of their energy on learning roles, singing what they could, but they've been using voice, voice, voice." The singers say to me, "Miss Lee, you say don't learn whole roles, but I go and make an application for a contest or for an opera house, they have down there *number of roles.*" I say, "Well, if you know three, fine; you write that. If you don't know any, you write none. They're not going to judge you by the number of roles you say you know." Once upon a time, way back there, thirteen or fifteen *repetiteurs*—men who aspired to be conductors at the Met, working in the basement—they were to teach those roles and beat them into the heads of people. They liked a singer, he was told to get *Parsifal* out and report to Mr. So-and-So in the basement and start working on it. No, no. I mentioned this system to Mr. Levine and he said, "We can't have them now because we can't afford them." I was told that Leonard Warren took two years to learn *Rigoletto.* Now it may take you today two years to learn *Rigoletto,* but you're not going to learn it in the Met basement. You're going to learn it on your own the best way you can. They tell you to prepare it; and then you have rehearsals, maybe six months later; and they expect you to know everything.

WC: Your statement about Leonard Warren makes me think about Rosa Ponselle. I'm sure there are many others who were spoon-fed, but Ponselle had never heard an opera and had never even set foot in an opera house. [Enrico] Caruso heard this operatic voice singing vaude-

ville, took her to the Met, and she became not only the first American-
born singer to perform there, but a diva of phenomenal impact. I once
heard Marilyn Horne say that opera today is losing many singers
[who] could make great contributions because there is no longer the
kind of system or nurturing that was there for people like Ponselle, that
everyone was now in it for themselves.

SOL: Yes, very different today . . . And this practicing voice three and
four hours a day. And the poor singer who majors in voice at most universities is required to be in their chorus. There should be a law that
they can't. I don't care what the choral director needs. I incurred the
enmity of a man in Cincinnati. They had a wonderful chorus; but when
I said these voice major kids have no business having rehearsal with
you an hour every day—they then have no voice left to work on their
own technique because they're supplying you with the second soprano—he had a fit, and they all feel this way. If you're a good singer,
yes, you should be in a chorus—first, to get experience—but hopefully
something more than singing second soprano in the Verdi *Requiem*. I
said to Jessye Norman, "Girl, you were in the Howard choir for a
whole four years. How did you end up with a voice to sing?" "Dear
Dr. [Warner] Lawson did look for me to be the backbone of his chorus
because there were many kids in there who could not read music.
They had good ears but they came from other departments of the college, and so I was supposed to supply them with pitch. Many times
he would be up there conducting, looking to me at a difficult place,
and I'm sitting there mouthing—looking right straight at him and not
making a sound—because I wouldn't have had a voice." If I could
only get them to print it, because I'm for going to the United States
Department of Health, Education, and Welfare . . . with the federal
government making it absolute. Potential voice stars, classical vocal
stars, opera or anything else, shouldn't be allowed *in* a chorus—only
as a periodic soloist—shouldn't be allowed. I'm sorry to say that, and
each voice is different. We've got trumpets, and we have honey, del-
icate ones; but they don't know how to sing yet and so they're singing
anyway, throat and all, and doing damage. Some of it is repairable,
and some of it is not. The only reason Kathy Battle reached a point
where she had some voice to sing with is that they didn't think enough
of Kathy at the University of Cincinnati to require of her. She was in
a corner all the time, being shy, and they didn't pay much attention to
her. I was there and I watched those jumping ahead of her to get the
parts; and so they sang them. She graduated and taught for a year or
so; so she had her voice. If they had known that she was going to be
the Kathy Battle of today, they would have worn her out at Cincinnati;
because they wore out others. I know their names. Isn't that something?

WC: It is. What about the voice teacher and the vocal coach? How do their roles differ and interact?

SOL: One is a technician whose main job is voice building. Some of them—teachers—are great artists, and I think that all of them should have had vocal performing experience. Now, as to whether they stopped before they had to or not, that's none of my business; but they should have a good method of carefully building a voice. Once upon a time—I feel bad that it is no longer true—voice majors got two half hours of teaching time each week. You got checked Tuesday from what you did Friday, and you were corrected in case it wasn't quite right. Now it is the thing: you get one lesson a week and it's for one hour; and you're probably singing too much during that hour; and then you have six days to go ahead. As Mattiwilda Dobbs says, "Singing all wrong and not knowing it, and working it in." So when you go back for the next lesson you're in sort of a bad situation. It is so pathetic; but it comes out of the commercialism of most conservatories and colleges. Each one tries to see who has closer to the ideal with the revolving stage, and all the lights, and the big pit, and orchestra—that is gorgeous. Most of these orchestras in colleges are simply fantastic. They are go great! They have fifty, sixty people, and they have to put on an opera. Now they may put on a musical comedy, which, thank goodness, they do, some of which is really fine, and this gives performance activity. But that's not getting into the classics. So we must put on the Verdi *Requiem,* and we have to put on *Rigoletto,* and the rehearsal hours are enough to kill you. Then you have big orchestral rehearsals the day before, and then you go on and sing. They say, "Oh, yes, she's young; she can do it." They wouldn't dare in a European opera house, or at the Metropolitan, or Chicago Lyric, have rehearsal the day before a complete opera. Singers at the Metropolitan would say, "Well, you know I can't do it because I will have had dress rehearsal Thursday. I'm performing Saturday night so I don't sing all day Friday and Saturday." They don't open their mouths, and those people know how to handle their throats and sing sotto voce in rehearsal. The young singer is ambitious, and he feels that he can rehearse on Friday morning, go home and eat lunch, come back and sing—and does. But within a few years, the voice is murdered.

WC: So the voice teacher is a voice builder.

SOL: A voice builder. Watching the instrument with well-placed vocal exercises and emphasis on strengthening the torso where the lungs and diaphragm are really controlled, where most of the bulk of singing would happen—below the collarbone, not in the neck and throat.

WC: And the coach?

SOL: The coach's job is to do the printed page of whatever literature is being sung, and it would be hoped that he knew about style. You

see, there are some "pop" singers who have had vocal training, like
Frank Sinatra and Roberta Flack; I think Dionne Warwick. They
have had the training, so they're not completely out of it. There are
some who hit right off and they've never studied, but they don't have
to because vocal deterioration isn't going to matter. They're going
to be all style. Their thumbprint is how they do certain numbers.
That person who works with them is called a stylist. Now, in our
field a vocal coach is supposed to be a stylist. Some of them of
course are not well versed in it, and they will just make sure that you
sing correct rhythm, correct pitch, that your language pronunciation
is right, that your breaths are taken correctly, and, it is hoped, dynamics—soft and loud. But you very seldom get that; most people
get up and sing with the same dynamics throughout the piece. But
the vocal coach, I call myself an interpretation teacher because that's
what they call it abroad. A *repetiteur* [is] one who plays the piano
and shouts the cues and sees to it that you come in on time, and we
cannot have opera without that, you must have that. These people are
invaluable. But I'm not good at that—my singing Rudolfo while you
come in as Mimi, and playing it, and conducting. I can't do that. I
could do it with some scores. I know some operas from memory; but
I can't be called upon to do that, the role of *repetiteur,* skillfully.
That's a real talent. But often they, *repetiteurs,* are not interested in
how it's being done. A *repetiteur* might tell singers what the translations are and not see to it they dig it out for themselves. "Oh, you
know my boyfriend knows this language. I don't have to worry about
the translation. I'll get it from him." Getting the translation from
your boyfriend is not going to help you at all. He can be invaluable
once you've looked it up in the dictionary yourself and written out
the translation above the notes. He can be invaluable in helping with
shadings of pronunciation; but as to your knowing what you're doing, you have to do that yourself. And a lot of vocal preparation is
done quietly, lying down in bed—without sleeping—looking up in
the dictionary, and actually photographing what you have to do. I tell
the students—I don't have music here so I can't show you how I tell
them—"You are responsible for knowing thoroughly. It doesn't
mean that you have to do things just exactly as you find them; but
you are responsible for knowing everything but this print that is
marked down here: page 402. That's the only thing you don't have
to know."

WC: At what point do the roles of the teacher and the coach overlap?

SOL: They should go hand in hand. I have felt many times, down through
the years, that students brought material to me that was vocally un-
healthy for them. But who am I to say that? I then say to the student,
"Honey, but, 'Pace' . . . the Verdi operas . . . this is a little heavy, I

think. To bring this to me. I'm going to work for the ultimate, dramatic portrayal. I don't know why she gave this to you. She could be working on something technical, and she knows why; but if I'm going to coach this, I don't want to do it unless she is around so that she keeps you in line vocally."

WC: What about operatic characters? You know a lot about operatic characters and I would like for you to identify some of the most complex personalities in the opera, the most villainous, and the most stable, the whole psychological bit. And how does this come through in the music?

SOL: I don't know. Villains are villains no matter what, and certainly the romantic person is romantic. He may have a villainous moment or two. Most of the characters however have many sides, but certainly not always. There are some operas where heroine or hero, the character is just a normal guy, just a nice guy, or she's the girl next door and dramatic things happen to them. But to have somebody . . . Iago, of course, from *Otello:* he is villainous. And of course villains are not standing there twirling mustaches. They are masquerading as good guys a lot of the time. They have ways that make them very amenable and very helpful while they are only weaving a web, as Iago does and finally confesses. But for complex characters: Porgy. Thank goodness *Porgy and Bess* has been established in this country where it was conceived; after fifty years, it has reached its full glory of being classified as what the composer said—opera. It has been all over Europe. It has been translated and performed in different countries in their languages. The Finns early on had a translation. The Scandinavians have had translations since the forties, and they put on the opera with their natives, and they work very hard. They will do it sometimes in English, but they will also translate it into their languages. Porgy, the character, is one of the most complex in all of opera, he really is, and to have him handkerchief-headed and grinning all the time, or feeling sorry for himself throughout the opera, is a mistake. The libretto doesn't bear it out. He is a magnificent good guy. He just can't walk. He is looked up to by the whole colony there in Catfish Row. He's a preacher, a consultant, a counsel. He is a fighter, and he is also a lover. I just wish that more of those who do Porgy would realize this. There is nothing pathetic about Porgy. There isn't. I consider it a mission to make everyone realize that Porgy is a man to be reckoned with.

WC: What about the flip side of that? You say that Porgy is one of the most complex characters in opera. What about a character that is probably the least complex? You sing it, and there's not much more to do in the way of development.

SOL: Oh, I don't know of any of those. Maybe Clara in *Porgy and Bess,* who sings "Summertime." . . . But she gets dramatic at the end. She runs out, going after her husband, and she never comes back. She's going to search for him in a hurricane. All of those people in *Porgy and Bess*—Sporting Life is the only one who is obviously one-dimensional all the way through. He's a villain. He is the villain: a very wonderful part, sneaking up from behind and offering dope. A wonderful story. I'm so glad that the work has been given its rightful place; and I don't care what any bunch of Negroes, blacks, or African-Americans decide. They don't like it because it's in dialect, and it's holding us back. No. Dialect will never hold any people back. White dialect, Dogpatch, Appalachian dialect is not gonna hold people back. It's what you do with your accent and your dialect. You learn; and we should not be ashamed of anything in dialect. Those European operas that are done in dialect, they don't look down on them.

WC: What were the stimuli that triggered your interest in opera?

SOL: Maybe because my mother [Sylvia Ward Olden] was an opera singer, a recital singer, had trained for it. She was very Caucasian-looking, blond. She went to Fisk University. She sang in the choir and had this big voice. Mr.—I never met him—Cravath, Paul Cravath—the same person that I spoke about earlier—his father, Erastus Milo Cravath, at the time Mama went to Fisk with Daddy [James Clarence Olden] and Roland Hayes, was university president emeritus. The chapel at Fisk is named after him.

WC: Is it true your father sang with Roland Hayes in the Fisk Quartet?

SOL: Yes. That is correct. My mother said those abolitionists who came down to the South to found those schools gave up everything, home and friends, loved ones, to do their mission. It was just like a missionary going over to Africa. Mr. Erastus Cravath was a Quaker who went down to Nashville from Oberlin and founded Fisk. So when they got old and retired, they had no place to go back to. They just stayed there on the campus. Mr. Paul Cravath, son of Mr. Erastus, became a young Donald Trump. He left Nashville, went to New York, and made millions in no time. In about the twenties and thirties—Mr. Cravath loved music but he wasn't musical himself—[he] was on the board of the Philharmonic in New York and also the Metropolitan Opera. Got to be president of the Metropolitan's board. He would come home every holiday to see his folks. Mr. Cravath heard Mama sing—Mozart, Gounod, Bach, Haydn, and Beethoven—singing in the oratorios. Mr. Cravath was on the board at the Met, and he offered her—Mama never told me this in her whole life, but a lady came and told me ten years after Mama's death, "I was there when your mother was offered the Metropolitan Opera by Mr. Cravath at Professor Faulkner's home one Sunday afternoon. Mrs. Faulkner had told Mr. Cravath, 'She comes every Sunday to tea with us, and we'll ask some of her good pals to come also.' Sylvia, I was one of those friends. I heard that man offer your mother the Metropolitan. 'We need you. We need your type of voice. Come right up. We'll have an audition for you. The only thing [is] you've got to forget about being colored.' Your mother didn't say anything. We knew how much she loved to sing. Your mother looked around and finally said, 'I certainly appreciate this offer.' She had tears in her eyes saying, 'I want to sing, but I can't leave James.' " That was my Daddy. They were engaged.

WC: This is really a historical revelation. What year was this?

SOL: The year: 1912. And everybody who knows Harry Belafonte, that knew Daddy, says they looked like twins. In the fifties and sixties when Harry made it on Broadway, people would walk up and ask my brother for autographs. That is the way Daddy looked—very handsome, but certainly Negroid. "I told her," Mrs. Myres said, "Oh, honey, go on to New York and take your chances. Postpone the wedding for a year. Up there, they aren't so bad. You can marry James and live on the other side of town, and nobody will be the wiser. Go on, take your chances.' My mother said, 'No, I can't leave him.' Mrs. Myres said she then told the others, 'We can't do anything with her. Let's go talk to James, tell him the story, have him encourage her to go and take this opportunity. James, give this girl a break. Encourage her. She's got a chance to sing at the Metropolitan Opera. She can marry in a year or two. She's such a great singer. You tell her to go and she'll do it.' He said, 'I won't do any such thing.' And that was the end of that." I never heard any of this during Mama's lifetime; but she did continue to work, went to New York, Washington, got in the school system there. She gave recitals and went to Europe, all of those avocational things. Mama was a double major: piano and voice. I heard her playing Beethoven's *Appassionata* sonata and other major piano works. . . . [She was] vocalizing and singing great vocal literature from the time before I was born. I became a piano major. People thought that I would sing, but I really didn't desire to be a singer. My voice was so small, and I had this indoctrination from hearing Mama that if you didn't have a voice of good size you could forget about it.

WC: How did you become the Metropolitan's first black staff member? It's really ironic that your mother had an opportunity, decades ago, to sing there, and fate decreed that you become the first black staff member.

SOL: When Miss Anderson was offered and contracted by the Metropolitan and went into rehearsals, Mr. Bing said, "Sylvia, I'm giving you the first box because it was your input that first raised the issue about bringing a Negro singer on board." I let the box go to our friends—loaded it with people—and didn't save a seat for myself because I knew that I could go backstage. I was backstage all of the time, and I planned to come to the performance and just stand back there. A special notice came from Mr. Bing that day: "Due to the historical occasion of tonight's performance, there will be no one allowed in the theater who is not immediately connected with the opera. Please do not make it necessary that I enforce this." I saw that and I just . . . I went to Mr. Rudolf immediately and said, "Now I've let all of my seats go, I've waited forty years for this. Way before I was born, I was waiting for this night. Now do you have a legitimate way for me to get in, or do I have to trick myself in?" "Well, I don't know," he said. "I tried to get a ticket for Mrs. Rudolf and I couldn't get it." All right, I then went and talked to the lady on the desk. She had her earphones on when she wasn't on the telephone, being very busy buzzing people in, we talked. Robert Merrill came in. Mr. Bjørling came in. They were going upstairs to the roof to have dinner. I'm there in plenty of time. In talking with Mrs. Berry, I said, "You know they aren't going to let me go through here because I'm not necessary to tonight's performance." "Oh, I wish that I could help you." So you know what? The next time that one of those people came breezing in with his theater party, I just walked right in there with them. Went up to box one and sat on the ledge. I wasn't going to let them cheat me out of that performance.

WC: Then how did you become the Metropolitan's first black staff member?

SOL: Mr. Rudolf talked with me a lot. My husband would be studying symphony and opera with him. My husband is a violinist. He doesn't play piano, so I would be playing. I had done a lot of work with singers privately. Todd Duncan sent me his pupils for four or five years. I worked with them on arias and duets. Sometimes I had even played for Duncan, and then Mama. Mr. Rudolf took notice of my work with Everett. We both went to Tanglewood because Everett got the Serge Koussevitzky scholarship to study with Boris Goldovsky. Boris had been Everett's teacher at the Cleveland Institute of Music; he was then head of the Tanglewood Opera Department. The war was over and they had renewed their friendship. "Why don't you come to Tanglewood?" Boris said to Everett. "I'll see what I can do about it." Everett's scholarship was to be with Boris in the opera department and then to go over and do some work with Koussevitzky in the symphonic literature and [to work with] Leonard Bernstein. Everett had conducted *On the Town* for Leonard Bernstein the season before. Boris said, "Everett, you don't play piano, so bring your wife to be your hands and do your coaching." I had all of that training. Mr. Rudolf knew all of this, so he asked me to come in and join the Metropolitan staff in the Kathryn Turney Long department. I could only be there six weeks before the season and six weeks after the season because they had not allowed women in during the season. Mr. Rudolf brought me [there for] two seasons, and one of them was the season that Miss Anderson first performed.

WC: You have not only pioneered for blacks, you have also pioneered for women.

SOL: I've been back to the Metropolitan and done work with James Levine. Everett and I lived abroad—for seven years in Munich and for about eight years in Sweden. Then I was invited for one year to the University of Cincinnati. Mr. Rudolf, by this time, had left the Met and taken the Cincinnati Symphony. We had kept in touch with him, and when I was invited to Cincinnati, he said, "I have a season ticket for you, and not only that, I will fetch you every Saturday." I didn't even want to go to all of those programs, but I had to. Mr. Rudolf was with the Cincinnati Symphony for ten years. When I got to the university, it was his tenth year with the orchestra. "Sylvia," he said, "I'm leaving. Rudolf Serkin has asked if I'd come in and take the opera department at Curtis Institute. I want to, and I can have two assistants. One I'd like to be a man who would conduct when I'm not conducting, and the other I'd like to be you." I was surprised, but I went. He's still a good friend, and I've put in twenty years at Curtis. As I said earlier, I have gone back to the Met periodically. James Levine has consulted with me, and I've worked with some of the singers—privately and under the aegis of the Met. And even if they were private people, if they were [the Met's] property, I could always go to the Met and work with them. Myra Merritt comes to mind. Kathy Battle has had me do quite a bit of work with her, and Jessye Norman I knew from Howard University. Kathy and Jessye are two of the biggest Metropolitan names that I've worked with recently. Something, isn't it?

WC: Yes. We were talking about Marian Anderson. We know that Miss Anderson turned down many opportunities to sing opera in the major houses of Europe. I feel that had she taken advantage of those opportunities to sing opera in Europe, the Metropolitan could not have have kept its doors closed to her until 1955.

SOL: Even if Miss Anderson had sung opera in the houses of Europe, I believe that the Met could have kept its doors closed to her until 1955, because we had people taking advantage of European opportunities in opera: Lillian Evanti, Caterina Jarboro, Florence Cole Talbert. These people had careers over there.

WC: Yes, but what I'm thinking is that those people, none of them had the symbolic presence of Anderson in Europe or America, particularly after 1939.

SOL: They kept everybody else out. You know with Mr. [Ralph]—Dr.— Bunche, having freed those folks, whatever he did for Israel and got the Nobel Peace prize, [he] came home, couldn't build a house where he wanted to. They said, "We don't care how much money he won and what he did for Israel. We aren't having him here in Forest Hills, Long Island." What are you talking about? He certainly was a symbolic presence. But I think that we are just so glad to look back on it and see that it's gone. There's no longer a hold, symbolically, I guess, yet there are people still having difficulty. There are black singers, reportedly, from the Metropolitan's very beginning, from the time of the old house, that have had the doors closed in their faces. Now, when blacks go there to audition, I don't know whether it's all true, but some of the black people who have tried say they were told, "You are auditioning for *Porgy and Bess,* aren't you?" "No, not necessarily." "Well, we're not going to have you for anything else. There are far too . . . We have quite enough blacks at the Metropolitan." I don't know if that is true, but three or four people have reported that such happened before the last production of *Porgy and Bess,* which was a year and a half ago. That has been told.

WC: Very unfortunate, but it is not too difficult to believe.

SOL: I do think that you must go into the Metropolitan from the outside, like Jessye Norman who made her debut in *Tannhäuser* as Elisabeth at the Vienna Staatsoper (State Opera), 1970, in Berlin. Thereafter she came into the Metropolitan. But she really had to establish herself as a visual presence twenty years ago. We just don't know. The main thing, though, I want to tell all of the beautiful talents who have been studying opera and learning opera for years is that they have not really gone about it in the right way. They are not really equipped. Most of the time they are not truly equipped. An example: a boy we heard perform here at the [1991 National Association of Negro Musicians] convention was just so marvelous with his talent, and he's a decent musician, but he didn't know what he was singing about. Now, your audiences are not going to know German or Italian—couldn't care less. A small percentage of the audiences will know the foreign languages; but you're not fully able to interpret if you don't know yourself. You're just singing pretty with everything mezzo forte or forte. It is just skimmingly prepared. It makes me feel so bad. I had begun making lists of such singers: the dramatic sopranos and mezzos. Certainly we must be concerned about men's voices too, but women— [some say] that black women get by easily because they don't have the stigma of being black, of being handled by white people, because it's a white man handling a black woman—but I do have a list that has about eighteen singers on it. Two of them are white, the others are black, and they are living. If they are in Soupcreek, Arkansas, or some other place way down behind the sun—singers are in those places, too—geographically, they often have things against them. And sometimes [they suffer] monetarily. You just can't do it in some places because usually the people to provide training aren't there. But when they live in New York, New Jersey, have wonderful jobs, are struggling but continue to pinch to get those voice lessons every week . . . You ask them to sing a number at the Alpha Kappa Alpha luncheon, the Rotary Club, or even at the White House, they could come and do two or three numbers beautifully. But to be really prepared? They are not prepared. Why are they spending money and really getting the voice building done? These coaches who charge like mad, with contracts and everything. [Singers] often think that if they once get one of these big name teachers or coaches to take them on, they have got it made. You've got to know. You've got to be a thorough musician. There are many bad musicians among the whites who are in the opera houses in Europe and at the Metropolitan. You can sit with the score and see many, many, many mistakes. You don't have to do everything perfectly down to the last sixteenth note or get every accent right. Sometimes when we get Italian, it's hard converting to French. You just have to know more about what you should be doing. People often say, "Why doesn't she get a chance? She sings far better than Miss So-and-So at the Metropolitan." True. The voice sounds pretty; but it's just not at the level of dedicated scholarship. You've got to be unimpeachable as far as the printed page. I was floored when I heard a boy recently who had the most beautiful voice. He sang in the right key, three-four time, slowly and all. That's where it all ended. It was decently sung with rhythm and pitch. He didn't have a voice that was greatly divided and failing in technique. His breath support was all right, but [he] didn't know anything more beyond that. Now if he were white, he'd get away with it. Not us. All of those people who are there, at the Metropolitan—I don't know if I said this before or not—but [of] all of the black singers that have been there since Marian Anderson, there has been only *one* disappointment, and that was just a bad night for that one person. All of the rest have had beautiful voices. Whether you and I agree on every one of them is not the issue. They have at least had operatic voices. They have been trained. They have all been out of this world as far as interpretation goes. They may not have all been great actors or actresses, but they have all known what they were singing about. The story and the character, the mood of the person and how old, where the character is leading and what went on just five minutes before the aria. You don't have to buy the whole score. Go to the library and look and see and know. I don't understand why we are still dragging feet with preparation.

WC: What about the years that you spent working and studying in Europe? I'd like to hear more about that.

SOL: Oh, my. That's another whole session. I went over simply because I was Mrs. Everett Lee. I never wanted to go abroad because I don't have performance aspirations. I love accompanying and I was doing a lot of that here. I had been at the Met for a while, but I didn't ever intend to go abroad. My husband had to go there because of his area of emphasis, conducting. He was told to go abroad, so I went and took advantage of opportunities while being there. I was drawn right on in. It seemed that in many countries they were short of people who would work with singers. Also, I was called upon to work with people in concert performances and in the opera houses—in Italy when I was [on] a Fulbright there, and then in Germany where we had expected to be for only one year. The Germans told us the grant was for one year only. "Don't expect to get it renewed." It was only because of the shortness of time that I agreed to go. We got over there and everybody on the grant got an apartment by Thursday. We were two-and-a-half months without a place in Munich. No one would give us an apartment because we had children. We lived in a pension. Bonn heard about it, apologized, and told my husband that he didn't have to return to America so soon, they would give him another year. I was busy as all get out. He was busy conducting a traveling opera company, so we stayed. We were there seven more years. I was with the two opera houses in Munich [and] worked up and down Germany, spilling over into France, into Italy, Scandinavia, Yugoslavia, [performing in] some four hundred concerts.

WC: We hear a lot about typecasting. Is there any difference in the typecasting in American companies and in the European companies?

SOL: I don't see typecasting so much now. Yes, in some instances they still insist on having blacks in visible black character parts; but typecasting no longer holds true. As I said, Jessye Norman made her debut in *Tannhäuser,* not in some walk-on like the companion in *Lucia.* She was a symbol of spiritual love; and they're very particular about those things, that you look the part. Now if they put on *Aida* and have a blue-eyed blond in the title role they'll darken the complexion [and] the eyes. But then nobody cares because the singer is one of them. But with blacks, "Oh, you're not Nordic!" Jessye Norman made a beautiful Elisabeth. They had been in the habit of chalking up the faces of blacks when they were doing white parts. "Jessye," I said, "I hope they're not putting that ugly clown makeup on you." "No," she said. "I got that straight. I make myself up." She made herself up rather high, but still a good brown. . . . She went out there as Elisabeth and made a huge success and was well accepted. Blacks now are doing all parts—even here. Leontyne [Price] has done about everything—all parts. Mattiwilda Dobbs was in several operas here. Of course [Mattiwilda], she doesn't have a hue of skin that is too difficult to make look light under the lights, but you know the lights bleach out so terribly.

That's why the whites try to use a dark makeup, so they will not look like ghosts.

WC: Is there a relationship between support from the black community and opportunities for the black classical musician?

SOL: That was once a great, horrible burden. You, we blacks, had to work hard at getting help from whites. And of course, any kind of help, if we want it today, will largely come from whites. We must remember that there is not a great call for opera. People are not opera crazy, even in Europe now. I was so surprised to see in the *New York Times* about twenty years ago that only 1 percent of Italians today are truly avid about opera.

WC: That is astounding.

SOL: I said it's sad, but I guess it's true. They love opera, but not in the main like they did before. I think the world is getting smaller and they are more swing, rap, and rock crazy. They're just like right here in America. You've got people here in the metropolises who are tolerating it only because Pavarotti's doing it. It won't last long and has a certain appeal, and they can always flip it over. But to be standing in line to get in at the opera houses, it's not as much as before. It really isn't. Certainly for the size of the population. And, of course, if whites are that way, where does that leave most of us? Who invented all of the contemporary styles—rap, blues, swing, rock, bop, jazz? The world has gone crazy about that, and of course we have very little patience. When, however, you get people with a voice like Leontyne, it spills over; and the pride that we have in our own will bring us out. You can hardly make a career, though, without those big houses—crowds of whites and blacks. I must say also that we're not teaching enough black history anyway—not just in music, but in the sciences, across the board.

WC: And the black experience as it relates to the classical art forms—not just in music, but in dance, theater, film—has been largely left untouched by systematic research.

SOL: The wonderful contributions that blacks have made in this country since 1619. You see, the first blacks studying classical music didn't start right after the Emancipation Proclamation. Those planters in the South had everything going. They had string ensembles, and they were often manned by slaves. If you had a flair for classical music, and if the planter found out, he saw to it that you were educated in a certain way. Sometimes they truly loved them [the slave musicians] and would help them get going. There were many black persons doing wonderful classical music—singing, playing instruments—before the Emancipation. And this is a matter of record. We notice that [in 1992] Mr. Francis Johnson, the first professional musician in this country white or black (Mr. Johnson is, however, black) [was] hailed with a bicentennial. He supposedly composed, performed, and did a lot for the army during the War of 1812—all kinds of classical music things. He did this way back, before the 1800s. We just have to be a little bit more resourceful and let the "kids" know.

WC: The last statement really leads me to ask what other kinds of steps in the resource process can we take to make the system work more effectively for the black classical artist?

SOL: Support young blacks. But to the issue of being black: I'm one of those persons trying to get the world to be not so definitely brandish about black. It has been said that we're black if there is in blood content even a drop, or a quarter, or an eighth within the mixture of racial lineage. If we could just get "whites" to admit that there is really a very small percentage of real white, white people today. A University of Chicago president got on television and said he wondered when this world would stop fighting and making a difference in color—not color, but blood content, because there were probably, out of the whites in this country, [reputedly] only 30 percent that were *truly,* genuinely white. Now with our being proud of and supporting . . . We're not all in ghettos. There's nothing wrong with the ghetto, just see to it that you get out. But certainly if you are a moneyed black—no matter what your color is, if you're moneyed—it behooves you to see that somebody is being helped along the way, to open up doors, and support, and fight for rights, so we can get prepared along with the whites. That's all. I find so many of us who are affluent blacks . . . and now there are how many black millionaires?

WC: Quite a few.

SOL: About a thousand.

WC: Yes . . .

SOL: So what's their story? Some of them are very lovely, and they do help. Others don't quite have the money because you see the wives must have these three thousand dollar evening gowns. We have to fly orchids from Hawaii; and we have to try and compete with these gourmets and fly chitterlings and cream puffs to our resorts, and that wanton, absolute extravagance for frippery—because that's what it is—just think of what you could do to help young people who are just not in singing, but in piano, and painting, and drama. Drama is the one that's really suffering. They are still out there in Hollywood just suffering because they come and go. They've studied at these places: Yale drama school and Northwestern [and in] New York City. They've prepared and they've done the best delivery in college. What do they do when they come out? They can't get anything to do. You've worked like mad with the Greek and the Shakespearean tragedies, and you just aren't going to get a chance to do it. We need to make opportunities that way. We had the Lafayette Players in the thirties. Now

we have the Lafayette Players of the West still trying to give opportunities in drama. . . .

WC: A lot of black composers have written operas. . . . Yet, I don't know
of a single opera written by a black composer that has made it into the
mainstream of operatic repertoire. Why have we not been able to . . .?

SOL: Because no one is pushing it in there. These people are not studying to do the black idioms, styles.

WC: I'm writing an opera right now, and I'm trying to write it so that it
will be reflective of mainstream operatic writing, not ethnic opera—
not ethnic in story line or whatever, but just an opera.

SOL: You should not have to write on *Little Black Sambo* to get your
work published. We now have *Blake* [Leslie Adams, 1986]. Didn't we
have *Malcolm X* [Anthony Davis, 1985] put on by the New York City
Opera?

WC: Yes. I don't know how many performances were done.

SOL: We just have to keep on pushing. There was a Mr. Freeman. Do you
know anything about him?

WC: Yes. Harry Lawrence . . .

SOL: Wrote fourteen operas. Very romantic things.[5]

WC: He established an opera company: the Freeman Grand Opera Company.

SOL: A bunch of us put his operas on in Carnegie Hall about thirty-five
years ago, in concert version. I don't know if anybody's fighting to get
William Grant Still's *Troubled Island* [1941] put on. His *Boyou Leg-
end* [1941] was videotaped for PBS in 1979. The premier was in 1974
by Opera South.

WC: The world premiere of *Troubled Island* was done by the New York
City Opera in 1949. It was also the first of what has become that company's many American premieres. Robert McFerrin was in that production.[6]

SOL: But it wasn't taken up. Ruth Steward, my pupil, was also in that
production. Lawrence Winters had the lead.

WC: There were only three performances.

SOL: It should have been taken up from there into black communities
and put on in a big style in other cities and then forced into Chicago,
San Francisco. . . . I don't think they have anything against it—producing operas written by black composers. They might, however, look
at you, if the issue were raised, and say, "We don't put on the con-

5. See Eric Ledell Smith, *Blacks in Opera* (North Carolina: MacFarland, 1995), pp.
138–39; and Eileen Southern, *Biographical Dictionary of Afro-American and African Musicians* (Connecticut: Greenwood Press, 1962), p. 138.
6. Smith, pp. 178–79; and Southern, pp. 359–61.

temporary operas today of *white* composers either that much. It's usually the romantic—the kind that 'crowd please' from the nineteenth century." They'll throw that at you; but then they'll put on *The Crucible* [Robert Ward, 1961]. What are some of the others? *Mourning Becomes Electra* [Martin David Levy, 1967]. I'm not so quite up on it. [You see] *Susannah* [Carlisle Floyd, 1954] a lot. We just have to keep on plugging. Didn't Mr. Ulysses Kay have his *Frederick Douglass* [1983] produced recently?

WC: Yes, and Ulysses Kay has composed other operas. I have heard that some of his operas suffer because the story lines are not powerful.

SOL: Could be . . .

WC: I've heard that about the operas of several black composers. I studied screenplay writing before doing the libretto for my opera.

SOL: And you know Bob Owen of San Francisco?

WC: I know that Mr. Owen has composed at least two operas.

SOL: He's an expatriate. He lives in Munich. He has gotten his operas put on in Germany. His operas haven't been on black subjects, I think.

WC: That's interesting, and also very revealing.

SOL: And you see there were operas by black composers way back there: Mr. Saint-George . . .

WC: Chevalier de Saint-George, of course, composed several operas.

SOL: Portions of them we've performed; but very rarely have they been performed full scale. But we don't put on that many operas full scale anyway. We should put them on.

WC: It has also been recorded that Saint-George was offered the directorship of the Academie Royale de Musique, later known as the Paris Opera. The opportunity was withdrawn because he was a mulatto.[7]

SOL: I tell you, the closer we come to realizing that we're brothers, the better off all of us will be. But this sitting back, waiting, and saying, "You know she has to be good. Mr. So-and-So took her and now she's in the Met." True, but you can count them on one hand, those who can come away from the Met and keep going on with opera in other places. . . .

WC: Why isn't more written about you in the literature?

SOL: I don't know . . . I don't know. . . . But, honey, what got me was how they had a big spread in *Ebony*[8] about classical conductors, and not *one* mention of Everett Lee. Anyway, there were two people who had done a lot who were not mentioned, and Everett Lee pioneered in so many ways. They didn't even mention him. . . . He blazed trails and took a whole lot, and they didn't bother. . . . I wrote to them. The magazine is very nice. . . . I was very happy to see that they're doing things.

7. Smith, p. 164; and Southern, pp. 330–31.
8. *Ebony*, February 1989: 54t.

. . . But how could [they] have stepped over—Is it Henry Lewis or Dean Dixon that they didn't mention? And there was a Mr. Dunbar. Maybe it's because Dean Dixon is dead. Everett Lee, though, is still around, and he's still doing good work. He is the first black to conduct opera in full performance in a reputedly established house; he is the first to conduct an established symphony below the Mason-Dixon line—the Louisville Symphony. That was thirty years ago. [He was] the first one to conduct a leading hit Broadway show that was not black—on Broadway. Never said anything about it. I think because it's classical music nobody really gives it attention. The person who wrote that article on classical conductors deserves all the credit in the world; and Mr. John Johnson deserves credit for even putting it in because I'm sure they wouldn't be able to see many magazines if that was all they had. . . .

WC: I've asked a lot. I'm wondering if there are other concerns that need to be addressed.

SOL: Just trying to be in the classics, getting to a certain level and being encouraged by people who don't know—which is good, any kind of encouragement is good—but to get all of a sudden like a diva, phony and all, let that occupy your mind. That you are fooling with a medium that the ordinary man on the street can't understand. If you can't get the man on the street to understand what you're doing, as closely as you can possibly do it, then you're not going to make a career, and shouldn't. I mean if you're overgrand . . . You can be talented and also very learned, but if you get so grand that there's something mysterious about you, it doesn't work any longer. The world is getting more educated. Television has made it possible for everyone to see all the performing arts. If they put on good or bad presentations of opera, there are at least people who will have their curiosity enflamed. And phoneyness isn't going to go. It's not going to help you at all—that you're so grand, and you can't think of how to say it in English, and all that kind of . . . that's pitiful, and it's also contemptible. . . . Just learn as much as you can about the craft. Be humble about it. Be respectful for the composer, the author, and do as much as you can to bring it to what it was first conceived to be. Not, "I'm sorry, but Sylvia, I don't feel it that way." You don't have to feel it my way; but you've got to explain the phoney delivery that you're giving. Is that what the composer wanted? People don't conceive through the infinite of great works in a phoney fashion. It comes from a true being. That's just the way it is. To have it set down in a wonderful fashion, then have somebody come along and be very overgrand—thank goodness today that approach is failing. There's no place for that kind of diva any longer—diva or divo.

References

Borland, Carol, ed. 1983. *Who's who in American classical music*. New York: R. R. Bowker.

The maestros. 1989. *Ebony* February: 54t.

Smith, Eric Ledell. *Blacks in Opera*. North Carolina: MacFarland, 1995.

Southern, Eileen. *Biographical Dictionary of Afro-American and African Musicians*. Connecticut: Greenwood Press, 1962.

Dorothy Rudd Moore. *Courtesy of Dorothy Rudd Moore.*

5

Dorothy Rudd Moore:
With Whom the Score Begins

The compositions of Dorothy Rudd Moore have been performed throughout the United States, in Europe, in South America, and Asia. "The most arresting feature of Ms. Moore's music is an original and often intense lyricism that pervades even the most complex harmonic and contrapunal textures." *The New York Times* has additionally said of her music, ". . . a gifted and creative mind at work."

Born on June 4, 1940, in New Castle, Delaware, Ms. Moore is a 1963 magna cum laude graduate of Howard University, where she studied composition with Mark Fax and piano with Thomas Kerr; majored in music theory and composition; and minored in voice and piano. After graduation from Howard, a Lucy Moten Fellowship made it possible for her to study composition with Nadia Boulanger at the Conservatoire de Musique in Fontainebleau, France. Ms. Moore, upon her return to the United States, studied composition privately with Chou Wen Chung of Columbia University in New York City. Currently teaching voice, sight-singing, and ear-training in a New York studio, Ms. Moore has also held teaching positions at Harlem School of the Arts, New York University, and Bronx Community College.

In addition to the Lucy Moten Fellowship, Dorothy Rudd Moore has received grants from the American Music Center, New York State Council of the Arts, and Meet the Composer. A cofounder of the Society of Black Composers, Ms. Moore served on the music panel of the New York State Council of the Arts from 1988 to 1990; the Wisconsin Arts Board, in November 1990, composer competition; the Illinois Arts Council, Composer Panel, November 1987; and two National Endowment for the Arts panels, music recording 1986–1988, and composer panel 1988. Dorothy Rudd Moore is a member of American Composers Alliance, BMI, New York Singing Teachers Association, and New York Women Composers. Ms. Moore resides in New York City with her husband, the cellist and conductor Kermit Moore. In this conversation, Dorothy Rudd Moore, from a very keen perspective, talks about the world of a composer in general, and the world of a black composer in particular.

Wallace Cheatham: Many operas, from the time of Chevalier de Saint George, have been done by black composers; yet there isn't a single opera of a black composer in the active repertory to my knowledge. Also, there are not that many concert works of black composers performed; yet many have been written. Why? Is it just racism?

Dorothy Rudd Moore: I know many black composers, including myself, whose works have been performed over a long period of time. As one of the founders of the Society of Black Composers in the late sixties, I became aware of the activity of black composers across the country. Of course, there are many white composers whose works are not in the "active repertoire," if by that you mean works performed with the frequency of eighteenth- and nineteenth-century composers. So far as opera is concerned, companies basically stick to the well-known operas for a variety of reasons. Racism, of course, exists in all aspects of this society. So does fiscal conservatism, as well as the comfort of the tried and true. Opera is a huge, costly undertaking, and given the financial support the arts receive in this country, it is difficult for any composer to get a commitment from a company to commission and/or perform an opera.

WC: How has the "super nigger syndrome" been reflected in opportunities for the black composer?

DRM: I have no knowledge concerning this question. In any case, I would give the term no consideration.

WC: Would you speak to the kinds of creative qualities that a composer must have to write a work for the lyric theater?

DRM: The most important aspect, initially, in undertaking such a monumental task is the *desire* to do it. After that, is is all hard work. One can't delineate "creative qualities." Whatever the medium, one brings her, or his, own creative energies into play. It goes without saying that to write an opera requires knowledge in several areas: the voice, theater, orchestration, etc. Musical training, research of subject matter, and a sense of drama are essential elements, of course.

WC: I know of one opera that bears your name as composer: *Frederick Douglass.* Would you speak analytically to this work and to its performance history?

DRM: *Frederick Douglass* was commissioned by Opera Ebony and was premiered in New York City in June 1985. It is full-length opera in three acts, for which I wrote the music and libretto. It is based on Douglass's own "Narrative," as well as other books on his life and works. It covers the period from his life in Massachusetts as an abolitionist to the Emancipation Proclamation. It consists of many scenes, and includes a ballet. The opera has been very well received, with favorable reviews by *The New York Times, Opera News,* and *The Amsterdam News.* Opera Ebony continues to perform scenes from the opera, here in the United States, in Europe, and in the

Caribbean. The cast is large, with black and white characters, and racially mixed choruses.

WC: What were the stimuli that motivated you to become a composer?

DRM: My interest in music began as a child. My mother was a singer and played piano as well. I had piano lessons and sang in school and church choirs. I also played clarinet in the band and orchestra in high school, where I also had music theory classes. During high school, I continued my piano lessons at Wilmington School of Music. I also attended concerts of the Philadelphia Orchestra, which I greatly enjoyed. I majored in music theory and composition at Howard University. My composition teacher was Mark Fax. I also sang in the Howard University Choir under Dean Warner Lawson. After graduation, I studied at the American Conservatory in Fontainebleau, France, with Nadia Boulanger.

WC: If one hopes to get any real recognition as a composer, are there certain genres that must be explored and conquered?

DRM: A composer should write what appeals to her or him. The emphasis should be on the composition, and the integrity of the work. No matter what the genre, or how large or small the medium, one should not think in terms of "recognition," though one always hopes for performances. Often, composers are prompted by commissions, and the interaction between performers and composers is important. I don't think in terms of "conquering" genres, as such a notion is antithetical to my concept of artistic creation. It does seem, however, that the larger forms—orchestral works, opera, etc.—command attention.

WC: In composing *Frederick Douglass,* what aspect did you find most difficult? Why? What aspect did you find easiest?

DRM: My opera *Frederick Douglass* was a long project, and a labor of love. The man himself has always interested me, and I had read his autobiography long before I ever knew I would write an opera about him. Altogether, from the research, to the writing of the "book," to the libretto, composing, orchestration, etc., the project took eight years. Creating is an organic process, and as such, its components cannot be divided into "easy and difficult." It is all work. The only "easy" thing would be sharpening the pencils!

WC: What about other genre? The score that was most difficult to compose, the easiest.

DRM: My cello sonata "Dirge and Deliverance," which I wrote for my husband, Kermit Moore, and was premiered in Alice Tully Hall in New York City in 1972, was a challenge because I do not play the cello. Of course, I studied the possibilities of the instrument. The work is virtuosic for the cello and the piano. However, I consider every composition to be a challenge.

WC: You have composed in many genres. Do you have a favorite medium of composition? Why?

DRM: I like writing for strings. In addition to "Dirge and Deliverance," I have written a string quartet, a duo for viola and cello, a piano trio, and a work for violin and piano. I also enjoy writing for the voice, and have composed several song cycles with strings and one with oboe. I also have written a clarinet sonata and a theme and variations for piano. In addition to chamber works, I have also written a symphony and a work for symphonic wind ensemble. There is also a work for chorus and orchestra. In essence, I enjoy composing in any area.

WC: Has your proficiency as a singer influenced your approach to composition?

DRM: Being a singer has given me an understanding of how to write for the voice and to set texts. In general, it aids in the writing of melodic lines, as well as development of thematic material.

WC: Is there a kind of typecasting for the black composer? If so, how is it played out?

DRM: There is no such thing as "the black composer." We are all different. I am not aware of any "typecasting" in any case, and no composer that I know would permit such a thing.

WC: Is there a relationship between support from the black community and opportunities for the black composer?

DRM: African-Americans, like any other group, are vast and various in their musical tastes and appreciation. In the "classical" field, black organizations and performance groups that show interest in the work of black composers can provide opportunities for performance. In the final analysis, composers must continue to find opportunities for performances and should not be limited by race.

WC: What steps can be taken to make "the system" work more effectively for the black composer?

DRM: Composing is a solitary undertaking for any composer. First of all, one has to write the music and then have contact with performers and presenting organizations. As in any field, one must continue to work and make opportunities for the music to be performed. Also, the composer must know how to apply for grants and be aware of arts organizations. College and university music departments could do more to make the works of black composers known.

WC: What can we expect for programming the scores of black composers as we approach the twenty-first century?

DRM: It is important that black composers not be ghettoized. Unfortunately, certain forces are intent on polarizing our society, and creative people are affected as much as anyone else. Funding on federal and local levels must be increased, and audiences must be cultivated. Music in the schools is essential so that children become aware of the many kinds of music that exist, and not only what they hear in the popular medium. In other words, the programming of works of any composer depends on the health of our musical institutions and financial support that mandates inclusion of all whose works have artistic merit.

WC: Is there a subject, play, or novel that you would particularly like to set as an opera?

DRM: I have begun working on another opera, based on the story of "Phaedra," set in nineteenth-century America.

WC: Is there a concern or are there concerns dealing with the African-American experience as it relates to the classical arts that you would like to address?

DRM: "The African-American experience" is too narrow and limiting a term. There are many black artists in all disciplines, and each is an individual with his or her unique experiences. We must not allow others to dictate what we should create nor succumb to the notion that black artists have legitimacy only when dealing with the pathology of what politicians and bureaucrats like to call "the inner city ." Such myopia deprives people of their humanity and unique vision. African-Americans, like anyone else, should be free to express their art through the prism of their own creativity, and to celebrate their totality, without self-consciousness and without imposed restrictions.

New York, New York
1994

Benjamin Matthews. *Courtesy of Benjamin Matthews.*

6

Benjamin Matthews and Wayne Sanders:
And the Dream Became Reality
to Dwell with Us

Opera Ebony represents the greatest single success among opera companies that have been founded by African-Americans. Much of this phenomenon can be attributed to the instrumentalities of two very highly distinguished black men, Benjamin Matthews and Wayne Sanders.

Born in Mobile, Alabama, Mr. Matthews studied at the Chicago Conservatory and received his operatic training under Boris Goldovsky. In recital, concert, and opera, Mr. Matthews has performed around the world to critical acclaim.

Born in Chicago, Illinois, Mr. Sanders studied at the Chicago Musical College of Roosevelt University and the Chicago Conservatory. An impeccable pianist, Mr. Sanders has coached, performed in recitals, concerts, and opera, and recorded with many international personalities.

In this conversation, these two very knowledgeable and artistic black men speak to the very soul of what makes the African-American experience as it relates to opera so very unique. Bravo!

Wallace Cheatham: Your advertisement describes Opera Ebony as "An American Dream Come True." What would you like for this dream to be in 1998, the year of your twenty-fifth anniversary? I find it to be "sweet irony" that this milestone will be reached two years before the beginning of a new century.

Benjamin Matthews: I would like to see Opera Ebony be a repertoire company. By that I mean a company with a set season of three or four operas, with three or four performances of each, and a full permanent staff—administratively or otherwise. We have not quite accomplished all of that yet. We still have great difficulty with funding. We still have many things to overcome. As a black opera company, we have our unique problems with the funding agencies and so forth. So we haven't quite come to that yet. But we're working on it. And I would like to see that part of the dream come true.

Wayne Sanders: And along with that, I would like to see the center, the building, the places where we could continue to practice our craft, and to find our truth in our own wonderful surroundings.

Wayne Sanders. *Courtesy of Wayne Sanders.*

BM: And what do we mean by seeing Opera Ebony have its own center? We're speaking of our own orchestra and a permanent cadre of singers that we can identify as our own chorus. In the meantime, we're like many of the opera companies. We go into the community. We call the experts and the contractors. We get what we need and put on our productions.

I would like to see us permanently have a space that we call our home. A space that belongs to us, housing our offices with all of our business transactions there. I can even visualize a small performing theater being there. Not necessarily one where we would put on our big productions, but certainly one that would allow us to do productions on a certain scale.

If a larger theater is there where we could put on our big productions with orchestra, all of the lighting and equipment, that would be fine, too. The year of our twenty-fifth anniversary might be pushing it a little bit; however, there are angels out there. And maybe one will come along who will give us this. There are certainly people out there with the kind of money to establish us in this way.

WC: When the histories of opera companies established by African-Americans are studied, we find that Opera Ebony is the brightest light among them in longevity and productivity. What did you do? What have you done? And what are you doing that was, has been, and is being overlooked by others?

BM: Perhaps in many ways, we have done nothing that was so different from some of the others. I would think that our main difference has been the willingness to sacrifice. The willingness to personally sacrifice. For instance, it is very difficult to start a company like Opera Ebony, to have a dream, to understand and visualize what you would like to accomplish, and not put yourself first on the payroll with a high salary. We didn't go about it that way. We were willing to sacrifice. We had a certain expertise. We knew how it could be done. And we set out to do it. We put the production first, unselfishly first in every respect.

WS: And I find that unselfish part is crucial for me. It allowed us to have a singular vision. We agreed and disagreed. But we had a singular vision. We kept this in mind at all times. We gave priority to what was good for the production along with what was good for the artist performing in the production. This always stayed in the forefront. I find when people are not afraid of each other, and when they trust each other, something very important happens. I might even say something very spiritual happens. This allows us to bring who we are to bear on the music. I think that's what we've really done. It's a coming together in an unselfish way. And having a joy in what you are doing. Without the joy, the sacrifice becomes too heavy and very hard to do.

BM: One of our first priorities has been to keep the company with a good name. I've always felt that this was so very important. This goes back to the unselfishness and the sacrifice; paying the artists so that they won't gossip and talk about you, and spread your name all over town. Not only all over town, but, telephones being as they are, it would be from coast to coast within days. Make sure that your orchestra is paid. We put those priorities above carving out a salary for ourselves. This is what we did. We protected the company's good name. When the production is over, pay the orchestra. When the production is over, pay the people from whom you have rented your space. Keep a good reputation for your financial responsibilities.

Money has torn up most of our fine organizations. Most of them that fell apart had to do with money—either by not paying the bills, or the money getting mixed up and not being properly accounted for. Accountability! Maintain a good name so that you can be trusted with the artists and those people who are supporting you. This has been one of the main things that we have been very careful about. Perhaps many others did not quite take that kind of care. But this has certainly been our priority.

WC: How did you come up with the name Opera Ebony?

BM: When Opera Ebony was founded, we naturally had to come up with a name because we have to be incorporated. We came up with several names. And of course, we chose one.

Sister Elise [Sister Mary Elise was a Caucasian nun: a member of the Sisters of The Blessed Sacrament. Sister Elise, for many years, was a professor of music at Xavier University in New Orleans, Louisiana] impressed upon me that she wanted us to have a national company, and that "National" should definitely be a part of our name. Of course, many names were already out there. An organization can so easily be rejected when applying to the Secretary of State for incorporating a company. We sent in the first name and it was rejected. So we chose another name. And I said to Sister Elise, "Why don't we call it Opera Ebony." Then she chimed in, "National Opera Ebony." I think that's a good name.

I had thought of something that would identify Opera Ebony as a black company. And ebony being so beautiful and black, I thought of the beauty of the wood, the beauty of the thing that we were doing, and the beauty of these things that we were doing, and the beauty of these things we wanted to accomplish, and so I came up with the name Opera Ebony.

We could not incorporate the company as "National Opera Ebony" because somehow they found some conflicts with the word "National." So we incorporated as Opera Ebony, Inc. Since we no longer have any ideas about spreading Opera Ebony all over the country as

National Opera Ebony, we are known by our founding name, as Opera Ebony. And it was I, Benjamin Matthews, that came up with that name for the company, as one of its founders.

Interestingly, even without the name all over the country, we find that people are taking it anyway. Using the name when it has nothing to do with us. They have never contacted this office about using the name. People who are certainly not a part of our organization. We've been given the understanding that some of them are presenting things on the level of very amateurish workshops. But since this is being done from California to Texas, to Virginia, and all around, we certainly cannot spend all of our time running around trying to put a lawsuit against all of these people. Perhaps some of them will succeed and find an identity for themselves. And the others will just eventually diminish and no longer be around to give us a bad name. We are not of the financial means to sue everyone who wants to attach Opera Ebony's name to what they're doing. So for the most part, we just let it be and hope all things will take care of themselves.

WS: Yes, at first I did find it very problematic for me that we would spend the kind of time, energy, work, and money that it takes to present high-quality productions from the ground up, and then have other people, our folks, our black folks, just lift the name, change it around slightly, and put "Guild" in front of it or after it. It's more than bothersome. But again, what has gotten us through is the uniqueness of what we are doing, and what we have done, has shown the world that it can be done. It is just a little bit unfortunate that a lot of people are not willing to start from the ground up and to do the sacrificing. It's an interesting phenomenon; maybe at another time we'll talk more about that.

BM: There's one thing that I really would like to touch upon and clarify with Opera Ebony's name being scattered and pulled in so many different directions. This is one of the reasons that we fought so hard, and even went to court when the Philadelphia group wanted to basically disassociate themselves from the founding company and still maintain the name of Opera Ebony. This came about after Opera Ebony had put on ten years of productions in Philadelphia under the name of Opera Ebony Philadelphia.

When they decided that they wanted artistic autonomy, to have no connection with the New York group, and keep the name at the same time, then of course we fought that. It was an unfortunate and extensive court battle trying to get those things settled and we eventually did. The Philadelphia group changed its name after we went into court and put forth a lot of force and effort. This was a very unfortunate event. We maintained the name, but so far as anyone winning anything, there were no winners.

The only thing that was realized out of it was the fact that so many times our black people can come together and be one and form something good and something strong. But there's always some one to two people in there to mess it up and to tear it up. They let their personal egos get in the way and just tear down and destroy something that is very beautiful. This kind of thing among us is still very unfortunate.

I feel that whenever there are black people, and wherever there is a community of black people in this country, somehow I feel that I am a part of that community and I can identify with that community. Whatever good, and whatever expertise I have, I am willing to share and to be a part of what is going on there for the uplifting of ourselves as a people, as one unified community throughout the country. Many don't feel this way, and it is their prerogative to feel however they feel, or do what they do. I just want to be on the record as to how I feel and how Opera Ebony feels about the oneness that we should have in working together and cooperating with each other.

WS: Right. I think that's important, Ben, to say the least. And I think you should know that every production that has gone on, from the very beginning since 1973, has been under Ben's artistic direction, and myself as music director. I think that says something too—that we as black men can hang in there for so long together and work for something that has proved to be a force that the world over is now recognizing.

WC: The four founders of Opera Ebony, how did you meet and formulate an idea for something so unique?

BM: We met Sister Elise. Sister Mary Elise. A nun who, interestingly, founded the music department at Xavier University. She was one of the nuns who belonged to the Sisters of the Blessed Sacrament, founded by Mother Katherine Drexel.

The sisters of the Blessed Sacrament dedicated their lives to the purpose of educating blacks and Native Americans. They, having founded and established Xavier University, sent Sister Elise there to Xavier in 1935 to form a music department. Out of that music department, Sister began to produce operas on campus. From those campus operas, they began to grow so big that each year she began going to the big auditorium in New Orleans for the production. Upon her retirement around 1970 or 1971, she was quite an energetic person and was not going to give up. She was not near ready to retire. So she went to Jackson, Mississippi.

There she formed Opera South and stayed there and worked with Opera South until 1973. In 1973, she retired. Something happened there and they forced Sister's resignation. That was the kind of retirement that she got from Opera South. In other words, they pushed her out.

She came to the Mother House in Philadelphia and to New York to visit Wayne Sanders, myself, and her friends here. She told me the story of what went down at Opera South. So I suggested to her, "Sister, why don't we form an opera company here in New York?" She asked if I thought we really could do it. Of course my answer was yes. I think we can. This was in the summer of 1973.

Sister went home for a month or so, and then she returned to ask me what I felt the first steps should be in getting the opera company going that we were talking about. Then she and I met with Wayne Sanders and some others: Mr. Ernest George, Margaret Harris, and Alfa Floyd. We had a big discussion about it, and decided that we should incorporate. But we met Sister at Opera South. I was there singing as one of her artists. Wayne Sanders went there as one of the pianists to help her prepare the singers, and Margaret Harris went there as a conductor. We got together here in New York after Sister left Opera South, and we formed Opera Ebony to carry on the work here in the North. Our idea was to have a sister company to the one that was there in Jackson, Mississippi. That's how we met, and that's how we came about formulating our company.

WC: How is a season for Opera Ebony planned?

WS: As you can imagine, because of financing we have to find many unique ways to do it. Ben and I were just discussing our mission. Keeping that in mind when we plan a season is important. For me, that means not only the standard operas, but a lot of the minority operas that have not been done, and a lot of the black operas like those by William Grant Still. In fact, one of Mr. Still's operas was used for our debut here in New York. Our very first opera here was William Grant Still's *U.S.A. Highway 1*. We definitely are committed to minority composers, American composers, period, but a special emphasis on our minority composers. So we always keep that in mind when we're planning a season, and try to incorporate that.

If we don't put on a main opera, then we will do scenes and excerpts with orchestra in between some of the bigger works. Because we're reaching out to a very wide and diverse audience here in New York City and the surrounding areas, it's important that we have the kind of works that will pull and embrace the entire community. Works that will have great dramatic flair. We do a lot of our productions in English, not all of them, but some of them to reach out to that diverse audience. Many times if we have a tragedy, say for instance like Menotti's *The Medium,* then we'll balance that later with a witty something like Mozart's *Cosi Fan Tutte* so that we keep it very much in check. Ben, do you want to add something?

BM: No, no, you covered that pretty well.

WS: That's generally how we plan it. We have *Young Artist Concerts* that we do every year with a lot of the up-and-coming artists. We take excerpts from five or six different operas. We bring in a stage director, choreographer, and orchestra, and do staged scenes. These have become real highlights, and audiences seem to really like them.

WC: Who are some of the technicians, designers, choreographers, and conductors who have been engaged by Opera Ebony?

WS: There was Janet Bookspan who directed *Carmen* and *La Traviata* for us. There was George Faison who in 1990 directed our world premiere of *The Outcast.* Also Ward Flemming, who passed away about four years ago. Ward Flemming was a black choreographer and dancer who had his own dance company in Germany. We met him through Felicia Weathers. Ward decided to stay here in New York and to help Opera Ebony. We introduced him to full-time stage directing. So we feel very special about him. Ward directed Opera Ebony's *Faust, Sojourner Truth* by Valerie Capers, and the special show that we do with spirituals and dance called *Journin'.* He also directed our world premiere of *Frederick Douglass.* Felicia Weathers, who is living in . . . Where does Felicia now live, Ben?

BM: Munich.

WS: Felicia had her directing debut here. She had never directed anyplace. Am I right, Ben?

BM: Yes!

WS: We gave Felicia her debut. She directed *Il Trovatore,* for Opera Ebony in Philadelphia, and *Madama Butterfly* in New York. She also directed *Porgy and Bess* with us when we participated in the Rio de Janeiro production. She is quite a wonderful director. I think I mentioned George Faison directing our world premiere of *The Outcast.* Henry Miller directed our *Lost In the Stars.* Darryl Croxton directed our *Impresario* at the Beacon Theater. Duane Jones directed our *Medium,* Menotti's *The Medium* at the Beacon Theater.

A very well-known director, James Lucas, directed our *Figaro.* Franco Gratale directed our *Carmen,* and there are many, many, many more; but these are some. Frank Gentelesca directed many productions for us, including *Rigoletto* and *Traviata.*

Some of our lighting persons have been Bill Grant and Ron Burns. Ron Burns is the resident lighting designer; he is also an incredible set person—he builds sets as well, at Aaron Davis Hall. He's on staff there. Ron has done many of our things there in the Hall. Also, we're very proud of Hope Clarke, who began her opera stage directing career with Opera Ebony directing many performances, including *Cosi Fan Tutte, The Impresario, The Medium, Porgy and Bess,* and many others both in the States and abroad.

One particular costume person that we're very excited about because we introduced him to making and designing costumes for the opera world is Larry McClammy. We introduced him to it and now he's making costumes full time. He's really quite wonderful and we consider him one of our discoveries. Conductors, of course, there's Everett Lee, who still is conducting for us and has conducted many, many of our major productions. Everett will be going with us to Iceland in November to conduct our Heritage Concert with the Iceland Symphony. This will be a return engagement.

Henry Lewis conducted *Carmen* for us. Margaret Harris conducted our debut performance here in New York of William Grant Still's *U.S.A. Highway 1*. Byrne Camp, who is deceased, conducted many things for us, including Mozart's *Figaro*. Paul Freeman conducted Menotti's *The Medium* and Mozart's *Impresario*. Leslie Dunner has conducted many things for us, including a lot of our Young People's Concerts, and most recently he conducted our full production of Mozart's *Cosi Fan Tutte*. Warren Wilson has also conducted many productions for us as well: *Samson et Dalila;* he's conducted *Figaro*. Did he conduct *Faust,* Ben?

BM: Yes, he conducted *Faust* and the world premiere of *Frederick Douglass*.

WS: Oh! I want to mention Eri Clas. He is from Estonia, and he made his American debut with us in Harlem conducting Opera Ebony's *Verdi Requiem*. He is a world-class conductor and known all over the world. But he had never conducted here in the States. He also conducted our *Porgy* when we did a coproduction with the National Opera Company of Finland. We met and things went well. He wanted to come to the States. We wanted him, and it was quite a wonderful evening.

WC: Would you speak to the role of music director? What are the steps of preparation?

WS: I think perhaps I go about it . . . somewhat differently from other people in that the music preparation has so much to do with the total preparation of the artists: the mind, the body, and the spirit. It's not just learning the notes or talking about the phrasing. It's helping the artist to dig underneath the character, being able to honestly, if need be, correct some things that they are doing vocally or musically.

So I spend actually many months meeting with the singers, talking through the part, and breaking it down very slowly. That slow depth preparation is crucial. The artists must have lived with the role, slept with the role, eaten with the role. They must know it inside out. They must know what they're capable of doing and what they are not capable of doing in order to bring the best of what one has to offer. That way it is not overwhelming.

WC: How does the role of artistic director differ from the role of music director? How do you prepare to be artistic director of a production?

BM: The music director is in charge of, and is responsible for, all music—all of those things that pertain to music and the music delivered from the stage. He is responsible for choosing the repertoire, including the person who is chosen to conduct the repertoire. That person is chosen to be in charge of the orchestra. He's in charge of choosing the musical staff that will help to coach and musically prepare the artists.

The artistic director is in charge of all artists, at least he's supposed to be, from the singers on. It can be rather touchy sometimes and problematic between the music director and the artistic director. Many companies have resolved this problem by making the music director also the artistic director, hoping they will make out better and run into much, much less conflict.

To give you a good example, a music director would be in charge of the conductor. He would be the one who basically chooses that conductor. An artistic director would be in charge of the stage director. Then if there is conflict and disagreement as to what is going on with the music and what is going on with the staging, it's not so easy sometimes to have two people resolve that in the same manner. It can even come to the point that one may want to leave the production if the problems cannot be resolved. This could bring the music director and the artistic director into conflict. Because the artistic director can say, "My stage director is not going to leave!", and the music director could say, "Well, my conductor is certainly not going."

This can be a very touchy thing with the artistic director being in charge of the artists. He might find reasons to find a certain artist very weak in his artistic opinion. That artist may not be prepared and is messing up the production, or cannot memorize and is throwing off everyone around them. Then one would have two people very much in agreement, working very, very closely together. They would have to come together on how to solve these problems. So the function can be very interrelated, so interrelated that it can cause lots of conflicts within a company. It can, depending on how powerful they are.

It's like having two gods reigning over one heaven; two bosses over one big production. It also can bring conflict within your board of directors. This kind of thing can interrupt an entire organization. It's very tricky. Yet these two functions are different.

Your location can determine what those responsibilities and job descriptions are. In the old European tradition, the artistic director was basically chief. In the American tradition, that is not necessarily so. The music director can be chief and in charge of all. Unless these differences are clearly outlined and these job descriptions are very well in place, you need a knowledgeable board to know what to do in case of conflicts. However, it is dangerous for a board or administration of business to try to tell the artistic director or music director how to do their jobs. Such actions will surely cause a company to fail!

As for preparing to be artistic director of a production, one really does not prepare to be that. You're either an artistic director and you have the knowledge of your job and know how to be an artistic director, or you just don't know. This comes through experience, knowledge of repertoire, knowledge of artists, keeping an ear constantly open for artists, even for things that you don't even plan to do yet, knowing how things work backstage, knowing who's to be in charge of what happens backstage.

The artistic director has to know his way through the entire production in every artistic sense. This, of course, is his job. He must know how to do it! The good one gains a lot of understanding from being on stage in performances. Having an idea of the whys and wherefores; having knowledge of things that can be done and things that cannot be done; a knowledge of things that ought to be executed, and knowing his way into exactly how they can be executed.

He needs a very sharp eye for resolving problems. He needs a very sharp eye for discerning when a particular member of his staff is lost or stuck. He needs the temperament to know how to talk with that person. He needs to let that person know that he is there for him or her in case he is needed. An artistic director is supposed to have the intelligence and the knowledge to choose his staff, put that staff in place, expect that staff and these directors to do their job, check to see that the job is being done, and then stay out of the way. Stay out of their way. Do not try to tell a director how to direct. Only if the artistic director is called upon because of a problem in a certain area, only then should he step in to give any suggestions in any way.

This is how I have done it. And this is how most artistic directors do it. This is how we find success in putting on the productions that we put on. I guess that's enough about that.

WS: And let me add one other thing. I think what makes Ben and me as music and artistic directors work so well is that my background is also dance, drama, and voice. I have performed in all of those areas. There's a lot of good give-and-take between Ben and me. We know enough about all of the facets. We know when to sometimes release one. Not everyone can do that. It's not about what the book says music and artists directors will be or should be. But somehow we've managed to not let egos get in the way. It works for us that way, with a kind of flexibility.

WC: Of the many operas that you have prepared, which one was the most difficult musically and artistically? Why? The least difficult musically and artistically? Why?

BM: That might appear to be a long question. But it's really not a difficult question at all. The most difficult operas that we've mounted were naturally the world premieres and new productions. These are the ones that test your creativity and your expertise because there are no models. There is nothing to be copied from anyone else. These are yours. You make it live. It will either succeed or it will falter. We did not find *Frederick Douglass* or *The Outcast*—which were extremely different, not only in their story lines but in their musical structure, in their style—difficult at all. We found them the most interesting creatively because we had to create everything—the sets, the costumes, the lighting designs. Everything to come from scratch. Naturally, these gave us the most artistic and musical challenges. The least difficult were those that we have seen over the years, some that I have even performed in over the years, even though, for the most part, I did not perform in Opera Ebony productions.

I knew my way through these operas, and we would have a very keen sense of who we should put in charge of mounting or conducting these operas. We have not run into anything that was beyond our reach, beyond our imagination, or beyond our knowledge as to how it should be done, how it should sound, and how it should look.

WS: And I think, adding to that just a little note, the reason that I didn't find it difficult, in the sense of the word, is that both Ben and I took a lot of time and care in choosing the artists who were right for a particular role. Just because an artist has a voice, even a beautiful voice, does not mean that he can sing every opera; for instance, Noa Ain's *The Outcast*. A jazz opera requires trained singers, but they must be flexible singers who can improvise, but have the vocal range. If you put the right people in the right roles, it eliminates a lot of problems. I think that's one of the keys to success.

WC: How would one define black opera?

BM: Now that's a tricky one in my opinion, because people have been trying to define black music and black opera, particularly black music, for the past twenty-five years. I have never seen a definition of black music or black opera that you really could not punch holes through, depending on which direction you were coming from. An opera written by a black composer, on black subject matter, and performed by a black company with black artists, and everything black from back wall to the entrance door, this would come closest to defining a black opera for me. I haven't run across that even with Opera Ebony in my lifetime.

WS: *Sojourner* would be the closest, *Sojourner Truth*.

BM: *Sojourner Truth* would be the closest, on Black subject matter.

WS: Orchestra was black, singers were black.

BM: . . . with the orchestra black and the singers black, and the conductor black, and the composer black, that would be about the closest thing we could come to in defining black opera. Then someone might come and say, "Well, did you play it on black instruments?" What is a black instrument? How can you have a black opera with a piano involved? The piano came from Europe, you know. There are so many different directions you could take it, and then say the only way you could make *Sojourner* a black opera would be to do it with a few African instruments and some bongo drums. Then it's black and only then is it black. There are lots of arguments to be made so far as black opera is concerned. I even wonder if a "black opera" could really come out of our multicultural society. I wonder about that. If I really wanted to get technical about it, and if anyone else wanted to really get technical about it, they could also question these things. But as I said, *Sojourner,* our description of *Sojourner,* with its subject matter and all of the aforementioned considered would come closest to what we consider a black opera.

WS: Right. You've covered it. Another way perhaps to look at that, something that you probably wouldn't see but you would feel, as we discussed a long time ago with Sister Elise, Ben and I. Don't lose the soul and spirit of the black man, no matter what the opera is that is being done. Let that come through. That can be many, many things. But don't lose ourselves, don't lose our sense of inflection and rhythm, those special things that make us black persons. That's one way to look at it. I know that's not defining black opera. But for me, it's not losing ourselves, no matter what the work is.

WC: How has the life of the black opera singer changed since the founding of Opera Ebony?

BM: There have been some changes since the founding of Opera Ebony. Many things have been done through the years that have made it a little bit better, or created a little bit more work for the black opera singers. We were founded in 1973. And in mounting our operas, in getting reviews, very fine reviews, our work was very strong and highly successful. We found many of the established opera companies wondering, and even coming to us to ask how we put on productions like that. How could we generate that kind of excitement? Interestingly, many of the established companies began to put on operas either utilizing more blacks or putting on all-black productions of this or that opera. They would put on all-black productions within their seasons to see what they could generate and if they could get some kind of response, or if they could get that kind of excitement going.

It is since the founding of Opera Ebony that *Porgy and Bess* began to take its place in the standard repertoire. This was one of the operas that they would use to involve blacks in their seasons. They would tour it all over the country. It is since the founding of Opera Ebony that the established companies began to take an interest in and revive

Treemonisha and to tour that all over the country. Year after year since about 1976, the established companies have been going from *Porgy and Bess,* to *Showboat,* to *Treemonisha,* and some other works. So I feel, yes, I pretty much know for a fact that these things were done and created work and outlets for the black artists due to the success of Opera Ebony.

Our national companies began to hire more black artists and mix them in because they would come and see that once the artist was involved with the music and the character, one really does not see black on the stage. I as artistic director of Opera Ebony have sat and watched our productions without thinking black at all. When we put on *Figaro,* we saw and heard *Figaro.* When we put on *Carmen,* we saw and heard *Carmen; Il Trovatore,* we saw and heard *Il Trovatore; Madam Butterfly,* we saw and heard *Madama Butterfly.*

The drama, the music, respect for the style, the characterization, the costuming, we were transformed beyond a color line. Opera Ebony's productions caused the established companies to see and to realize that there's basically no black and white once the curtain is raised. The performers are the character. There have been lots of changes, and there have been doors opened more freely to black artists. Because of Opera Ebony, there have been some very positive changes. Wayne . . . .

WS: Just a little bit. You said a lot of the things that I was thinking. A lot of artists have been heard in our productions by people who were in a position to also hire them. We've had singers get recording contracts from people who heard them in our operas. We've taken singers who had never been outside of the States to Europe, and other jobs have followed.

It's really quite exciting to see that Opera Ebony has made a difference that way, too, in the lives of these singers, in their employment, in the connections to other people that could help them further. It makes me feel really good to know that something starting from a dream has affected so many lives in so many ways.

It's really quite something to reflect upon. Even as I'm talking about it, because I don't normally stop and reflect on that. As Ben was talking, I thought of Rita McKinley who made her debut with us in the role of Bess in *Porgy and Bess* in Finland, Estonia, and Moscow. She had started out in the chorus in Philadelphia and worked her way through and received incredibly wonderful reviews. They called her the young Leontyne. I think that is quite a change in a life.

BM: And, too, many of the artists that have worked with Opera Ebony learned stage right from stage left, upstage from downstage, by being involved in Opera Ebony productions. Some of them who came to us did not know, figuratively speaking, that you could chew gum and walk at the same time. They learned how to sing and how to act at the same time in Opera Ebony's chorus, and by taking small roles that demanded them to act. From there, they went on to bigger things. Many of the artists who were more professional learned big roles and performed them first with Opera Ebony and then went on to other houses to perform them later. It was a great opportunity for them to have this advantage because so many times an artist can go for an audition and will sing a role for a conductor and a stage director. But if they have not done that particular role, regardless of how good they are, the conductor and stage director will not entrust the role to that artist.

Many times the conductor and stage director have the time to hone an artist into having some kind of idea about what they're doing. Sometimes the conductor and the stage director have only two weeks of rehearsals, or three weeks of rehearsals. They don't have that preparation time to devote to the singer. But when the singer can walk in, as has happened in many instances, and the conductor and stage director say "Have you done the role?" and they can say "Yes." "Where did you do it?" "Well, I did it in New York. I did it with Opera Ebony." "Who was the conductor for that production?" They can say, "Warren George Wilson," or "Everett Lee." "Oh yes!" They would know that the artist had been under good musical direction. "Do you have any reviews for that?" "Yes, I have reviews from the *Times, The Daily News,* and *The Amsterdam News.*" The artist puts the reviews on the table and shows that he or she has mastered that role to the point where he or she can sing it and act it, everything will not have to be put into his or her head. Because of this, the artist is hired. Here in the United States and in Europe many of our artists' roles were prepared and sung with Opera Ebony first! They went on to sing them other places. This kind of involvement has made a great difference in many lives, and contributed to their development and their work as artists.

WC: Can we expect to see more black opera companies into the next century?

BM: I certainly hope that there will be more black opera companies as we near and move into the next century. I'm not sure that there will be. But just in case there are other opera companies, I certainly hope that they will do well and find a definite identity for themselves. By all means, if they should need to counsel with us, we will assist in whatever way we can—talking with them, and sharing our experiences. I hope that there will be more black opera companies in the next century.

WS: Ben probably doesn't want me to say this, but to the issue of future black opera companies getting their own identity, for me, Wayne Sanders, I find it crucial that we as black people learn to share with each other and not take from each other. In other words, we are here for each other, and because we need as many black opera companies as we can put out there. Let us not assume the identity of a company like Opera Ebony because it has been successful, and try to ride on its coattails when individuality and diversity would generate more and different kinds of opportunities for all artists. I feel very strongly about this, as you can probably tell. Do it! Come not only to us. But go to other people that have done it. We're more than happy to share whatever in every way. But don't try to take it!

BM: Mr. Sanders is just saying come to us for help if you need it. But don't steal our good name and good reputation.

WS: Yes!

BM: Don't just steal our name without contacting us, at least get our consent. Who knows, depending on what it is, we might even be willing to share it with you. At least give us that respect. That's all we're saying.

WC: Is there a kind of vocal instrument and personality required for opera that is different from the kind of vocal instrument and personality required for concert and recital?

BM: Let me take the vocal instrument first. Basically, there is no different kind of vocal instrument required for opera than for the recital stage. There are probably people on the recital stage who have some superior abilities that could be used for the operatic stage. But for one reason or the other, they just absolutely have not done it. The voices do not necessarily require anything different. For the personality part, that can require something a little bit different.

A singer can have an operatic temperament, but not necessarily have an artistic temperament so far as acting and coming forth with that powerful personality on stage. The temperament and the personality requirements are a little bit different. I will make a personal example. I did concert and oratorio first. I was trained as a recitalist.

My first professional jobs came on the recital stage and on the oratorio stage. I was by no means in those early years an opera singer. I had not mastered and, for the most part, had not even been introduced to the techniques of singing on the operatic stage. The two are different. Yet, once I trained in opera, acting, and singing projecting over an orchestra, this addition brought about a refinement of my work on the recital stage. And also brought me into the awareness that to a great extent I had been singing opera, or drama from the dramatic point of view, all along. I just wasn't aware of it.

Each song and each piece of music that one sings is a drama within itself. A fine recitalist must be able to understand and project and share that drama with his audience. Yet, one can do this and not have the techniques in place or the understanding of how to project over an orchestra and act at the same time. So there is a difference in the styles of the two. I would say that they are very much interrelated and yet they are very much different.

WS: In essence you're saying that with the training and with the opportunity to explore the operatic world, it is possible for singers who thought that they couldn't sing opera to become proficient in the genre.

BM: Yes, yes.

WS: We have had singers with the company, some who have never been in an opera, and with slow, careful work, with the right dramatic direction and the right staff, it's been rather amazing to see a lot of these singers unfold. It shocks everybody. They say, "I didn't know she could do that." I think all of us are capable of exploring opera. Many of us find out that we can sing the opera. A lot of people, a lot of artists find out that they don't want to do opera, that they would be more comfortable in musical theater, or in recital, or on Broadway. And I think that it's very important to find that out. Only in working with top people, and allowing oneself to be open to opera, would one know whether or not opera is for them. Because it boils down to an individual kind of sensibility.

BM: Yes, and the individual personality. I would like to add that in my experience, I know, understand, and realize that an opera singer does not a recitalist make. There are many great opera singers who cannot sing a simple Italian song. They cannot sing a simple hymn. They can't do it. And yet, for the recital stage, so many times, in wanting a great name, a great operatic name, these people are called upon to come and sing recitals and to appear on the recital concert series. They're not very good recitalists. They are just simply not attuned to that, and attuned to the fine art and delivery that a recitalist has to make in his presentations; much the same is true also for the recitalist. They are two different schools calling for two different types of mastery and delivery.

WC: In our time, it borders on being impossible for a singer to have a major career without an identity with opera. Would you speak to this phenomenon?

BM: This is true, and it has been true for quite some time. The glamour and the fascination of a classical singing career is in opera. With most of the general public, whenever they hear a classically trained voice, even if it's in church and the singer is singing sacred music, they always refer to that singer as an opera singer.

I can only relate to the experience that I had when I first came to New York. I went for big management. I spoke with this gentleman who was very famous. He handled many big-name artists. He said to me, "Mr. Matthews, in order to have a career, you must gain some operatic experience. You must do some opera. When people call us for a recitalist, they ask us for an opera singer." He said, "And, of course, you and I know that an opera singer is not a recitalist. Most of them aren't even prepared to sing a recital." He said, "Mr. Matthews, we send singers out to sing a recital, and they go and sing a couple of songs and then do eight, nine, or ten arias." He said, "You and I know that is not a recital. But the public out there, and particularly the public outside of New York, Chicago, San Francisco, feel that they have had a recital, and by no means did they have a recital. They only had an opera singer to come and sing some arias and a couple of songs."

So the classical careers seem to center around opera. Before I could get out there—even in oratorio, and to a degree to even have a recital season—I needed opera attached to my name. That's why I really got into singing opera. I couldn't get management, and I couldn't get jobs without it. So this is very true. A singer needs an identity with opera. It was true then, twenty-five years ago. And it is true today, even more so.

WS: Yes, and I think it's just that opera is bigger than life to most of the public, also to the presenters. I think people find it exciting to hear a voice doing all of the athletic things that are required in opera, the histrionics. It's just something that is, and if one wants to have a career, classically, one has to really deal with that.

There are a few singers who have gone against this phenomenon and have made it. But nowadays, especially as we go into the twenty-first century, it seems that one has to do both if he/she really wants to have a major career. There are singers who are having recital careers, but most of them are in Europe. The Europeans really love the art of the recital. It's starting to come back somewhat in the States, but not really enough to have a career or support oneself.

WC: What were the stimuli that triggered your interest in opera?

WS: My interest in opera did not really trigger until I was in college. I grew up in the projects of Chicago, Ida B. Wells Projects, and opera was not a part of my experience. But I've always loved the voice. Then when I got to college and started listening to recordings, I had never been to an opera. I heard these voices and it was thrilling to me. Then I found out that you had to act. Acting has been a part of my life since childhood from about five or six. Growing up in the Catholic schools, I was always either acting or dancing or singing little things. When I found out that opera was a combination of all of this, I knew that it was something for me. It was like a food for me. It was like a tonic. I then embraced opera, because it did something for me that was very special.

BM: I've always been interested in the classical voice. When I was very young, I thought that I was interested in opera. I didn't know what in the world an opera was, but we did get the Metropolitan Opera broadcasts on Saturdays at home. My mother would always listen, and whatever my chores were, I was finished by two o'clock in the afternoon so that I could listen to the Metropolitan Opera with her.

I would try to sing along with them, and being young, my voice was a soprano voice, and whatever notes the sopranos would hit, I could imitate and hit those notes. I found it great fun, and I found it very intriguing. I loved listening to the opera. I didn't particularly care what they were saying. I was just fascinated with that sound, and with that orchestra, and what I could imagine was going on as they sang to one another. So I have always had an interest in that classically trained voice, which like most people, I just considered opera.

We had the other radio programs to come, The Bell Telephone Hour and the Voice of Firestone. The great singers, and the great opera singers, would always be guests on these programs. This, too, was a part of our entertainment in the home. We would tune in, and we would listen and we would enjoy those wonderful programs. So I always had an interest in opera from that standpoint.

Of course, when I began to get my training, understand, and was introduced to and learned what an opera really was, and ventured in that direction, then I became even more interested in opera. But I have always—from as far back as I can remember, when I was five, six, and seven years old—had an interest in the classically trained voice and in operatic singing.

WC: Why has there not been a black male to become a "real" operatic superstar—a parallel to Leontyne Price?

BM: This is a question that has been tossed around for at least fifteen to twenty years. There are many theories out there, and these theories seem to change as times goes on. The bottom line is nobody really has the answer. One can speculate on what the answer might be. I've tried to answer this question before in other interviews, and so many times I felt that I had given a good answer.

My answer was almost always totally different from the answer of other black singers and those involved in classical music. It's the type of thing that one really cannot pinpoint. However, we can still continue to try to come up with a rational reason why this has not happened. I think first we must look at the fact that no one is born a superstar. Superstars are made. It has to do with opportunity. It has to do with experience. It has to do with trusting an artist on stage with a role to get that experience. It has to do with so many things.

I strongly suspect that racism also plays its part. And the level of racism directed against the black male that is not necessarily directed against the black female. The fact that in so many instances the black man is considered the "real threat." Threat to what? I cannot tell you what really makes many nonwhites feel that black men are a threat. It can be carried into many directions. But the bottom line is, in order to become a superstar one has to be assigned the superstar-type roles; has to be put in a superstar-type setting; has to be invested in so far as putting money into their publicity; has to get the press behind them to impress upon people that a superstar is here. Here is a superstar!

This has not been done for the black man, and the black man, for the most part, those who are singing opera, don't necessarily have the money to do it for themselves. There are very few black male singers who can put a hundred thousand dollars a year into publicity. There are very few who can buy the cover of *Time* magazine, or the cover of some of the other popular magazines so that people will see his face. Or to pay writers to declare that he is a superstar. Then to get those people who have the power, make the inroads to put it into the newspapers or to put those statements into the magazines. This is how it was done for others and this is how it will have to be done for the black male "superstar."

Until a black man comes along who is financially able to do this type of thing for himself, publicity-wise, it is not very likely that there will be a black male elevated to superstar status. Until a black man is assigned the major leading roles in the opera houses, and then have someone to put together and to package him into an image, and then to go and buy advertising space and persuade people to print it, nothing will be done. And what I have learned is that it doesn't make any difference whether it's true or not. If *Newsweek* or *Time* say that you're a superstar, and it's there for fifty million people to read, then people are going to get it into their minds that you are a superstar, even when there might be five people around the corner who can sing rings around you. I have seen this happen all of the time. So there are many reasons why there are no black male superstars in opera.

The basic ones are the assignment and entrusting of the roles in a major opera company, in a major glamorous setting, and then that major money will put it out there to the public in the news media; and have people to buy it and begin to consider him as such. That's the only thing I can come up with that would make any kind of sense to me in this year of 1994.

WS: You've said a lot, Ben. And I think you're right on the money. Just a little extra word on it. Until the black male singer in totality, his sound, the person, is nurtured with regularity and given the roles as they do with the black women, he can get out there with a role in *Porgy and Bess*. But if that is not followed up with other roles in other major works, superstardom will not happen. He becomes a superstar in *Porgy and Bess*. It is as simple as that.

I also have a feeling, and it's my own personal feeling, that the black male sound is different. I know that I am opening up a whole hornet's nest here. But I feel that it is different, and somehow for the most part, the sound of the black male has not been embraced like the black female sound has been. That's connected to many things, Ben, that you were talking about. But I find that a lot of people don't understand our sound, don't want to understand our sound, and try to eventually make us do something else with the sound. And that in its own way can destroy, and has destroyed, many of our voices because a lot of us as black singers, especially black males, even when the voice is very light, there is a darkness in the quality of sound. We have many colors and timbres that are innate to us as black people. It is a basic way, innate way of singing, added to the training, of course. But if that innate quality is tampered with, we become homogenized and sound like everybody else. It does not work for the most part for most of us. Then we're dropped from the opera company. It is said that we can't sing. This is my personal observation. Ben, I don't know if you've found this to be true; but I have. I have experienced this from my just being out there.

BM: Yes, I have found a lot of that to be true. Back to the *Porgy and Bess* syndrome. I find it interesting that one can be hired—I've sung that role of Porgy many, many times, and I'm sure that many of my other black colleagues have had the same experience.

The fact is, many of them are refusing to sing Porgy anymore. We baritones and bass baritones can go on stage and sing the role of Porgy, which is one of the most difficult roles to execute while crawling around on your knees. We can sing the role magnificently. And anyone with any kind of open judgment can hear that our voices are operatically trained. Anyone who knows his way through that score knows that we have pulled off a very difficult feat. And once we have finished, management will come to us as if to say, "Oh!, you're such a wonderful Porgy." "You're a beautiful Porgy!" "Oh!, you were just magnificent!" "Now, let me hear you sing."

This is how they treat us. Yet, they can take Bess, Serena, and Clara, and any of the females and carry them on through; make them a part of the regular season; assign them roles; but not the men. We are looked upon differently.

The females are assigned roles in regular operas. But the Porgys, Crowns, and Jakes, are left out. This sort of double standard the black man still has to deal with. It has gotten to the point where most of the black baritones who can really sing the role of Porgy with any kind of credibility will say to management—fortunately, they're still able to eat after taking this stand, and I admire them for this—"I will sing your Porgy, but what else are you giving me in your regular season." If nothing else is offered, they will refuse to sing it.

I think more of the black men who can sing Porgy should take that stand. I became very sensitive to the fact that I could go places to sing the role of Porgy and they would take the newspaper and begin to publicize me as a Gershwin expert. I was not there as a Gershwin expert.

I was there to sing the role of Porgy. Most of the other things that Gershwin wrote are too much in the Broadway style for me to be an expert in those areas. It is a very tricky thing and something that most of the black men who are not hungry and have a roof over their heads really need to think about. How much of it, how much of Porgy they will sing, and what advantages should come to them as they go out to sing this role. After they have studied for ten, fifteen, and twenty years to be a classical or an opera singer. It's something very interesting.

WC: How has the "super nigger" syndrome been reflected in opportunities for African-Americans in opera?

BM: By the "super nigger" syndrome, I understand that you mean how is it that black Americans should be expected to do any and everything above everyone else in order to gain acceptability in opera and into the regular operatic seasons. A lot of the expectation is still around.

I think the closest example I can give you is one of my dear friends and a singer who I asked what had happened when his contract was terminated at the Metropolitan Opera House. I had heard many things, and I wanted to know directly from him what actually had gone on there, and what had happened to him. He said some of the problems were his own fault because he was assigned to cover many roles that were too big and too heavy for his lyric voice. His voice is basically a full lyric and in my opinion where the most beauty in his sound comes out. Then he told me, "I felt that I had the burden of the black man in opera upon my shoulders. I set out to prove that I could do it; that I could sing whatever was assigned to me. And with some of those roles being too heavy for my voice, I really sort of messed myself up. When there was a cancellation of the things that I was covering outside of the roles that I was already assigned to sing, Ben, I would just walk in and do it. And, it finally caught up with me."

That's a good example of what it means to be pushed and assigned to the point where you just have to be "super nigger." Singing, and covering, and doing whatever is thrown at you, and being able to pull it off. It can begin to wear on you to the point where you'll be out there trying to pull it off regardless of how it sounds. You pay a tremendous price! You shorten your career. Your voice changes to the point where you cannot handle it. And instead of developing into the *superstar* that you deserve to be, you wind up at the point of ruination, and almost total destruction being overassigned, overworked, and having those inhuman expectations played upon you.

Some of that is still out there, even today, where in order to get the opportunity to do one thing, you have to do three or four things, sustain them, and be ready when you're called upon, after all of your energies have been depleted because you've been concentrating on something else that now is less important.

The African-American singers, any singers, who should read my comments about this should be extremely careful. You have only one voice. It is up to you to protect that voice, to be intelligent about what you will do, what you will not do, what you can do, what you cannot do, what you can sing, and even those things you refuse to sing. And it is crucial for black artists to understand that once you reach a certain point in the development of your career, half of the answers should be "Yes, I will do it"; and the other half should be "No". You reach the point where you grow as much on *no* as you do on *yes*. It is crucial that our singers and artists understand this.

WC: I have asked a lot and you have certainly said a lot. Is there a concern, or are there concerns, about opera and the black experience that you would particularly like to address?

BM: No. I think in all of the above comments, we have pretty much addressed our concerns, and we have pretty much addressed mostly everything that we would like to say. Everything that we can say for this time. As times goes on, we hope that we will have the opportunity to speak and to go even deeper into some of the things that we have talked about during this conversation. Thank you.

WC: Thank you. The operatic landscape in general, and the African-American experience as it relates to opera in particular is indeed richer because Benjamin Matthews and Wayne Sanders dared to have a dream and dared to make that dream a reality. And there is no doubt in my mind that there will be upcoming opportunities for the two of you to go more deeply into the things that you have talked about today.

New York, NY
1994

George Shirley. *Courtesy of the Lyric Opera of Chicago.*

7

George Shirley:
a Renowned Divo Speaks

George Shirley represents the consummate professional. His entire life has been devoted to achieving excellence in the performing arts and in teaching. From early on, unfolding events seemed to propel him toward an ultimate identity: the first black man to achieve international distinction in opera, that most grandiose of art forms.

I first met Mr. Shirley in the 1960s, when he came to Knoxville College (in Tennessee), where I was a music student, to present a recital as part of our lyceum series. By no stretch of the imagination could I then have believed that some thirty years later this conversation would be prepared through our joint endeavors. In 1960 Mr. Shirley made his operatic debut in Milan, Italy, at the Teatro Nuovo, singing the role of Rodolfo in Puccini's *La Bohème*. How appropriate that this interview be published in 1990, marking the thirtieth-anniversary year of that momentous event.

George Irving Shirley (b. 18 April 1934 in Indianapolis, Indiana) grew up in Detroit, Michigan, where his family moved when he was six years old. He obtained his music education at Wayne State University in Detroit and through private study. Today he continues to sing around the world, and is professor of music at the University of Michigan. He is also on the faculty of the Aspen Music School. Our conversation took place over a period of several months: we began during the summer of 1987 and continued intermittently through 1988 and into 1989. In the spring of 1990 we edited the tapes.

Wallace Cheatham: Why is it that a black male has not become a "real" operatic superstar, a parallel to Leontyne Price?

George Shirley: Superstars are a big investment. A lot of money goes into creating a larger-than-life figure. Superstars can be controversial. A mystique can be built around those controversial elements in their nature.

WC: Would you speak more about the meaning of "controversial"?

GS: Some of the time-honored subjects that a good press or media person might take to build a mystique or aura for a superstar—certainly one of them is the person who lives on the fast track—a lady's man, a woman who is perceived as being of somewhat loose morality. That kind of mystique has attended many movie stars, and has been built upon by media persons, which makes these individuals that much more interesting in the eyes of certain major segments of the public.

Someone who lives close to the edge: A movie star or performer who, in his or her free time, likes to involve himself or herself in dangerous activities, such as auto racing—sports that have a certain element of danger about them. Someone who builds his or her life around astrological charts. Someone who spends his free time trekking off to poor areas of the world, giving of his time, sharing his wealth.

These kinds of things are controversial and help to build an aura, enhance the attractiveness of the person. A good media person makes great mileage out of this. We also have examples of people who are known to be temperamental. The late Maria Callas was one, and this became a major part of her attractiveness so far as the general public was concerned. The media took this and enhanced it—I think, completely out of proportion—but it became something that made us much more interested in her.

Superstardom must be marketable; consequently, race does not necessarily ensure that people who invest the kinds of money required for building an individual into a superstar will reap a benefit. Black males have proved to be marketable items in areas where white society expects them to excel: in sports and the popular and jazz music genres, but less so in the classical-music genres. The power structure in music is dominated by white males.

WC: How does this affect the black woman as an opera singer?

GS: Women have made some inroads, but still the power rests with the white male. Artist managements, those that are run by white males, are still in dominance. There have been, and there are, successful women managers of performing artists. Ann Summers, my own manager, is one. Ann Colbert. But most of the powerful managements, like Columbia, are dominated by white males. The managements of orchestras are still in the hands of white males, although the Detroit Symphony is now managed by a woman.

WC: The Milwaukee Symphony now has a woman manager, Joan Squires.

GS: But I think that women are still in the minority there. There are a couple of successful opera companies run by women—certainly Sarah Caldwell in Boston, Ardis Krainik at the Lyric in Chicago, the late Carol Fox, who was at the Lyric. I think it is safe to say that the boards of directors of opera companies and symphony orchestras are dominated, at least in terms of leadership, by white males.

So again, music is the microcosm of the macrocosm. Black women who find themselves able to enter doors that may remain shut to black males will no doubt feel the pressure. They know that they're out there alone in a sense, and being the first one in the door does not necessarily ensure access to all the roles that the singer may be vocally equipped to perform.

I remember a young black woman who was successful in getting employment in Europe. She wrote me a number of times about her frustration at being denied roles that she knew she could do, roles that in the eyes of the Germans were roles that she couldn't possibly do because she didn't really look the part. They would give her Mimi [in *La Bohème*] because after all Mimi is French; but they wouldn't give her an Annchen in *Der Freischütz,* for instance, which she knew that she could do, or Blonde in *The Abduction from the Seraglio.* They would look at her and think she couldn't possibly be blond, but Mimi just might be black. I'm sure that's the way they thought of it, and they were right. Blonde and Annchen were out of the question! So even though she was accepted on one level, and was able to perform in a house where possibly—I say possibly because I don't know this, but I'm fairly certain that there were no black tenors singing there—she was still limited.

Persons in that situation never really know to what extent they've been accepted for their talent and ability alone, and to what extent their acceptance hinges also on being visually, ethnically or racially, unique. From my own point of view, I would hope that in the areas where I have worked, acceptance has been based on talent and ability, not [on] my being black.

I'm sure it's true of majorities, too: how much of this is acceptance because I happen to be a good-looking, attractive woman, and how much of it is because I have talent and ability? A black woman must add to this, how much of it is because I am really unique in this situation—unique among women, as well as possibly having unique talent? A black woman has these questions, I think, looming over her head.

In opera it has been easier for black women to gain acceptance as a physical presence, [to gain] star and even superstar status because white males don't see them as a threat to their male base of power. It has been a "feather in the cap" of opera managers who have discovered and nurtured exceptional black female talent. I think it a reflection of male chauvinism that no one has asked any of the white female singers how they feel about seeing many of their black sisters achieve superstar status. But when a male enters the picture, black or white, there is a sense of threat on many levels—real and imagined.

WC: Such as?

GS: Any singer who becomes a star stands to gain more power to dictate terms, both artistic and financial. So if I enter an opera company, and I really become one of their bright lights, then I am better able to sit down across the table and demand the terms that I want financially, and demand the casting with which I would like to surround myself. This puts the manager in a position of having less clout. A singer may, over time, even become a contender for that person's position.

Edward Johnson became manager of the Metropolitan Opera. Placido Domingo is in a position of artistic direction in California. A singer might gain influence over certain members of the board of directors, which might possibly lead to an erosion of the present artistic director's power. So these are very real areas, possibilities of the acquisition of power on the part of a star performer that I'm sure haunt managers when they're dealing with superstars. A male singer might also be seen as a contender for the affections of females; or as they say today, "significant others," in a manager's life. With men, that is certainly an area of concern that we see across the board in this society.

It is of interest that two former artists, who have become very powerful managers that males now have to worry about, are women: Beverly Sills and Ardis Krainik. So not only do the male managers have to worry about the male singers with whom they contend, they must worry about the possible takeover of power from some of their female superstars.

So there are many fears that dance, I'm sure, through the minds of managers when people walk through that door; and given the way society is structured in the United States, certainly one of the biggest specters looms when the black male comes across the threshold and places himself in a position that has to be dealt with by the white male manager, whether it's in music or other areas, such as commerce, business, or what have you. A male in power does not look forward to defending his position against another male who may be in a position to upset that power; those in authority don't welcome someone on the scene who might be a potential challenger. Herein lies one of the reasons why it has been difficult for black men to become "real superstars" in any area of classical music.

The males who achieve superstar status, like Placido Domingo and Luciano Pavarotti, wield real power—they can name artists with whom they want to perform, and indeed, if their conditions are not met, they can just walk out of a situation, thus creating a loss for the presenting party. Another problem—at least for the tenor who has the vocal capability of doing romantic leads—[is that] many white people still have a problem accepting black males in romantic roles opposite white females. Thirdly, the darker in complexion the performer, the more difficult it is for whites to accept that person in costume and makeup playing a "white role," such as Rodolfo or Des Grieux. There is less problem with white artists playing ethnic personalities: Aida, Otello, or Cio-Cio-San.

WC: How has the "supernigger syndrome" been reflected in opportunities for the black male in opera?

GS: I will respond to this question from two points of view: role assignment and workload. On my first trip to Italy, at the beginning of my career, whenever people saw me they wanted me to sing Otello. This wasn't a negative response made out of hatred. It was just that the Italians saw and immediately made a judgment on what they saw rather than what they heard.

WC: Is there a black tenor who has been acclaimed for this role?

GS: Charles Holland sang Otello in the 1950s in Germany and in London. Holland had a beautiful, lyric, spinto voice. It really wasn't an Otello voice in terms of weight and size, but it had a wonderful clarity and heroic ring, a manly quality, unique quality. He told me that on one occasion in Hildesheim, a small house in Germany, he sang two Otello performances in the same day: an afternoon matinee, and then an evening performance!

WC: He lived to tell the story!

GS: He came out of it retaining his voice, which was certainly a compliment to his ability and understanding of technique.

WC: A compliment also to his emotional stability and inner faith.

GS: You're right.

WC: Just having the nerve to undertake such an endeavor—that alone is significant.

GS: Charles also sang Otello for BBC television, Televised Kinescope, in the early 1950s. To my knowledge he is the only black tenor who has performed the role on that level with success. [Born in 1910, Charles Holland died on November 7, 1987, in Amsterdam.] During those early days in Italy, 1960, I met a black tenor from California who had been studying in Italy for some time—Nat Boyd. A couple of years later I heard a broadcast of Otello from one of the provinces featuring Nat Boyd in the title role. This was a voice capable of doing the full lyric, and maybe some of the spinto roles. He probably was not happy doing Otello, but Otello and Radames [in *Aida*] were probably the only roles available to him. These are basically dramatic parts. I got the sense that because he was black, these were the roles with which he would be saddled. He looked the parts, so he had to perform them.

WC: Have you heard of Mr. Boyd in recent years?

GS: No, I have not heard of Nat Boyd since the early 1960s. I don't know where he is or what happened with his career. That year [1960] I was offered the possibility of getting management and staying in Italy. Had I elected to do that, I probably would have been stuck with "ethnic roles," regardless of voice suitability.

WC: Is there a black tenor who has been acclaimed for Radames?

GS: Radames? Charles Holland performed the role, I believe, in

Amsterdam and possibly in Germany in the fifties and sixties. I think
that Lawrence Watson, a tenor from Detroit who eventually had a fine
career on Broadway, might have performed Radames abroad. I'm not
sure. I think that he gave a performance of Otello also, with the Pitts-
burgh Symphony in the fifties. [Lawrence Watson died some years
ago at a home for actors in New Jersey.] I heard Mervin Wallace sing
a very fine performance of Radames in the debut performance of National Opera Ebony in Philadelphia in the 1970s—an excellent
Radames: right voice, handled the role vocally with great acclaim; no
problems. This was a voice that I think should have had a major career. For whatever reason it didn't happen.

He had been promised the role of Don José [in *Carmen*] a few years
ago—I think in the spring opera production in San Francisco. They decided not to follow through because he was, in their reasoning, overweight—which under the circumstances seemed groundless, to me at
least, for refusing him this role. He was very upset about it, and I can
understand why. Vocally, he would have been absolutely right. In
terms of his weight, he would have been absolutely right when you
look at some of the tenors who do the role. But Mervin's Radames was
exceptionally fine. [Approximately two years ago, Mervin Wallace
met with a most unfortunate incident. Mervin, as he was leaving his
Harlem residence to perform in a production of *Porgy and Bess,* was
robbed and very severely beaten. Death was the result.]

WC: I would like to hear more about the "supernigger syndrome."

GS: Yes. Another part of this is seen in the fact that early on in operatic
history, if a black soprano came along she had to do Aida. The late
Florence Cole Talbert made her debut in 1927 at the Commuale Theater in Cosenza, Italy, as this Verdi heroine! I came across an old
Black Swan label recording of Mme. Talbert, which I donated (with
the consent of her family) to the Rodgers and Hammerstein Library at
Lincoln Center. *This* was a voice, according to the recording—a very
high, light, coloratura instrument. She sings the "Bell Song" from
Lakme, and an aria by Arditi [*Il Bacio*]. This was not an Aida voice.
She had high notes, but certainly not the heft that Aida requires. Nevertheless, she was black; her debut had to be as Aida.

Otello, Radames, Aida—these are spinto, dramatic roles; every
black person is not a spinto or dramatic singer. I've done everything
from *Il Barbiere di Siviglia,* which I'm sure wasn't exactly right for
me, to heavier roles—Apollo in *Daphne;* Bacchus in *Ariadne auf
Naxos;* Herod in *Salome.* I've been called everything from *lirico leggiero* to dramatic. I suppose the truth lies somewhere in the middle.
Herod was done at the Festival of Two Worlds in Spoleto, Italy
(1961), in a production staged by the late Luchino Visconti. After that
production, Visconti wanted me to do Otello in the worst way! It
would have been thrilling to work with him on the score, but at that

time I was nowhere near being ready to sing such a role. Maybe never.

After my La Scala debut in 1965 singing the Mozart Requiem, I received a telegram from Visconti: *Su presto in Otello* ("quickly in Otello"). I was singing Mozart, but he still had that fixation of me doing Otello. As the English say, "It just wasn't on." I'm also glad that I had the good sense to turn down Tristan when it was offered.

When I first went to the Metropolitan Opera, I was asked by Sir Rudolf Bing (Mr. Bing at the time), on the afternoon of the opening night of the season, if I could make my debut on the following evening in *Così Fan Tutte,* an opera that I had never even seen before attending a Metropolitan rehearsal. The tenor had fallen ill; I was young and fearless. I said, "Sure." I really didn't know the final ensemble. I went home; took the recording that had been made by [Richard] Tucker and [Eleanor] Steber (it was in English—we were still doing *Così* in English at that time), walked through my paces in the living room the rest of the afternoon while listening to the recording. The next day I repeated the procedure, walked out on stage that night, walked through the performance, got through with no mistakes.

WC: You are really an overwhelmingly quick study and tremendous musician to have pulled off such a feat!

GS: That was my Metropolitan debut! Not my official debut—that came about a month later as Pinkerton in *Madame Butterfly.* The *Così* performance got me off to a certain start and into a kind of groove at the Metropolitan. Management saw that I was someone upon whom they could rely to learn things quickly and come through with an acceptable and solid performance.

Everyone at the Metropolitan is closely scrutinized, but because I was the only black male singing leading roles at that time, and the first black tenor, I felt in my own mind that there was an especially powerful telescope focused on me. I was determined to do my best; I was determined to prove that I could not only achieve a level of excellence in my assignments that was going to be impressive for me as an individual, but a level of excellence in my assignments that would declare to management, critics, and everyone that black men can do this job! Black men are worthy! Black men should be a part of this institution! I imposed the "supernigger syndrome" upon myself. However, it is doubtful that I could have done otherwise in that situation. That worked fine, I suppose, for a number of years; but after a while it became a kind of load that was too heavy and unrealistic to bear. In my last year at the Metropolitan, there were fourteen roles for which I was responsible.

WC: Fourteen roles! Mind-boggling! Do you have a photographic memory?

GS: No, I don't have a photographic memory. I've developed over the years a method of study that enables me to recall quite rapidly, within a rehearsal or two, what I need in order to go out and do a performance, but no photographic memory by any stretch of the imagination.

WC: Those fourteen roles—the assignment process?

GS: Some of those roles I was scheduled to perform. For some of those roles I was "first cover," which means I had to be prepared to jump in at the last minute in case someone fell ill. For some of those roles I was "second cover," which means that the first cover would probably be called upon if the scheduled artist fell ill, but I also might be called upon if they were roles that I had done successfully, or roles with which the first cover may have had less experience.

Here I was with fourteen roles, ranging from Strauss to Mozart, that had to be ready: about twelve too many. Additionally, at the last minute I was asked to jump into performances of *Romeo et Juliette*. Because of difficulty with the role of Romeo, one of my colleagues just didn't show up!

I repeat: nobody insisted I carry that kind of load, but it was part of my desire to prove once and for all that—yes, black men can triumph at the Metropolitan. Look at me! I'm leaping from tall buildings! I'm filling this position! Bullets are bouncing from my chest! By this time, however, they weren't bouncing off my chest. They were lodging in very sensitive places. Indeed, that season I was not singing too well.

I was beginning to pay the price for doing too much. Management did not believe it when I went to them and stated that there were fourteen roles for which I was responsible. The administration member with whom I was speaking, after checking my contract, said, "You're absolutely right." So in my eleventh Metropolitan year, after victimizing myself with the "supernigger syndrome," I said, "Let's eliminate some of this stuff." With hope, those coming on will be wiser and not feel that they must carry the aspirations of a people on their shoulders. Doing your work and dealing with the situation as an individual is quite enough.

WC: What can you say about the operatic instrument: criteria for identification, training, technique, qualities of a good teacher, qualities of a good coach, role preparation, vocal endurance?

GS: One looks for an instrument with special qualities—an identifiable sound that is immediately recognizable as belonging to a particular individual. A beautiful sound. There are people having operatic careers who don't have beautiful voices; nevertheless, a voice of beauty should be a criterion for a career. Flexibility, exceptional range, size, enough power through the purity and clarity of timbre to deal with operatic orchestras and the physical dimensions of theaters one is called upon to perform in today. Security of technique, stamina—good health, good habits, physical strength, staying power. Training and technique should produce a voice capable of sounding as natural as possible while dealing with the material it is required to perform.

A good teacher should be aware of all the latest scientific knowledge that is available. A good teacher must have a superior ear so that healthy sounds are easily identified. A good teacher should be able to communicate clearly and have enough flexibility to put students at ease. A good teacher should know about relaxation techniques. A good teacher should be able to spot wrong tension in the body and know how to release these tensions, thereby making energy that is being blocked available for the singing process.

A good teacher should be a superior musician, should have an excellent command of languages, should be compassionate, and at the same time demanding. A good teacher should be able to ascertain the potential of a student before too much time has elapsed.

WC: That is quite a list of qualifications! Am I correct in thinking that there are not too many good voice teachers?

GS: The incompetent doctors, automobile mechanics, and television repairmen are probably larger in number than those who are competent. The same is true with voice teachers. Woefully inadequate training has produced a mixed bag: people opening studios who tried to sing a little bit and were not successful; people who have been successful singers but have difficulty communicating their understanding; those who have analytical minds and are able to articulate with a great degree of accuracy what they feel and what they have grown to understand through empirical and theoretical study.

There is no licensing of voice teachers. Anyone, even someone who has had no experience at all, can hang out a shingle and declare himself or herself a teacher of voice. The proliferation of vocal pedagogy courses in colleges and universities today is an attempt to correct that situation. The vocal pedagogy courses are becoming more sophisticated, more focused. Today, someone with a graduate degree in voice, masters or doctorate, has been exposed to the latest scientific knowledge; he or she has benefited from practicum in their course work, has been observed by the faculty in teaching students, has had an opportunity in observed situations to really put the theory into practice.

This is fairly new. I would say that young people hanging up their shingles today are certainly much better equipped than were their predecessors—in the manner of the young medical doctor, the young psychiatrist, and I suppose the young automobile mechanic or television repairman. There are still areas that, I believe, fall to absolute talent: the ear, the ability to synthesize material; the wherewithal to analyze and to communicate abstract ideas to students, to make proper use of all the technological advances. This kind of profile will come together only in the most talented people. Consequently, we will always have a situation where the talented few will be few, and the less talented majority will be the majority.

WC: The role and qualifications of a coach?

GS: A good coach should certainly have as much knowledge as possible about the vocal process, but should have the good sense to not try teaching voice! A good coach should have a wide command of standard repertoire, should be conversant in all of the singer's performance languages, should be a solid pianist and good reader. A good coach should be sensitive to the needs of various singers and voice types. A good coach should be supportive: pianistically and psychologically. A good coach does not obstruct the ideation process of a singer. A good coach should be able to communicate clearly. A good coach should be a provocateur: processing the ability to draw out of the singer the singer's own truth, and the wisdom to help the singer to see how that truth fits with or differs from the truth of the composer, to see where it melds and where it does not quite join.

WC: Would you agree that there needs to be a proliferation of courses in universities dealing with the techniques of coaching?

GS: Yes.

WC: I know that there is one such course at the Juilliard School, taught by Alberta Masiello. Certainly the teacher and coach are different animals. There are areas, however, where the two meet and even merge.

GS: You are quite correct. A good coach and teacher should teach the singer how to study most effectively. The coach and the teacher should impress upon the singer the fact that vocal and artistic progress take time and perseverance. The singer must be patient with himself, and at the same time insist upon forward movement—a balance difficult to achieve.

WC: Are there steps that the singer can take to bring about this equilibrium?

GS: Most people never take full advantage of the available resources—the opportunity to speak with people who possess wisdom about life and living: teachers, spiritual leaders, psychological counselors. Our parents are willing to share their insights, if we decide to take advantage of their presence. I suppose that the most important thing is reaching a point of being unafraid to reach out, unafraid to let someone know that we are going through a vulnerable period, unafraid to ask for help.

WC: You spoke a moment ago about teaching the singer how to study.

GS: Too many singers try to perform something without having the slightest clue as to why the composer has put all of those little black notes on the page the way he or she has, and without having the slightest clue of the performance connotations in the score. It is amazing how many people attempt to sing foreign-language literature without first doing a thorough job of verbatim translation. Without such preparation they can only, once they get on stage, sing in a general way, worry about their clothes, have their minds wander to all parts of the room, or to problems of vocal technique—rather than being mentally focused on communicating the message of the song, or the life of the character they are being called upon to re-create.

Role preparation, how to study and how to approach literature, is of extreme importance: taking things apart, analyzing and putting them back together again; dealing with the words and music separately and in a meaningful manner, so that when they are rejoined, a picture of what the composer wants is firmly established. Poetry is imagery, and unless there is an understanding of that imagery as portrayed by the poet and translated into music by the composer, there is nothing to say.

WC: Your roles at the Metropolitan: The Metropolitan Archives list them as Almaviva in *Il Barbiere di Siviglia;* Rodolfo in *La Bohème;* Simpleton in *Boris Godunov;* Don José in *Carmen;* Ferrando in *Così Fan Tutte;* Don Ottavio in *Don Giovanni;* Nemorino in *L'Elisir d'amore;* Fenton in *Falstaff;* the title role in *Faust;* First Prisoner in *Fidelio;* Erik and The Steersman in *Der Fliegende Holländer;* Edgardo in *Lucia di Lammermoor;* Macduff and Malcolm in *Macbeth;* Pinkerton in *Madame Butterfly;* Des Grieux in *Manon;* Des Grieux in *Manon Lescaut;* Beppe in *I Pagliacci;* The Duke of Mantua in *Rigoletto;* Romeo in *Romeo et Juliette;* Singer in *Der Rosenkavalier,* Narraboth in *Salome;* Gabriele in *Simon Boccanegra;* Elvino in *La Sonnambula;* Alfredo in *La Traviata;* Sailor's Voice in *Tristan und Isolde;* and Tamino in *Die Zauberflöte.*

How are the character and personality traits of these men revealed through their music?

GS: I will comment on those roles that have special qualities about them in their musical characterizations.

Almaviva in *Il Barbiere di Siviglia.* The music is light, bubbly. There are moments of lyricism—the Count making love (vocally) to Rosina. He is sincere. The comic moments are reflected in the way the lines rise and fall. The whole work is indeed a jocular look at the foibles of love and life.

The long, soaring, sweeping lines of Rodolfo in *La Bohème* (the love music in particular) reflect his poetic character. Moments of drama in the third act are powerfully written. Moments of play between him and the Bohemians in the first and last acts are captured with short lines of conversational interjections. His poetic soul is most effectively captured in the sweeping lines of the aria, the duet, and the tragic moments in the last act. Extremely romantic writing for a romantic character.

In *Boris Godunov:* The purity and lack of malevolence in the Simpleton, plus his sadness at perceiving, as he does, the situation of his homeland, are all reflected in the pure lyric line and simple setting of the aria.

The many mood changes of Don José in *Carmen:* from his expression of tender feelings for his mother and Michaela in the first-act duet to the blending of harmonies without discord, except for the minor and diminished chordal structure that comes in the middle to identify his troubled state and reaction over what has happened with the gypsy; his joy at being a soldier, seeing Carmen again after his release from prison, reflected in the march that we hear off stage near the beginning of act 2; the wide ranging outbursts in the last act, the wailing, pleading [in] "Carmen, take me back"; the depression; the surging and repetition of rising lines. All of this reflects a very complex and unsettled character, a man who strives hard to "toe the line," but whose volatile nature makes it impossible. A man who loses his heart in spite of himself. This is all masterfully reflected by Bizet in music that manifests José's turmoil.

Mozart covers the range of Ferrando's feelings in *Così Fan Tutte*— from the cocky, angular aspects in the opening trio with music that is rather martial, straightforward, and energetic to calm assurance, when he is first convinced of Dorabella's fidelity in the beautiful, long-flowing and high-soaring phrases of *Un aura amorosa;* to the even higher phrase lines of *Ah! lo veggio quell; anima bella* as Fiordiligi resists his attempts at wooing, thus convincing him of her fidelity. Ferrando is definitely insincere in this rather difficult and quite often omitted aria; there is a sense of play here, and he is not at all serious about winning her over. To the very depths of despair when he laments Dorabella's unfaithfulness in the painful and dramatic *Tradito* aria, which alternates with very dramatic phrases, first short, then soaring and wailing—all set by Mozart in a not overly tragic, but painful, moaning way.

To me, Don Ottavio in *Don Giovanni* is one of the most fascinating characters in Mozart's operas. Don Ottavio is also one of the most challenging characters that I have sung, because more often than not he is seen as a wimp who accomplishes nothing. I see him quite differently. I always play him as an older man, which I think is valid. Even today in Latin countries, it is not unusual to see a young woman on the arm of a man old enough to be her father. I find nothing in the score that would negate that view as regards Donna Anna and Don Ottavio. One of the most superficial moments that could be used to bolster my argument is in the first-act duet when Don Ottavio says to her *hai sposo e padre [in me]* ("You have both husband and father in me"). Can you imagine a twenty-two or twenty-five-year-old guy saying that to a young woman?

It weighs more heavily if Don Ottavio is at least the age of Don Giovanni, who is no spring chicken when we encounter him in the opera. Don Ottavio and Don Giovanni are contemporaries, not young men, not in their twenties. I don't think that Ottavio is the age of the Commendatore Anna's father, but he is certainly not much younger. The music for me supports this point of view. I see the aria *Dalla sua pace* as the expression of a man who is mature: "My peace of mind depends upon hers." This is a view not of a young firebrand, but of a man who has been around for a while, a man who has lived by the Knight's Code of Honor for an extended period of time, and for whom that code of honor has become a way of life, a man who doesn't jump off the deep end without carefully thinking things through.

Dalla sua pace is a mature reflection on the situation. There are moments when passion intrudes (the sustained *morte* in particular) but it is controlled, as Ottavio is a very controlled individual. He has grown up according to the rules of knighthood and doesn't fly off the handle. I don't see *Dalla sua pace* as a weak aria or expression. It is perfectly balanced. It is the essence of controlled and mature reflection.

Il mio Tesoro intanto is also controlled, but there the emotions are controlled a little less successfully. I see the challenging runs and the long crescendo on *cercate* as being reflective of Ottavio's anger. He now knows that his friend and fellow knight is the perpetuator of misdeeds—murder and possible sexual attack on Donna Anna. His blood is boiling. This is a vengeance aria. The closest we see Ottavio come to losing his cool is in the long run, which builds to a climax and then tails off as control is regained. The music masterfully reflects Ottavio's strong character traits. I understand that *Dalla sua pace* was composed because the tenor for whom this role was written could not successfully handle *Il mio Tesoro intanto*.

If Don Ottavio is played as an older man, his response to Donna Anna's reply to his request at the end of the opera makes more sense. He asks her to end her grief and give him her hand in marriage, now that the culprit Don Giovanni has been punished by heaven. She pleads with him for an additional year to mourn the loss of her father before she consents to marriage. He grants her request with the words, "A faithful love must consent to the desire of the beloved." You don't expect a younger man to have that kind of patience and maturity.

Ottavio has to be a man older than Anna, a man who has been around and dealt with life in a very successful manner for a considerable period of time. His music adequately reflects that control.

WC: It is obvious that you are highly knowledgeable about theater and the subtle intricacies of playwriting. Have you studied acting as a craft?

GS: Yes, I have studied acting, but only very briefly. I know that in order to give a role its due, you have to look below the surface. It is the performance connotations that bear so much of the character's DNA material, material that has been given to us through the score, the written presentation of the written music.

A performer has to look beneath the surface of the notes, into the structure of the piece, in order to gain insight into the structure of the character. A lot of my feeling for theater has come as I have worked with directors who have helped me to illuminate the score. Boris Goldovsky was certainly one of the most helpful in that regard because he taught all of his students to be independent, to look at the score as the map, as the way to know that score, to depend on it rather than depending on the director and the conductor.

I haven't had a chance to do any straight acting. It's something that I've had a desire to do, but an opportunity has never really presented itself. But it is of interest to me. I studied acting during a period [when] I was recovering from an operation in 1974, while living in Montclair, New Jersey. We had a very fine theater company there, run by Olympia Dukakis and her husband, Louis Zorich. (Dukakis gained increased fame about a year ago when she won the Oscar for her performance in film). I knew them, and I took an acting course during that period of recuperation. It was revelatory! It gave me different insights and new techniques, which I subsequently applied to my work in opera and in teaching.

WC: I'm eager to hear more character analyses. They are masterful. You seem to have really lived these personalities.

GS: The music of Nemorino in *L'Elisir d'amore* is buoyant, full of energy, like Nemorino the man, simple in a beautiful way. The famous *Una furtiva lagrima* is a marvel in that everything about it reflects Nemorino's state of mind at that moment. He has been struck by the tear seen in Adina's eye, taken to mean that the potion upon which he has been guzzling has finally had an affect on her. Nemorino is awestruck; he has seen this manifestation of her love for him. The music also reflects his being tipsy; a wonderful rolling figure in the bass reflects his unsteadiness. Nemorino is not falling down drunk, but he is gently rolling from one side to another, like a ship reacting to the incoming lapping of the waves. The buoyancy, joy, and simplicity of the music all reflect his character quite clearly.

The musical purity that Beethoven gave the First Prisoner reflects that fact of his innocence. A young man who is a political prisoner, his expression and desire for freedom are beautifully captured, making for very special moments in *Fidelio*.

The music that Verdi gave the Duke in *Rigoletto* is for the most part always boisterous, very secure, and cocky. An exception is the second-act aria when the Duke has a little twinge of feeling for Gilda, but only in passing. There the music becomes longing and plaintive; the lines are longer, not as jumpy and choppy ("Parmi veder le lagrime.")

The aria of The Singer in *Der Rosenkavalier* [is] one of the most difficult moments given to a tenor by any composer—overly beautiful, overly high.

I always feel that this is Strauss's caricature of an Italian tenor aria: [it has] more than enough high notes to hold and play around with, and a melody that is surpassingly beautiful. It is a wonderful moment, and I am convinced that it is a musical caricature. With that in mind, I always played the character as a caricature, with padded belly and grand manner.

The music of Narraboth in *Salome* moves from sweeping, soaring phrases which express his passion for Salome, to short, choppy phrases when he realizes that Salome is ignoring his pleas to leave the Prophet alone, and that her fascination with the Prophet is everything. Through all of the pain in seeing the object of his affection throw herself at the feet of this wild, weird-looking man from the wilderness, Narraboth's music becomes wilder and wilder and more and more frantic, until he finally takes his life!

WC: You stated that Don Ottavio is one of the most challenging characters that you have sung. Which character has presented the greatest challenge, and which has been the least challenging character?

GS: In speaking of challenging characters, I would focus on the different reasons why a character can be challenging. Although I probably can't come up with one character or role that has been the most challenging [of those I have discussed] thus far, I can think of a number of characters or roles that have been challenging for different reasons, categorizing the challenges as physical, musical and physical, interpretive, or musical-interpretive challenges.

Probably one of the most satisfying roles for me of all—and it's hard to choose a most satisfying role because all of the great roles give great satisfaction—but I think one of the most satisfying experiences of my career was the opportunity to portray Pelleas in Debussy's *Pelleas et Melisande,* a musical-interpretive challenge. The music is not easy to acquire, but it is extremely satisfying. It was a challenge bringing Pelleas to life, a naive young man, to capture his innocence and to encapsulate his awakening to love. [It was] an interpretive challenge with which I enjoyed grappling.

Other roles that I would identify as being of this same kind of challenge [include] *Oedipus Rex* of Stravinsky, which was the first opera that I sang. *Oedipus Rex* is not a pure opera; actually, the score is called an opera-oratorio by the composer. The role of Alwa in the American premiere of Alban Berg's *Lulu,* which I sang in Santa Fe back in 1963 [was] an interpretive challenge. The role of Mozart's *Idomeneo* offers also this same type of challenge.

If I think strictly in interpretive terms, one of the great challenges for me was the role of Loge in Wagner's *Das Rheingold*. The roles of Tamino and Ottavio, both Mozart tenors, one of whom I spoke about earlier, both are often given little, if any, interpretation, quite often coming off as cardboard characters. For me it was a great challenge to breath life into these two personalities, which I think I was able to do successfully.

Herodes and Apollo, both Strauss tenors in *Salome* and *Daphne*, respectively—I performed Apollo in the American premier of *Daphne*, in Santa Fe, back in the 1960s—both of these roles were feverishly difficult from the viewpoints of physical stamina and musical challenge. The host of roles in my career that I found physically difficult? The music was not that difficult to acquire or interpret, but just the physical demands that they made on me were considerable!

I know that some tenors don't necessarily find the [following] roles physically demanding, but they are written in such a way that I really have to husband my resources in order to sing them, and sing them well: Romeo in Gounod's *Romeo et Juliette;* Edgardo in Donizetti's *Lucia di Lammermoor;* Erik in Wagner's *Der Fliegende Holländer;* Des Grieux in Puccini's *Manon Lescaut;* The Duke in Verdi's *Rigoletto,* particularly "Parmi veder le lagrime," just physically in terms of stamina. Elvino in Bellini's *La Sonnambula,* a role with a very high TessiTura, no doubt, one of the roles that I probably should not have attempted. It really wasn't something that fitted my voice, just vocally a great challenge.

One of the least challenging roles, interpretively, was Alfredo in Verdi's *La Traviata.* Alfredo, I find, is pretty straightforward, [there is] not a lot of opportunity for delving into the character. Alfredo's music is lovely to sing, but he is not one of the most fascinating characters that I've had to interpret.

WC: About your tenure at the Metropolitan: how were your relationships with management, singers, and other personnel?

GS: During my tenure at the Metropolitan I enjoyed very good relationships with all of my colleagues. This remained the case until the labor situation in 1969, when, as an officer of the union, I made some comments on a radio show that made some people unhappy. Relations with certain members of management became strained. In all other aspects, my eleven-year Metropolitan tenure was excellent. There were no problems that were not of my own making. I found people helpful. I really enjoyed working with my co-artists in the house.

WC: Typecasting: to what extent does it exist for the black man in opera?

GS: Heretofore, typecasting has not been a problem for me at any place where I've worked. My original debut at the Metropolitan was scheduled to be Pinkerton in *Madame Butterfly.* Fate decreed Ferrando in *Così Fan Tutte.* Since 1983 I have been at the Deutsche Oper in West

Berlin, where I think typecasting is somewhat of a problem. The tendency in Germany is to look at you and make determinations as to what would be appropriate. I am very much enjoying working there with the director, Herr Gotz Friedrich.

I have performed two roles over the past six years, Loge in *Das Rheingold* and Pluto in *Orpheus in the Underworld*. Both of these characters are somewhat devilish: Pluto is a devil; Loge is a half-god. They are both excellent, wonderful roles, but I think that my being asked to do them was certainly with purpose in mind. Friedrich, in his staging of *Der Ring des Nibelungen,* is, I believe, trying to deglamorize the gods, thus making his audiences see them not as worshipful characters, but as gods with feet of clay.

Loge is certainly the archetype of minorities in present-day society. Loge is used by those in power, who detest him; in return, Loge detests them. Although Loge has grudging respect for Wotan, the chief god, finally he gives up on Wotan altogether. I think Friedrich wants to get that message across to German audiences in no uncertain terms.

WC: About the current political change and social upheaval in Berlin: how will the arts climate be affected; will opportunities for American artists in particular become more plentiful or more scarce?

GS: During a recent conversation with Reri Grist, a much-beloved artist in Germany (Reri lives there with her German husband), she spoke to me about the changes in Germany today. She is of the opinion, and I would agree, that the focus in Germany now is going to be on Germans and on the citizens of the former Iron Curtain countries. That is not to say that American artists will be excluded, but I think opportunities are going to be lessened because the "wall" has been eliminated. This, however, may present opportunities for Americans in some of the Iron Curtain countries, where we were once prohibited from working. But with the possible reunification of Germany and the collapse of barriers with the Eastern Block countries, a tighter situation for American artists in general, I think, will become very real.

WC: Is there more that you can share with me about typecasting?

GS: When Simon Estes made his debut at Bayreuth, it was as the Flying Dutchman. I joked with Simon about that because The Dutchman is a ghost, or, in German, "spuk." We had something of a laugh. I did not see the production, but I understand that it was staged so that the Dutchman didn't come anywhere near Senta. She was in some kind of structure upstage, and the Dutchman was placed elsewhere. Simon has, since then, added another role to his Bayreuth repertoire.

It cannot be overemphasized that basses and baritones enjoy a wider range of acceptance and role possibilities because they usually play the villains, uncles, grandpas, and brothers, and not the romantic leads. In the area of romantic involvement on stage, you will still find casting limitations. The Germans tend to be rather literal in making decisions about most things, which to an extent explains the fact of their looking at someone and saying, "But you can't possibly sing this, you must sing that."

This is also true in Italy, but in Italy I feel there is no malicious underplay or intent involved in the decision, just a simplistic way of viewing life. Consequently, black men may be asked to do a greater range of roles in the United States. Black women are also affected by typecasting, but to a lesser extent.

WC: What about attitudes in other countries where there are major houses—France, England?

GS: My experience in France was limited to one engagement in the small town of Angers, where I was the male chorus in Benjamin Britten's *Rape of Lucretia*. So, I don't feel qualified to speak about typecasting, if it exists, in France. I sang in England a great deal, from 1965 through 1979. I was never typecast. I did everything from Tamino in *The Magic Flute* and Lord Percy in *Anna Bolena* at Glyndebourne, to David in *Die Meistersinger* at Covent Garden. So in England my personal experience was very positive; there was no hint that I encountered of typecasting.

WC: Is there a relationship between support from the black community and opportunities for the African-American artist?

GS: Absolutely! If the black community were more supportive of activities in the classical music area, pressure would automatically be brought to bear upon eliminating many of the barriers that still exist for black artists. But we who perform in the classical music field don't see many black faces in the audience.

Classical music is still considered by most Americans to be foreign, and support for it is still a minority support, among whites as well. In the case of black support, it is a minority of the minority who show interest. Moreover, in opera and concert, there is the added hurdle of dealing with foreign languages. People don't want to pay for something that they don't understand. Opera on television with subtitles, however, has made that genre more accessible.

WC: What steps can be taken to make the system work more effectively for the black male artist?

GS: Trying to correct any situation where prejudice exists requires exposing and keeping the culprit under constant attack. The other part of that is making sure that the people who are trying to establish themselves in a career are qualified, that their training takes a backseat to no one's, and that finally they are more than capable of doing the job and filling the auditorium. We can ill afford in any corner of society to allow a negative situation to persist without exposing, attacking, and hopefully eliminating its existence.

Artists who are working have to keep the public aware of the fact that there are still problems, because once people see a few faces they have a tendency to think that everything is "hunky-dory." Managements will often tell their young up-and-coming artists: "Keep your nose clean; don't get involved with controversial and political situations." If you happen to be black, you will be told to soft-pedal responses to questions concerning race that you may be asked by an enterprising journalist during an interview.

Young artists who have been struggling to make that dent, and who are on the brink of establishing a solid career and don't want to rock the boat, will then find ways of saying in effect: "I know that prejudice exists, but it hasn't bothered me." The truth should be told. If prejudice hasn't bothered you, declare it with conviction; but when a problem is discovered, one has the responsibility to make that problem public knowledge, and not to play it safe by sticking one's head in the sand, or looking in another direction, hoping that the dilemma will go away. The problem will remain unless and until it is actively eliminated.

WC: Organizations like the National Association of Negro Musicians (NANM): do they have a role in this drama? I know that NANM provides performance and workshop opportunities at their conventions; I attended a convention Masterclass in Chicago [focusing on] art songs by black composers. You were the clinician. My compositions have been performed at NANM conventions, but is this enough? Is there more that could be done? I feel that the presence of NANM should be powerful enough to command mention of its president among groups like Ebony's annual listing of the country's one hundred most influential black Americans. Convention activities should command attention from the news media.

GS: I do believe that the National Association of Negro Musicians has a much larger role to play as an advocate for black musicians. NANM has not played that role. As an organization, it is lagging behind the times on a number of fronts. I know that a movement is underway, started with the presidency of William Warfield, to bring NANM into the present day. NANM could certainly be a powerful force in this country, and I would hope that we will see a strengthening of NANM in the immediate future. Performances and workshops at NANM conventions are certainly OK and should be continued. But activities like lobbying for the arts in education, pressing for fairness in the publication of works by black composers, monitoring hiring practices of performing arts organizations so that there is just representation of black Americans in management as well as on stage—these areas cry out for a more powerful focus. And the National Association of Negro Musicians should be actively involved with them.

WC: Black male artists have been singing at the Metropolitan Opera House since 1955. If history is often used to predict the future, what can be expected for involvement of the black male singer at the leading opera house in the world as we prepare to enter the next century?

GS: The future is hard to predict. Our country is currently in a situation where people have the perception that it is again all right to express racial negativity. This perception will certainly have an effect on the progress that has been made over the past twenty years in opening doors. We already see a "slipping back" in many areas, and there is nothing to suggest that it will not happen in our area of interest.

There have been in the past decade an increased number of black men who have made their debuts at the Metropolitan Opera outside of the influx of persons involved with the *Porgy and Bess* production. However, it has not been overwhelming and certainly not representative of the available talent. Nevertheless, it has grown tremendously from the "one and two" of Robert McFerrin and myself that covered a span of almost twenty years.

When I left the Metropolitan in 1974, Arthur Thompson was in the "Met" studio. He was then offered a contract, partly because two black female members of the chorus did some extensive needling of the Met management. Arthur then became the third black male to sing roles at the Metropolitan. Most of those who came in as part of the *Porgy* cast did so without any guarantees of being offered other role opportunities, although there may be one or two who have been successful in getting assignments beyond the Gershwin score. It's heartening in one sense, but it's still disheartening in another.

WC: I find it very interesting that the Metropolitan was born in the 1800s (the first committee meeting in 1880, the first performance on October 22, 1883), because there was social-class discrimination in audience participation at New York's Academy of Music. Ironically, the Metropolitan, after this heroic beginning, practiced discrimination based on nationality (there were no American-born singers before 1918, the first being Rosa Ponselle) and race (there were no black singers until 1955, the first one being Marian Anderson).

GS: That proves that discrimination teaches no lessons. People who are discriminated against eventually seem to find themselves discriminating against others, without having learned any of the lessons that one might think they should have learned.

We must keep up the pressure, keep producing young black men whose voices and artistic capabilities are so outstanding that people see opportunities to make money through their talents. That is the bottom line. I remember speaking with the late Natalie Hinderas some years ago on my radio program. She said that during the time she was signed with major management, she felt like a can of soup being marketed and sold. It is that precisely. If managements feel that money can be made from your talents, they will do what is necessary to make that money. If you are exceptionally talented and well prepared, your chances of being accepted are heightened tremendously.

Sometimes prejudice, as we well know, is stronger than the desire to make money. Talent and preparation may not be enough. You must then find and create places for yourself, thereby creating a demand for your services that can't be ignored with impunity, realizing that your talent was given to you by the Creator to be used, knowing that there is something there, that you keep moving in spite of frustrations.

WC: How have your diverse experiences influenced your approach to teaching?

GS: Having a career certainly has given me a tolerance for the difficulties involved in preparing for one. That is expressed in the compassion that I feel for students who are trying to make the music, the art form, and the languages involved their own. It's not an easy task to acquire the vocal technique and linguistic facility that is requisite for having a major career. I find myself not being too lenient, but certainly understanding when students are struggling with the material that they must ingest in a school semester or school year. If I had not been extensively involved with performance, I might tend to be a bit less forgiving of some of the difficulties.

WC: Why?

GS: I know how difficult it is, so I am very aware of the struggle necessary to acquire what is needed. I think when someone attempts to teach something that he has had very little actual experience in doing he may tend to be a bit more dogmatic about it than he would be if he really knew from practical experience how difficult a task it is to bring it off. Having struggled for years to acquire functional expertise in the musical literatures of Germany, France, Italy, and other countries whose musical heritage is joined with my own in forming the core of my repertoire, I find that I can't dismiss in a cavalier fashion the often unsuccessful attempts of my students to achieve an acceptable level of mastery in a ridiculously short period of time. If I hadn't had the experience, I might just dismiss those efforts with, in terms of a mark— D, F, or C—feeling that they just don't measure up. But I know how hard it is.

I try to constantly be aware of the fact that young people are dealing with something that is not only pure music, but something that is foreign to their experience. Americans must acquire more facility than their cohorts in Germany, France, and Italy, in part because the Europeans are dealing with their own languages and traditions. Consequently, I have a great deal of respect and compassion for American music students, and because they must acquire much of what European music students inherit, my teaching approach is tempered concerning what I try to achieve and how I go about trying to reach the end result.

A career has made me aware of the necessity for discipline, dedication and commitment to the task. Therefore, I am not lenient when it comes to being prepared and being motivated to achieving the goal. I want students to know that the potential will not be accomplished if they aren't dedicated enough to slug it out every day, to strive as best they can to overcome the frustrations that all too easily set in when something doesn't go right. Students are very easily discouraged; I try to help them overcome.

A career enables me to relate events that happen in the studio and the academic world to things that happen in the "real world." I'm able to draw parallels when students are having problems with materials or personnel. I'm able to draw parallels to the professional world, and in some cases assure students they will run into the same kinds of problems on the outside, that they must utilize what they are going through at present to help them gain perspective and techniques for dealing with these kinds of problems, when they do encounter them, once they leave academe.

Difficulties with teachers and colleagues, preparing and memorizing material—these are concerns that will be encountered throughout a professional life. I want my students to begin putting together the arsenal that they can carry into the profession, the tools that they will need to build a career and help solidify positive relationships, so that the work of making music can go forward. Continuing my performance experience helps me to bring new ideas into the studio that have been tested in the performance arena. I think that if I wasn't still performing it would be too easy to come up with some cockamamy ideas that really wouldn't go very far, or have much of a relationship to actuality. But still being in the center of performance life ensures that the ideas that manifest themselves in the classroom are viable, and not conceived out of my own fantasy.

WC: Does this mean that retirement from teaching will come when you are no longer performing?

GS: No. I don't think that I will retire from teaching when I am no longer performing. I would hope that by that time I will have learned and gained enough from active performance to draw upon for the rest of my teaching career. That is not to say that I will not gain new insights and ideas; it just means that I will have to be very careful as to how I apply those new insights and ideas, not being in the performance arena myself to test them firsthand.

WC: One would not think the army a likely place for motivating a career in music. Yet, the literature reveals that you began thinking seriously about opera while in the armed services. Would you comment on the setting that triggered a desire within you to tackle something beyond the commonplace.

GS: My stint in the military was not something to which I looked forward. I had pursued a degree in education, majoring in music at Wayne State University in Detroit, and I started teaching on the high-school level a semester before I graduated. I taught for a year and a half, then Uncle Sam drafted me [in 1956]. I went into basic training a week after I was married. I really was not looking forward to being a soldier for two years.

I had heard of the United States Army Chorus in Washington, D.C., while I was still a student at Wayne State. I decided not to audition as some of my colleagues at Wayne had done because it just seemed too impractical a move. Being black, for one thing, made me feel that there wasn't much of a chance for me to audition successfully—plus, I didn't think that my experience, although I had been singing practically all of my life, was adequate. It just seemed too far away, another world.

I decided to go into the service as a foot soldier and try for a slot in the band. After eight weeks of basic training, I went into the band at Fort Leonard Wood, Missouri. After about two weeks of playing the flag up and down, I felt that I would go nuts doing that for two years.

Along with two [white] colleagues, I took a weekend pass and went up to Washington, D.C., to audition for the chorus. One fellow serviceman was a trumpet player, the other a tenor with a pleasant voice. We sang for the conductor, Captain Samuel Lobada, [who] eventually became the Commander of the United States Army Band. Captain Lobada told my colleagues that they were not accepted, but he told me to wait for a while, and he went into the office. About twenty-five minutes later he came out and said to me, "If this is what you want, we would like to have you." I knew what was going on because, at that time, no black had ever been associated in any way with the United States Army Band, which was formed by General Pershing in 1925 and known as "Pershing's Own." The Army Chorus was formed in 1955. If I accepted, I would be the first black member of that organization.

WC: Astounding that the United States Army Chorus was formed in the same year that black singers first became members of the Metropolitan; more astounding is that you, the first black man to receive international distinction in opera, would become the first black member of this choral organization. Sweet irony, indeed.

GS: I knew that Lobada was in that office fighting for me. He was that kind of person. He was interested in talent; color meant nothing to him. He prevailed, as he did so many times in the future about many things. I found myself in this organization, which was peopled with young men, all draftees, who had either had professional singing careers interrupted by the draft or who were planning on having professional singing careers when they got out of the service. [It was] a top-notch singing group, full of solo-voice material.

I was content to be a member of the chorus for my two years, after which I would return to Detroit and go back to teaching. One of these men, Jack Gillaspy, became a very close friend. Jack later sang professionally in Germany as John Gillas; he now teaches at Texas Tech University. Jack kept after me to come with him to one of his voice lessons. He was studying with a retired singer living in Washington, D.C., named Themy Georgi, who had performed extensively in Germany and Chicago early in the century. It was nearing my time for discharge in the spring of 1958, so I finally went with Jack just to get him off my back. He was bugging me so much!

I sang for Mr. Georgi, who said to me in a very impressive manner, "You study with me for one year, and I can guarantee that you will have a career." No one had ever said that to me before. I went home, talked it over with my wife (by this time we had a small daughter), and she said to me, "Whatever you do, it's all right with me." She has probably had ample opportunity to regret having made that statement.

I felt that I was young enough to give it a try. Now that someone had said with such assurance that a singing career was possible, I didn't want to take a chance on going back to Detroit, resuming my teaching career, and then some thirty years down the road bitterly denouncing that decision, thinking that I could have possibly had a singing career had I tried. Moreover, I figured that I was young enough to bounce back if the trial proved to be a failure. I decided to give myself two years to devote to the pursuit of a career. I extended my [army service] period for one year so that I could have an income to take care of my young family while I studied with Mr. Georgi.

I was finally discharged in the spring of 1959. I then began my career with a small opera company in Woodstock, New York. My initial contact with the company happened rather fortuitously. About two weeks after I had extended my period of service in 1958, I received a call from a woman in New York City named Sally Turnau. The basso Ara Berberian, a former Army chorister, had signed a contract with her for the summer season after getting out of the service. One of the two tenors who had signed for their season canceled on them at the last minute. They were stuck; for some reason Ara told them to call me. Ara knew that I was supposed to get out of the service that spring, but I don't think he knew that I had made a decision to study for a career. Reluctantly I told Mrs. Turnau that I had just reenlisted for another year, but to please consider me for the coming year of 1959. I'd be getting out about that time, and I'd be looking for a job. I was then told by Mrs. Turnau, "Come to New York in January for an audition." I did, and they accepted me. In a real sense, there was a job for me before I got out of the service, at least for the summer of 1959.

WC: How large was the Turnau Company?

GS: The Turnau Company consisted of two sopranos, a full lyric, the other a kind of lyric coloratura; one mezzo-soprano; two tenors, one *lirico leggiero,* the other, full lyric; one baritone; and one bass. There was an excellent stage director, and two coach accompanists, one of whom was music director. This was the nucleus of the company. The business manager was also the stagehand, and we had a very fine stage designer. It was a very tightly knit company, and it was a wonderful way to start a career.

WC: So your activities as an Army chorister were motivating?

GS: Being a member of the Army Chorus, an organization with so many really exceptionally talented singers, made me think about my own place as a singer, performer, and teacher. If the surroundings had not been as stimulating, I might not have taken the chance: leaving my job in Detroit (I had tenure) and going off to New York City, which was really stepping into the unknown.

I must say that until I started studying for an operatic career, I really was not interested in the genre. My musical tastes were focused mainly on recital, choral, and orchestral literature. I had no desire to attend the opera. When I was a senior in college we did Stravinsky's *Oedipus Rex,* a fully staged production that I thoroughly enjoyed, but it did not speak to me as a way of life. When I started studying for a career, naturally my interest in the art form peaked.

I joined a small opera workshop in Virginia, [in 1958] which was run in the living room of a private home by a couple who had no problems with having a black tenor. Most of the activities around Washington, D.C., at that time did not include African-Americans, but this couple welcomed me, and I began to become involved. When I walked out on stage in the little theater in Woodstock, New York, with the Turnau Opera Players, I knew that I was doing that for which I was born.

WC: If it were yours to do over again, armed with your current knowledge, what would you do differently? Which things would you not change?

GS: I would spend more time performing repertoire with smaller companies. The first time I auditioned for the Metropolitan Opera was in 1959 in Washington, D.C., before I really started my career, and it was not totally successful, although I received wonderful comments, which bolstered me along and helped me to know that I was on the right road. In 1961, when I auditioned in New York City, I felt that I was good enough to earn some money in the Met Auditions, but had no inkling that winning a contract was even a remote possibility.

I entered the auditions because I very badly needed some money. I was stunned when I won the contract! I found myself with relatively little experience, thrown into the arena with highly seasoned artists who had been doing their roles for many years. With very few exceptions, I was learning and performing everything that I did at the Metropolitan for the first time in my life. The ideal road to travel would have been to gain good experience over a number of years in smaller companies, grooving a limited repertoire, so that whenever I went to make a debut in a new opera house, I would be performing a role that I had been wearing like skin for some time, rather than taking on a new role each time, which begins to wear on the nerves. Obviously under such a plan I would not have gone to a big company like the Metropolitan as quickly as I did, following a scant two years in the business.

Experience declares that the best way to build a stable career in opera and ensure performance longevity is to develop two or three bread-and-butter roles. When you become known for these, naturally people will ask, "Can you do this new role or that one tomorrow, or yesterday?" The best approach is to say, "Thank you very much, but that's not currently in my repertoire."

Now you can make some enemies doing that, but in the long run it will save you a lot of grief. You can guarantee your durability by identifying a role that you would like to perform; if your advisers feel that it is right for you, take a year or two to learn it, to live with it, and work it into your voice. Once it's ready, announce to the small companies: "Yes, I'm ready to perform this role." Perform it over a period of years in places where the spotlight is not so bright, until it is yours, and you know that you can sing it if you have a temperature of 250 degrees and your mouth is swollen.

In this way you proceed at your own pace, and there is less anxiety involved. I would attempt to structure a performance schedule in a much less helter-skelter fashion than is normally done. Quite often singers are running from here to there, doing Puccini one week, Mozart the next; then off to do a couple of recitals; then back to the opera stage for Wagner; then off for a performance of the Verdi Requiem. It's such a pastiche! Instrumentalists, from what I can tell, handle it in a much more sensible fashion. Pianists will put together a program or two, and those are the programs they perform that season: a recital that they will play in a number of cities, and a concerto that they will play with orchestras. They are not running around from pillar to post. In so doing, they are really able to groove themselves into those works.

During my years at the Metropolitan, I sang Strauss, Mozart, Puccini, and a bit of Wagner—sometimes all in one season. That is a bit much, to go from one language to another, one style to another, one composer to another. I am convinced that the best way is, if you're going to do Puccini, then you do Puccini—maybe one or two roles of the same type and vocal demand. If you're going to do another composer, then give yourself an ample period of time to get Puccini out of the way, out of your voice. Give time to get the new composer and language ingrained before the performance, rather than working on Strauss for next week while performing Puccini, Verdi, or Mozart this week.

After the opera season, I would give myself enough time to get vocally and psychologically ready to meet the next challenge, recital or oratorio. I would not mix the two; I would set my recital tour well after the opera season. If there were opportunities for oratorio, I would wait until after the recitals. Moreover, if I were doing a Verdi Requiem, I would try to book several performances of that work, rather than go from the Verdi Requiem to the Mozart Requiem to Mahler's *Das Lied von der Erde*. I would structure performances so that they would make much more sense, because it is that kind of wild programming (I know this from experience) that causes tremendous difficulties with regard to fatigue and vocal confusion.

Most managers don't seem to understand this, and in some cases they don't seem to care. The artist must be made aware of these difficulties and be forthright in taking responsibility for controlling them in his or her professional life. I certainly would not change my decision to pursue a professional career as a singer. I've always had the feeling that I backed into, or was guided into, this career from above, since I didn't plan to sing professionally.

It does seem, however, from the way things have worked out, that there was no other choice. Therefore, I have no regrets whatsoever that I made the decision to sing, to pursue a career as an opera singer. It has been, and continues to be, richly rewarding on so many levels. I have learned about myself in ways that I think would have been impossible had I not gotten into this business. I know that it was absolutely the right thing to do with my life.

WC: In our time it is all but impossible for a singer to have a career of major proportions without having an identity with opera. Some classically trained voices are not appropriate for this medium, the recital or concert literature being more suitable. Some singers are effective in all three genres. You will be remembered as an opera singer. Your resume, however, lists extensive performances in concert and recital. Where does the vocal breakdown come? Does personality play a part in the equation? Since you have been effective in all three forms, which setting, for you, presents the greatest challenge?

GS: I have done a lot of recital and oratorio work in my career although, basically, I am an opera singer. I must say that, for me, recitals are the most challenging of the three performance settings, simply because of the artistic and vocal demands that can be built into a recital. In an opera, one deals with only one character and the development of that character throughout the work. You're dealing with one musical style, one composer, one language. The same is true in oratorio—one composer, one style, one language. The peaks and the valleys, the vocal high points are built into both the opera and the oratorio.

In a recital, you the artist are responsible for its construction. With a little of this and a little bit of that, the recital is a real kaleidoscope of musical events: different composers, different languages. Each song is a miniature opera within itself. In a particular song, you're dealing with (unless you're doing a cycle) the life of a character that you portray, and that song has its climactic moment. Each song is really a little aria, and if you're not careful in programming, you can kill yourself in the first half by overprogramming. You must be very aware of the fact that every song can't be a socko item.

You must build in the pacing very carefully, so that out of a group of songs, maybe one of them is really a demanding piece vocally, and the others give you an opportunity to coast a bit. So the recital is a tremendous challenge. When you change languages from group to group, you are really almost changing vocal techniques, because each language insists on your approaching it with a degree of purity so that it can be understood, and it makes certain demands on your vocal technique. Italian is different from German, German is different from French. All of these languages are different from English.

WC: Your statements reveal a fundamental difference in the recital program formats of European and American artists, particularly from the perspective of language content. It is not uncommon for European singers to present recitals featuring songs in only one language.

GS: Absolutely!

WC: Luciano Pavarotti, for instance, sings only Italian songs and arias in recital.

GS: Dietrich Fischer-Dieskau sings German songs in recital.

WC: In other words, song literature in their native tongues.

GS: Yes.

WC: It is not a common practice for American singers to present recitals featuring songs only in English. For the black artist, even more is expected in programming: American songs and a group of spirituals.

GS: This seems to magnify one of my earlier statements: "American music students must acquire much of what European music students inherit."

WC: You are not the first singer who I have heard say, "Recitals are not easy."

GS: In my experience I began to feel comfortable with the recital genre after the first two performances, but to make the switch from the operatic stage, where I was much more at home by nature, to the recital stage, from the grand to the intimate, was always a big adjustment. Oratorio was something of a combination of the two things. Recital was always the biggest and remains the biggest challenge for me. When I do a recital that I'm proud of, I feel that I really have something to take pride in.

Certain personalities are definitely geared more to one genre than the other. There are people who absolutely come alive on the recital stage: they love the intimacy of the art form; they are uncomfortable in the larger arena of opera, and vice versa. Many opera singers feel very uncomfortable in a more intimate setting, where all of their little insecurities are exposed to the world.

WC: "I feel so naked out there," Birgit Nilsson is said to have complained when asked about how she felt on the recital stage.

GS: Some opera singers have difficulty scaling their voices down to meet the intimate demands of recital literature: the lieder, the French melody, what have you. They're accustomed to the broader vocal spectrum that opera demands.

WC: Is there anything else that you would or would not change?

GS: I would not change my family situation. (I have a son and a daughter; I also have two grandchildren.) My family has been of immeasurable value. I'm grateful that the singing profession has enabled us to have wonderful experiences—traveling together and sharing occasions, both unique and gratifying, in locales we might only have dreamed of.

WC: In our time it seems that fewer African-Americans are seriously studying classical music. In far too many instances our black college choirs have become little more than cuts above church choirs, over-programming gospel music, while sacrificing the choral masterpieces and classically arranged spirituals.

A generation ago more classical music was done in black churches. A large number of black classical artists first made contact with great music in educational and religious institutions. Now, many of our black contemporary youth feel that blacks have no identity with the classical arts. A recent publication that I reviewed on "Outstanding Black Americans" did not spotlight a single classical musician. We have won the battle, are we losing the war?

GS: In the 1960s and seventies there was a tremendous backlash on the part of both majority and minority Americans against much of what had been considered to be correct, proper, and necessary in the upbringing and education of young people. As far as African-Americans are concerned, that backlash I think was especially understandable because there was little information about our past disseminated to us in our scholastic studies. When black Americans became more aware of their history through the publication industry, there was tremendous anger and resentment. Accordingly, the Lyceum series went out the window in black colleges; the recitals of classical music were eliminated; and the performing arts series on campuses, both black and white, became more entertainment oriented, rather than educational experiences that were hopefully also entertaining.

In the eyes of African-Americans, much of what was a product of the "white" western world became synonymous with everything that was negative about the white world and its repression of not only black people, but people of color all over the world. The rising interest in the more popular folk-music forms, seen in that light, is understandable; the elimination of the other side of the coin, however, is lamentable.

The elimination of the Negro spiritual, which was seen as slave music, from the musical life of black churches in particular, is greatly to be regretted. Gospel, the fusion of blues and jazz with religious themes, was seen as music that more truly reflected the black experience. Consequently, this music has become more prominent than western classical music in the lives of young black people.

We are now faced in academia with the task of trying to make young people understand that you don't throw out the baby with the bathwater, and that time-honored things of substance must also find a place in their experience because those things are of quality. I think that gospel music is probably closer to the musical experience of the African than other forms of music because of its structure, dance rhythms, and spiritual quality; it certainly deserves a significant place in African-American culture. I'm happy to see that spirituals are making a comeback. As regards classical music, it is up to us, the performers and teachers, to present this music in a different light, not as the only music, but as music of significance and importance. If classical music is presented in the right way, it does make friends, as it should and can.

WC: And that is one of the reasons why it is so necessary for black scholars to pursue more vigorously topics dealing with the classical arts experiences as they relate to the African-American community.

GS: There is a problem, however, with classics of any kind: the masterpieces of literature are being attacked as being of less relevance for today's world. For many years they were taught as being the only sources of wisdom worthy of study and veneration, which was just as shortsighted a view. We should dedicate ourselves to awakening people to the fact that greatness is found in all generations and ethnic identities.

It's unfortunate when one looks at the history of jazz in this country. I taught at the University of Maryland for seven years, where there was a very fine jazz band. But out of a band of about 35 there were only about three black students. A jazz band conducted by a black professor, who couldn't find young blacks who were interested in playing jazz! If, however, he had put together a rhythm-and-blues combo, he would have had no problem finding players, or people interested in hearing the music.

All parts of our musical heritage must be presented and demonstrated to young people in a manner that will make them see that, yes, this music does speak to the soul, the emotions, the intellect. They should become aware, they should be exposed, they should take from this music what it can give.

It is a very hard task, because most of what young people hear on the radio is of the popular genre, and it is that medium with which they associate most easily. There is a very real problem among African-Americans in particular, and Americans in general. Classical music has always been a minority art form. Today, it's even more of a minority art form, even for the majority.

WC: Becoming an opera singer is a formidable task for an individual of any race. The task is even more formidable for someone who happens to have black skin, particularly if the gender is male. Beyond talent and training, what kind of personality does one need to perform in opera? How is this made more intense for the black artist in general, and the black male artist in particular? Also, beyond your experiences in the army, what other influences have impacted on your career, including the positive and negative events that have sent you in a particular direction?

GS: An opera singer finds that it can be a somewhat lonely experience pursuing a career. There is the travel; there are times when one lives alone in a foreign country. I remember speaking with a young soprano in West Berlin a few years ago, who was there to perform a contemporary work at the Deutsch Oper. I think that she had just gone through a difficult point in a personal relationship, and she spoke of how hard it was and how lonely life can be. There are stretches of time when you find yourself dealing with situations that are extremely difficult: the challenge of a performance, the challenge of working with a colleague with whom you don't have a good relationship; and there you are, sitting in your hotel room all by yourself.

It takes a certain kind of personality to stand up to the exigencies of having a career. You must really want it to [be able to] put up with all of the stuff that you encounter: the disappointments; the frustrations of auditioning for something; doing your best and not being chosen for the part; or coming up against some kind of political situation that denies you (for whatever reason) a fair crack at an opportunity. There is a lot of anxiety in trying to live up to your potential, trying to put into perspective the expectation of the audience when you're on stage, especially after you have gained some reputation. Knowing what your colleagues expect of you; knowing that you're only human, that you're not a recording machine; knowing that a performance will not allow you to rerecord and rerecord a moment until you get it absolutely perfect; knowing that as soon as it's out of your mouth, it's there, perfection or imperfection, for everybody to hear. You must have strong intestines.

You must have some kind of spiritual strength, so that you can bounce back from moments that are less than successful in your eyes and ears. You must have a good deal of intestinal fortitude to deal with the criticism that comes not only from conductors and directors with whom you may be working but also from the media. When you get a negative review, it may be read by people all over the world, depending on the organ in which it is printed. Only a few of those readers would have been in the performance hall; consequently, the majority won't be able to form conclusions from firsthand knowledge. The artist has that with which to deal. If you're overweight, if you're black, if you happen to be a black male, then those problems, of which we are very much aware, are exacerbated.

In Europe it is especially difficult now because of the common market. People are looking to citizens of those common-market countries to supply their artistic needs. In countries where economics are tight, prejudices rise. If you happen to be a minority person, it is more difficult then to find a place for yourself.

I was speaking to a well-known artist, a black woman, who is married to a foreigner. She got together with a number of black women, who like herself have careers, and who are also married to foreigners, [and] they found themselves lamenting the fact that even though they have married very well, they will always be foreigners in the eyes of the natives—not only just foreigners, but black foreigners.

There are problems. An opera singer must have the guts not to be put off by those problems and their attendant hurdles. The artist is required to keep the goal in mind, and lean toward that goal without wavering. This takes a great deal of internal and spiritual strength. It is not for everyone.

WC: Also, we dare not forget that for the black classical artist, biting criticism can often come from the black community. Unfortunately, some African-Americans strongly feel that it is a renouncing of heritage and identity when one of their own kind delves into a classical art form—caught between a rock and a hard place!

GS: Adapting to foreign countries [is essential]; that is still where more of the opportunities are, in spite of difficulties. Acquiring a new language, new social ways of being, different foods—I know that for a lot of my black colleagues this is a big hurdle. They are accustomed to a certain kind of diet, and you just don't find some of those foods in foreign countries! They must do as best they can. These are very real problems. It does take a certain kind of strength and desire for success to achieve a place for oneself in the business.

I think of Jim Wagner, a fine tenor, who for years tried to find a place for himself in Germany. He finally did. There were many refusals, however: "Thank you very much." "We like your voice, but we don't have a position for you now." Jim says that finally someone just came out and told him point-blank, "I like your voice, but I won't hire you because you're black."

These are some of the hurdles and bridges that black artists (black men in particular) must get over and around. A lot of people just fall by the wayside because they don't have the stomach to deal with the rejection.

WC: Where is Mr. Wagner now?

GS: Jim Wagner is singing in a German house. I can't remember exactly where, but he is having a very good career. I heard him recently on a broadcast here in the United States. I believe that it was an oratorio, and he sounded fine. [Mr. Wagner currently maintains an active performance career under the auspices of German management (Hilbert). Wagner makes his home in Munich. He is also a part of the academic community in Lübeck.]

I must say that in the places where I have worked, my colleagues have always been positive and helpful. I have never had a negative work experience. I've been fortunate in that regard. The only negatives that I can think of have been my overwork, which I think in part was generated by my twin desires of wanting to prove myself and create a situation wherein anyone coming after me would find the door much more readily opened. I've come to see that, indeed, each person must open the door for himself. If I had known that earlier, I might have removed a bit of pressure from myself. But it was that way and I have no regrets.

WC: Each person must open the door for himself. Could this be why black artists are not thought of, certainly by the larger communities, as being social and political reformers?

GS: I think that in order to be seen as a social and political reformer, the performer has to reach outside of the performance arena and involve himself or herself in politics, or political reform movements, as did Paul Robeson. Movie star Jane Fonda would be a contemporary example. If you're just doing what you do, and it is not an activity that in and of itself is seen as one that is geared to the advancement of a group of people, even though you may be pioneering, it won't be recognized in a large way. Someone might state that you are the first person, or the first black to function in a particular arena. But it doesn't take on that larger weight that one finds attending a political figure, or that political figure's efforts to better the plight of a people.

My comments earlier about reducing my workload and focusing my repertoire really speak to those things that were negative in terms of my direction and growth as an artist. Nevertheless, it's all part and parcel of my experience, and because of it I've grown. I've found myself moved in different directions. One of the most positive is back into the classroom, which is something that I thoroughly enjoy. I've always known that I wanted to wind up my professional days in the academic setting, where I can make the most effective use of my experiences.

The opportunity came to start teaching again in the early seventies when I was appointed an adjunct professor at Staten Island Community College. Then in 1980 I was offered a position at the University of Maryland, where I taught for seven years; and now I am enjoying my work at the University of Michigan.

Teaching is very important to me. I neglected it for a number of years when I was singing exclusively; therefore, I knew that it was absolutely right to take those positions and move back into the classroom when the opportunities were presented. It is now the right mix. I'm having a ball with my students. I have some wonderfully talented young people. When we have good sessions, and I see them gain helpful insight, everything that I have experienced in my career, whether it be positive or negative, makes real sense. I'm grateful. In total, I am blessed.

WC: Is there a role, concert work, or piece of recital literature that you want to perform as a crowning achievement to your career? Perhaps there is something from each of these categories?

GS: I am at present enjoying the opportunity to perform a good deal of chamber music; having excellent faculty artists available is a tremendous boon, and I really appreciate being able to get into, to explore, and to know this very beautiful literature. There are a couple of things in mind that would be nice to perform, but I won't talk about those now. I won't share them. Maybe I'll do them; maybe I won't. I'm just grateful for the opportunities that I have had, and I trust that I'll make the most of them.

WC: Thank you, Mr. Shirley, for enriching our world with your talent.

Milwaukee, Wisconsin 1990

Shirley Verrett. *Photograph by Christian Steiner, courtesy of Shirley Verrett.*

8

Shirley Verret:
A Renowned Diva Speaks

The uncompromising artistry thorough musicianship and the powerful stage presence of Shirley Verrett have been acclaimed throughout the world: in concert; opera, in both soprano and mezzo-soprano roles; in recital; and most recently on Broadway in the musical *Carousel*. Miss Verrett, early on, became her own woman in matters that related to her career and took steps to ensure longevity and continued growth in all facets of the repertoire. I first became acquainted with the voice of Shirley Verrett when I was a music student in the 1960s at Knoxville College. I listened with great interest to a recording of a Carnegie Hall Verrett recital that was in the Knoxville Public Library. Additionally, Nathan Carter, the conductor of our concert choir, brought into one of our rehearsals a tape of Handel's *Utrecht Jubilate,* a score that we were then preparing that had been made at the Juilliard School during his days there as a graduate student. Dr. Carter, currently choral director at Morgan State University, was conducting this performance, and Miss Verrett, who was also a student at Juilliard during this time, was one of the soloists. In addition to hearing and seeing Miss Verrett on Metropolitan Opera broadcasts and telecasts, it has been my great pleasure to be in the audience at two of her recitals: on October 16, 1974 at Uihlein Hall in Milwaukee, Wisconsin; and most recently during the 1993 National Association of Negro Musicians Convention in Oakland, California. It was after the Oakland recital that I approached Miss Verrett about engaging in conversation with me for this project. To all of our good fortune, she most graciously accepted.

Shirley Verrett, born on May 31, 1931, in New Orleans, Louisiana, grew up in Los Angeles, California, where her family moved when she was a child. A graduate of Venture College and the Juilliard School, Miss Verrett, in this conversation, speaks candidly, eloquently, and passionately about opera and the African-American experience and the forces and philosophies that shaped and molded her into one of the world's most beloved artists.

Wallace Cheatham: Why has there not been a black male to become a "real" operatic superstar: a parallel to Shirley Verrett or Leontyne Price?

Shirley Verrett: The first thing that comes into my mind is the beginning part of our history in this country: slavery—the idea of the male black being a superstud. And I think, unfortunately, this has come down—I know for a fact, in most cases—this notion has come down to haunt us even in 1994, as I am speaking to you. That is one reason. Another reason that there has not been a real operatic black male superstar is that not too many black males of a certain quality of voice have gone into opera. There are possibly many reasons for this. One reason that we cannot overlook is many times males do have families to support. They marry. They have children. And the struggle that one must go through to make a career in opera, and the amount of money that one can make at the beginning of one's career, because it takes time to build up a reputation, and be able to demand a certain kind of fee, a good fee, a wonderful fee, a big fee, if you have a family, you cannot do this. I'm not saying that females have not had, or do not have, families also. But in many instances the female's salary is an addition to the family, unless the female singer is not married. From where I have sat in the old days, the late fifties and early sixties, when I went to the auditions, you did not hear the real top male voices. Now the voices are out there. I'm sure of it. They have always been out there. But they didn't seem to get into the auditions that I attended. So this is another issue. In fact, some of the times when I was at some of these auditions I was quite embarrassed at the caliber and wondered why the judges even allowed that caliber of talent to enter the competition. Not only from the black side, but because we're talking about the black male, I became—because I am black—I felt more upset when a black male would get up to sing, to audition, and it was not good enough. I must say that I was a judge last year for the Lola Hayes competition. I was very pleased. I've forgotten the young man's name because I didn't know him before. Beautiful voice. Beautiful training. He did not win the prize because of some reasons from the other judges. I liked him very much. We do have the voices around, but in my time a lot of these voices did not come forward to be tested. We have only to my knowledge one real male star today: Simon Estes.

WC: Yes, and he's not singing in this country right now, certainly not at the Metropolitan.

SV: There are others who are coming up and I'm hoping that they will get to this stature also, will reach the point in their careers where they can be called stars, but at this present moment, we do not have them, black male stars in opera. Many black males have possibly been afraid to go into opera, even those with the great voices, because they know how much work is involved, and how much they would have to bear, and how much rejection in many cases. I have seen some of the young ones in Europe, but they're not of the caliber of superstar or star quality. The potential possibly is there, but they have not reached that yet. I know also that it's not only possible, but it does happen, that when black males do get to the point where they can have leading roles in the opera houses of the world, they are not given the opportunities too many times; whereas the black females have been given these opportunities.

WC: How has the "supernigger syndrome" been reflected in opportunities for the black male in opera, and for the black female?

SV: I think that this is a very difficult question. I have not seen the black males in opera to be superniggers. You would have to play a role like Samson in *Samson and Delilah*—things like that. I know that in the German literature, I don't remember all of the roles that Mr. Estes has sung, but I don't really put him in that kind of category of being a supernigger because he's singing in an area, the Wagnerian area, where blacks have not been singing. And for that I give high praise to him, that he was able to break into the Wagnerian world.

WC: I'm laughing within myself because my definition of supernigger is something sociological, meaning that if you're black you can't be just as good, you must be better. You are dealing with this concept aesthetically. Thank you. Please continue.

SV: I would think that if an opportunity would be given to black males, now this may be black males on another level, the ones who have not reached superstardom possibly have been given roles that reflect them in not a very wonderful way. In the days when we, the black females, began I was told and I have read that the first thing offered to Miss Price by the Metropolitan was Aida. She refused, until she made her debut; as we all know, that glorious debut of hers was as Leonora in *Il Trovatore*. I was in the audience, and I'm sure you were also, or friends of yours, or whatever, and you know about this.

WC: No. Unfortunately, I was not there, but I have read about it—the forty-two minute ovation! I know that she was a sensation!

SV: It was an exciting evening! So she immediately leaped over that, and then of course after that, came back and did all of the roles. At a certain moment we can't be too particular. We can be particular, but at a certain moment, if the role is really a fabulous role and we can sing it, we should do it because this paves the way not only for ourselves, but for the future generation. When Marian Anderson made her debut at the Metropolitan, she was Ulrica, and this is a fortune-teller. You could put this into the category of here she is playing the psychic; but it was a great role. So I think our focus has to be on that: is the role great? We know that for white males to sing *Otello* they have to blacken down. The white female counterpart in Aida has to blacken down. So I think that if we stretch this point too far it is not very healthy for us.

WC: The operatic instrument: criteria for identification; training; technique; qualities of a good teacher; qualities of a good coach; vocal perseverance role preparation. . . .

SV: Quite a mouthful there.

WC: Yes.

SV: I feel that anyone who hears an operatic voice knows and can identify that operatic voice because of the quality of the tone; the fullness of the tone, even if it is a coloratura, or a light lyric, or a very light soubrette-type voice. You hear the training because you hear that the voice is even throughout its scale. There is a wonderful center to the voice: the quality of a centeredness to the voice. It is as it should be, an instrument that when we listen to it, it sounds very free. It doesn't make you nervous. I mentioned already that it is rich in quality. A fuller range, a larger range than someone who sings "pop music." A certain way of forming the vowels unlike a pop singer. The kind of phrasing that an operatic instrument will do. The range of the operatic instrument usually is at least two octaves, and some of us have three octaves, and possibly some voices that even go to three and a half: those very rare instruments. But it is the freeness and the color of the instrument that tells us it's an operatic voice as opposed to a pop singer's voice. We start to train . . . I'm still training. And I'm sure that most really wonderful singers, fabulous singers, train to the day that they're not singing anymore. I've just recently been in *Carousel*, and I must say that even there, singing another kind of music, beautiful music, well-composed music, music that was really written for people who also know how to sing, I studied because the music didn't set really quite well in my voice. And I almost did not do the part, but I took it as a challenge, and I went into it. And I dare say that by the end, the last months of the show, I was much better than I was at the beginning. So this meant that I had to go back to school, to my own school, my own training, to the beginning and say, What am I doing here; how can I make this better; because it doesn't really suit my voice, it's not really written for my voice at this particular point, what can I do about it, which brings us to the point of technique. Technique is most important in voice training, any voice training, even for nonoperatic voices. But you cannot last in the opera world if you do not have a very firm technique. Most of us came into the world with a good voice. Some singers' voices are absolutely perfectly placed when they come into the world. Mine was almost perfectly placed, but there was a lot of work that I had to do, but the voice was natural, as I'm sure you will find with many operatic singers. There are very few who say that their voices had to be built from scratch.

WC: Your statements make me think of my first experience with Robert McFerrin. It was my study of voice with Mr. McFerrin that provided the initial catalyst for my interest in doing research into the African-American experience as it relates to opera. He had invited me to stay in his home. I really knew no one in St. Louis. It was probably about eight-thirty or nine o'clock in the morning. I was sitting at the piano looking through and playing his music that was there. Mr. McFerrin came out of his bedroom, still in his pajamas, and sat in the chair that was just a few steps from the piano. A score of the Prologue from Leoncavallo's *I Pagliacci* was among the music that was there. I asked Mr. McFerrin to sing it. I had played this aria for a singer some years before during my student days at Knoxville College. And he gave a performance of that aria that any opera house in the world would have been honored to have had—never moving out of that chair. Afterward he looked at me and very firmly said, "I was born with a voice, but I had to learn how to use it." I will never, ever, forget that morning!

SV: I always felt that until I had a technique that I could rely on, I could not really be a singer. Like anything else in life, you wouldn't try to write a book if you didn't have skills; if you hadn't gone to school to study; to take courses in writing; and before that, the English language; or whatever your native language is, it has become so much a part of you that you can use it at will; and not be confined to, let's say, an octave or an octave and a half. So technique is very important. When you have a cold, or when you have something else happen to you, an allergy maybe, God forbid. You will know that it is not because you're not breathing correctly that the voice is not responding. The technique will tell you that you have a cold now; you have been hit; you have been invaded by an allergy; you have a sore throat, tonsilitis, sinusitis whatever. Many times people have cut off a career because they didn't have the technique. And when certain things happened, maybe allergies reared their ugly head, they would immediately think that it was something they had done, or that they had ruined their voices, rather than knowing that they had an allergy and couldn't do anything about it until it was over; or having technique enough to get by the areas that are causing problems. This is what technique is all about. Something that you can fall back on. It is a foundation. When we are young, we can do anything. But as we get older, sometimes the instrument will not respond to the commands we give it in the same way that it would when we were eighteen, or nineteen years old; when we get to be forty, fifty, and sixty years old, we have other things with which to deal.

WC: Yes. Physiological changes.

SV: That is not to say that the voice is not continually, possibly maturing and being more beautiful; but there are things that will begin to leave; that we have to continually work on; but you must have the basic technique to start with so that you can work on these problems. The qualities of a good teacher. Well, I used to think that a good teacher had to have been a singer. I'm still not quite sure about that. I think that it can be good, and then sometimes maybe it can be a hindrance. I'm not quite sure. So I will leave that, because it is something I am trying to come to grips with myself to this day. A good teacher really needs to have great ears. Perfect ears. Ears that can hear, because even if you don't know anatomy, you can to a certain extent, if your ears are good enough, and you're a good musician, and you know and have heard a lot of good singing. . . . So here we are, these are some qualities: knowing good singing, having a great ear, being a musician. I think you really do need these qualities. Also, having the ability to know, if not speak, at least know languages grammatically. But the first thing for me is to have good ears. I'm taking for granted the musical education and all that this implies. The good ears so that he or she can pick up those very slight differences in what the sound is and what the sould should be. Qualities of a good coach, of course, are also having very good ears. Being a musician, almost the same qualities as being a good voice teacher. I want to go back to being a good voice teacher.

WC: Fine.

SV: Having said good ears, good musicianship, a working knowledge of languages, it would be wonderful—I'm going back to something I said that I would not say—to know that the voice teacher has or had a voice, a good voice, or a well-produced voice. It wouldn't have to be, or have been, so beautiful, but well produced. I think this would add to the quality of a good teacher. Because, if one sings well, he or she knows how it feels, and this part can be given to the student. That one knows how it feels when one sings well, and is able to tell the student—not that it's going to feel the very same way—this is a very difficult area, that it's going to feel exactly the same in another's body, in another's anatomy as it feels in my body, my anatomy. But it would be a wonderful starting point to have the feelings of what it's supposed to feel like when you hit a low note, when you hit a medium note, or a high note, a piano note, explained. Going back now to the vocal coach.

WC: Fine.

SV: I would like for the vocal coach to be an excellent pianist, to know the differences in style, the different periods in music, that you would not sing the German lied the same way that you would sing Massenet or Puccini. He or she should know that. He or she should have a good ear like a voice teacher, so that when the singer is away from the voice teacher and is with the coach, particularly in later years, that coach can help keep the singer on his or her toes by also having that good ear to say and know when sounds are not what they should be. It would be great if the coach also could have had voice lessons so that he or she knows, even if the voice is really very terrible, what a singer goes through to get the sound that is called for, or hoped for, or looked for. Vocal perseverance: I would rather say preservation.

WC: No problem.

SV: Preservation of the voice is a very, very important thing. You cannot do foolish things with the voice. I'm not going to say that everyone can't drink milk. Some people can. Some people can't. I'm not going to say that you can't eat nuts. Some people can. Some people can't. Smoking: I still feel that singers should not, and especially if they are inhaling. I have been able to tell in colleagues of mine, whose voices were still lovely, but something happened to the quality, when I knew that they were smoking and inhaling. Some of them just used to have a cigarette in their hand in a social situation: that's one thing. I'm told and I've read that Caruso smoked a lot, and maybe that's why his career didn't last as long as it might have. I don't know that part of it. But I would say it's better not to smoke. If you seem to be allergic to milk, or milk does not set well with you, it gives you phlegm, don't drink it; or if you do drink it, not near the time that you're going to perform. Keep the head covered. My mother used to talk to me about it, because in the early days, and up to the time that I was quite getting there in age, even into the forties, I didn't want to become so tied into the voice that the least little thing . . . going around in the summertime for instance with scarfs. There are many big singers who did that up to the end of their lives, and I just couldn't see myself doing that. But again that's Shirley Verrett and not anyone else that I'm speaking for. Don't go overboard with the protection, but be wise. In my case now, I always have a cap, or a hat, or a scarf on in the wintertime because of the air, the heat escaping from the top of the head, or air hitting you in the top of the head; and sometimes you can catch colds if you are prone to colds. But again I'm speaking for Shirley Verrett. These are just tips. I can't eat nuts when I have to sing. I can eat them the day before. But if it's on the day that I'm going to sing, I cannot eat the nuts, and I love nuts. I tried it once before a rehearsal and I had a terrible coughing spell. Maybe it wouldn't happen again, but I don't try it. I cannot drink milk on the day that I perform, or on a day before I perform, because it seems to coat my throat. So being in good health, taking good care of oneself, trying not to catch colds: some of the things that I've said will help that. Taking vitamins. Not going to doctors and letting the doctors, when you do have a cold, give you antibiotics. Colds are viral, and you cannot get rid of a virus with antibiotics; but most doctors will give them to you anyway because they will make you feel better. The doctor has given you something. But this is not a very good idea. The best thing to do is to take good care of your health. I believe in vitamin supplementation because I feel that our soil is not the soil that it used to be. In some places it may be, outside of the really great big cities. But I don't take the chance. I don't say that you have to live on vitamins, but if you can find a good herbalist, wonderful. I'm also not saying to give up on our Hippocratic kind of medicine. But I think there needs to be a balance. Don't let doctors give you antibiotics unless they're going to also give you azulfidine to help the colon. This is all a part of my formula for preserving the voice.

Role preparation. You have a study period. You have to know the style. A lot of us like to read a lot about the role. The period in which that particular role, that particular opera, was produced. It's a good idea to go to the museums and look at the paintings of particular periods. This is very helpful. But the study of the role itself, you should know a great deal about the composer. Then you take it, as if you were reading a novel. This is what I do. I read all of the parts. I read all of the music. I play the music. I'm not a very good pianist, but I can hammer out the parts, the underpinnings, to find out what is this whole work about; because it is about the whole. It's not just two or three pages, or an act that one has to sing. So my approach has always been to know, even if I don't know all of the parts from memory, which in many cases I don't, but to know what they are all about. This helps you in the preparation of your own part. What has been said before you entered the stage, and after you have left the stage, and before entering again. I prepare this way because I am so very much wedded to the theater. When in need of uplifting, instead of going to the opera, many times I have gone to the theater and to the ballet, or to symphonic concerts.

WC: You have done many roles, both soprano and mezzo-soprano. Which one did you find to be the most difficult . . . the easiest . . . and why? How are the character and personality traits of those ladies, or maybe men (you have done "Trouser roles"), reflected and revealed through the music?

SV: As I think about it now, I would say that possibly the role of Delilah in Saint-Saens's *Samson and Delilah* was the most difficult. I love this part very much, but have not sung it since the last time I sang it at the Met. I had a conductor at the Met who was really not tuned into what was on the page for the person who was singing the mezzo part between those two huge voices up there: the bass, the priest, and Samson. It was difficult from this standpoint: it is a very low-lying role. The Met asked me, we talked for about a year before I decided to do it. I have done the role in San Francisco and also in London, but in those cases I had conductors who understood what the composer wanted. When the mezzo-soprano is singing, the other voices cannot just belt out and sing as they wish. It has to be an ensemble. And the last performances of Delilah that I did at the Met, I did not have this. We did not have ensemble, which meant that in some cases I would oversing to be heard, or just say forget it, and not be heard. Acting the role was great fun.

WC: I saw you once in a telecast of Samson and Delilah. I believe Placido Domingo was Samson. I did enjoy the performance.

SV: I like the role of Delilah ten times, a hundred times, better for myself and my personality than Carmen. Carmen and I were really not great friends.

WC: I'm surprised. I've read and heard great things about you as Carmen.

SV: The best time that I had with Carmen, I could always sing it, was in Florence, because it was done on a small scale. It was done like opera comique, and for me that's the way Carmen should be done. There are one or two big scenes where you have everybody on the stage, but it's a small, chamber music opera as far as I'm concerned. When I made my debut at the Met in 1968 as Carmen, it was not given this way. It always displeases me a great deal when this is done. When something is taken and put into something that it's not supposed to be put into: a big opera instead of a small one. And for me *Carmen* is a small opera, a chamber opera. But getting back to Delilah . . .

WC: Surely.

SV: It would not have been so difficult if it had not been for the conductor who I had the last time I sang it, and because of that I will not sing it again. It lies low, and then you've got to have B-flats, which I do have in my voice. And that part when it gets to the last chorus is quite sopranoish. That's fine. The first thing, when she comes out, the recitative, is not written very high, and the first aria especially is very low, and the trio is very, very low for the mezzo-soprano. So you must have a great conductor to do that role. The easiest? I don't know. I've had several that were very, very easy; but even in the easy ones you will find places where you will have to work. I remember when I was asked to do my first Lady Macbeth at La Scala in 1975. A lot of this work was very easy for me, but there were very difficult places also that made me have to really go back to the technique and work it out for my voice. Something that gives trouble, I think for everyone, is that sleepwalking scene. In those days when I sang it, that D-flat would come out every single time. I know that some of the greats like Callas used to have problems with this scene. She'd get so frustrated that she'd get off stage, as the story goes, and sing the D-flat over and over and over again. But that's all a part of it, being on the stage, and that tension there. And it's written, this scene, very, very vicariously for the voice. And either you have that D-flat in your voice, you were born with it; or you have it in the voice, meaning that you were not born with it but you've worked with your potential to get to that D-flat; but it is very difficult. In the production that I did in San Francisco, I did an A-flat instead; and many singers have done this in the past. I felt very guilty about it because I like to feel that I am always singing the notes as the composer has written them. The other arias, the duet with Macbeth—it's stamina that you work for at those particular times. You wonder, how often can I do this role in one week? I feel that Lady Macbeth is the heaviest role that I would ever want to do—that and Tosca.

WC: I saw you as Tosca in a Metropolitan telecast. I believe that Luciano Pavarotti was Cavaradossi. I don't remember who did Scarpia.

SV: Tosca is a problem in the second act. It's a lot of heavy singing because of what she is doing, and not only because of how she must be moving on the stage, but the emotions that are inside. You have to be very, very careful; and then you have the high Cs to sing in the third act, when you're describing what happened, and how you killed Scarpia. So that was difficult. But those really weren't the most difficult things. I think Delilah in *Samson and Delilah* was the hardest thing. The role that I should never have sung, except for the arias in concert, was Amelia in *Un Ballo in Maschera* by Verdi. Sometimes when I was talked into things, like Lady Macbeth, it went well. This, *Un Ballo in Maschera,* did not. Another reason: while I was at La Scala, where Amelia was initially performed, I was ill. It was during this time that I began to really know that I had a bad allergy, but did not know what the allergy was until I came back to the United States. While I was singing Amelia at La Scala, the Metropolitan asked me to sing it, and because of what had happened while I was doing the part while I was ill—I couldn't do the part the way I wanted to—I canceled it, at the Met, a year ahead of time. This is one of the reasons that I had certain problems at the Met. Doing things like that. When I felt it was not the best thing for me to do, I got out of it. I loved singing *Norma* very much. I loved singing Princess Eboli.

WC: I saw a film, it was probably more of a documentary, some years ago about you and your work in opera. Eboli's scene that features "O don Fatale" was a part of that program. I remember your performance of this aria being so powerful, musically and dramatically. That documentary also had in it the "Judgment Scene" from *Aida.* You, of course, were Amneris. I can't imagine, certainly from an acting perspective, anything more being done with that scene. You are a very powerful and convincing actress. You could make a wonderful contribution to opera as a director. And your statements in that documentary about how well Verdi wrote for the mezzo-soprano voice were so enlightening. And if I remember correctly, you used a term in that documentary that I had not heard before and have not heard anyone else use: middle soprano.

SV: I've been asked year in and year out to sing Elisabetta in *Don Carlo,* but I really do like Eboli very, very much. The role was written for a voice like mine: not truly a one hundred percent mezzo, and not one hundred percent a dramatic soprano; but somewhere in between there, which has allowed me to sing many different parts; parts that had to do with mezzo-soprano or soprano. And *Norma* for me . . . I have a library that I started while I was at Juilliard. I've collected biographies all of my life. I have several biographies of Lilli Lehmann. I remember somewhere that she said that she would rather sing—I think I'm quoting her correctly—three Brunnhildes to one Norma.

WC: I have read the same story.

SV: I always say it is very dangerous for statements like that to be made, and for it to come out to be that you should not sing *Norma.* If you can sing *Norma* because your anatomy lets you, permits you to do it, you sing *Norma.* I feel this way. I would much rather sing three Normas to one Samson and Delilah! The notes are in my voice. I love the way Bellini keeps the voice moving, even if it's in the middle range and it gradually goes up. It's a wonderful, gradual, ascension. It's never jumping from the bottom to the top. Hardly ever does Bellini write like that. It's a wonderful way. I love to sing Donizetti in the same way. Donizetti can hop around and skip around a bit. But the line of Norma, I like for my voice. I'm not saying this for anyone else's voice, because for other people it might be hellishly difficult. But for me, I feel that even on certain bad days, unless it is a sore throat or something like that, because of the high Cs, the role would be wonderful. I also love the role of Adalgisa. I love it very much, and I would like to go back and sing that role again. It was a very rewarding part.

WC: I remember hearing the recording of *Norma* with Beverly Sills doing Norma and you doing Adalgisa. And I read somewhere that you are the first singer in the twentieth century, and only the third singer in opera history, to have sung both Norma and Adalgisa.

SV: In many ways Norma is rewarding from the standpoint of the many-faceted character that she is: a lover, a diva, the leader of her people, a friend, a complete tyrant, jealous, everything. She is a very, very well-rounded human being. For this reason I love her very much, and also because of the way that the part lies. I also like Bellini; and Adalgisa, a very beautiful part. One role that I don't think I would ever sing again is Leonora in Beethoven's *Fidelio.*

This has a lot to do with the kind of breath required. Because of my allergies, I always had to work on the breath. A lot of times people came to me saying, How do you do such long lines? When you do Leonora in *Fidelio,* it can be very, very difficult. The aria "Abscheulicher," has some very, very long lines, and they have to be supported, full and rich. I did it at the Met. I was going through allergy attacks, two of them. I had to give up singing the role. I don't think that I would do it again. I was talked into this role also. There are other roles—ladies and men, I've done Trouser roles—that I loved much more. The music itself of these personalities . . .

WC: Yes.

SV: In the case of Eboli, Verdi started to bring in the leitmotiv, similar to what is in the Wagner operas. In the Verdi operas, you know pretty much what the characters are going to be like most of the time. You know by the music because the man who wrote the music was a genius. I think this is always reflected in the music of the great composers. I hope that I'm not being too flippant with this.

WC: No, not at all.

SV: I feel that I would have to go back and take down the scores of all the roles I have done, and go through each of them point by point to give you the characteristics, how the personalities come through in the music. I'd like to speak a little about *Trovatore*. In this opera I like the role of Azucena very much.

WC: Azucena is one of the roles that I heard you do on a Metropolitan Saturday broadcast.

SV: I know that I play her a bit differently from some of the ladies who I have seen before and after me. I have a thing because of how I feel that she lived, how I feel that she walked, and how I feel that she looked: not like Shirley Verrett. I even wore a false nose in this part because I wanted to give the audience a picture of what this gypsy was all about. Her music—Verdi again, of course he was a great composer . . . a great, great composer. You know from the "Stride to Vampa," the way that *um pa pa um pa pa* is articulated, you know that this is not going to be the music of a soubrette, or of a great lady, the soprano lead in the opera. You know that's not going to happen when you hear the underpinning of the notes, before Azucena even opens her mouth to sing. A very forceful character. You hear this incredibly so in the duet with Manrico. I like the music. I love the music.

WC: As you are talking about Azucena, I can hear your laugh at the very end when I heard you do the role on that Saturday Metropolitan broadcast. Nothing comedic, but something emotionally strong and revelatory. One could tell and feel and know that Azucena was now finally at peace psychologically. That laugh just put emphasis on the depth of Azucena's hate for the Count and added to the intensity of what she tells the Count: that he has killed his brother! I say again that you would make a tremendous stage director!

SV: I go back to *Norma* again. The notes sort of follow one another very naturally. Something that the voice likes to do: scalelike passages;

skipping thirds; not doing too many skips and jumps. I feel very good when I'm singing in this way. Not that I have not done the other, but I am much happier doing vocal lines that move in a very gradual and wonderful, flowing way than skips and jumps.

WC: Are there roles that you would like to do, and roles that should not have been done, and why?

SV: I said earlier that Amelia in Verdi's *Un Ballo in Maschera* is a role that I never should have done. I did not, however, say why. You don't usually find characters or roles that suit you one hundred percent. And if you're offered a part in a play, or role in an opera, it is much more difficult to do that part or role if you don't have any kind of feeling for the character; if you don't have an acquaintance with a lot of the characteristics of the part. If this is the case—unless you really want to study a lot, or for some reason you've got to do this because you're trying to learn, or it's another discipline that you've placed upon yourself—I think that you should stay away from it. And Amelia, for me, was one of those. I did feel that I loved the music. I still love the music, but I never felt that I had too much in common as a stage personality with Amelia. To be caught in the kind of situation that she's caught in, that kind of love situation. With Norma it is something else. Norma has been the one betrayed, not the one to betray. She's been betrayed by Pollione, and even by Clotilde; so Norma is very innocent in all of this. I don't think of Amelia as a grand lady. And maybe I did my best when I thought on the scale of a Lady Macbeth, a Tosca, roles like that. There was a time when I thought about doing Lucia. Friends of mine, a very dear friend, John Arden, wanted me to do it; in those early years when I had started to do Donizetti. When I made my debut in Florence, I did Queen Elizabeth I in Donizetti's *Maria Stuarda*. And of course it was the soprano version. I had great fun. I heard the tapes recently and said, Did I do that? Yes, it was really great fun to have done that. People then heard things in my voice—maybe I didn't hear them myself, or maybe I didn't want to hear them—and felt that maybe I could do Lucia . . . Lucia as it was written. I think there is a version of the opera without all of the added coloratura notes. I was supposed to have gotten a score of it, but I never did. But I don't regret not having done Lucia. Claudio Abbado who was a very dear friend at that time; we both started to come upon the scene at about the same time. I did a lot of singing with him, and he was the one who actually persuaded me over a three-year period to do Lady Macbeth. Another part that I like very much, I've done it only one time in my life, and I'm very happy to have sung it. That was with Sarah Caldwell in Boston, Desdemona in Verdi's *Otello*. Loved it very much. Enjoyed it very much. Loved singing that last scene. I sing it now in concerts. I've done it with orchestra. "Salce Salce" and "Ave Maria." I love it very much.

WC: When you ended your recital at the 1993 NANM Convention with "Salce Salce" and "Ave Maria," I said to my wife, only a great artist could or would end a recital with a prayer. Tell us of your tenures at the various houses, relationships with management, singers and other personnel.

SV: I haven't sung at all of the opera houses in the world because my career was very strongly tailored to make room for my family. I wanted it so, and it was also a promise that I had made to my husband, who also wanted it, that I would not forever be gone from home. Why get married if you're going to be on the road all of the time? So I made a deal, I made a compromise, that I would try to keep the career down to six months of the year. Meaning that I would go to sing at the different houses, or for concert tours, recital tours; and usually for the amount of time that I had away, I would then come home and spend that same amount of time. It didn't always work out that way, but usually it did work out to be six months of the year that I would be at home because in the summers I would always take off. I would take three months off in the summer to go up to our country place. I would allow myself only maybe two weeks of that three-month vacation to make a stop at Tanglewood, or Ravinia, or to the Mann Center in Philadelphia, things like that. I would try to do those summer things that would not take more than about two weeks of my time at the beginning of the summer so that I was not in and out of my summer vacation; and the rest of the time I was just at home. But the houses I sang in . . . Covent Garden was the house that I called my home, and they called it my home. I went in there under Sir David Webster, and I stayed there through the reign of Sir John Tooley. I did all of my roles there. I called it my home house because all of the new roles that I learned, at that time during my career in the sixties, were done first at Covent Garden; and then at the Metropolitan Opera. La Scala was another place where I did new roles. I sang in Florence, especially at The Maggio Musicale. Vienna: I've only sung in the opera house there once. I've done many recitals there and appearances with orchestra, but I have not gone back to sing in the opera house. I was asked to go to Bayreuth in the early sixties. I didn't go there because I felt that I was not ready to do that. I had a theory about what would happen if I sang German a lot. There was a time when I studied the role of Brangaene in Wagner's *Tristan und Isolde* for Covent Garden, which I never did because Miss [Birgit] Nilsson became ill and they didn't want anyone else to do Isolde. So it was canceled. When I was studying that role, a different quality began to come into the voice, and I didn't want that quality at that particular time. It was lovely, but I didn't want that. I don't know how many other singers have gone through that, but that's the way I felt about it. Therefore, I did not latch on to the German operatic repertoire. I've sung a lot of German in recital, lieder; and I've done, in concert, the *Wesendonck Songs* of Wagner.

WC: I heard you sing "Isolde's Liebestod" in concert. I believe Zubin Mehta was the conductor. And of course I've heard you do lieder in recital: Brahms and Schubert.

SV: In France, I sang at the Paris Opera, of course. Not only did I sing at the wonderful Paris Garnier—I'm sorry that the opera house is not there anymore, it was a great house—but I was one of the singers to open up the Bastille, the new opera house in Paris. Where else? Oh, yes. Small places in Sicily. Not too many of those. Monte Carlo. I've sung in the Soviet Union, both in Moscow and Kiev, Russia, at this time. Performing in all of these houses because of my commitment to my home meant that I would go to Covent Garden, for instance, in a season, and then I might go to La Scala in the same season, but not back to a house. Only once did I do a back-on-back as I would call it. While I was still at La Scala I went to do my first Trovatore at Covent Garden. I didn't do it after that. I never did that kind of stunt again. I am this kind of artist: I love to do what I'm doing now and then when I've finished that, go on to the next thing. I think for me that has been a very, very good thing. I would be at Covent Garden, maybe I would sing at Covent Garden and La Scala, and then the next year I wouldn't sing there. When I started singing at the Met, I would be there a lot. Then I would go sing at Covent Garden one year. Then I would be at the Met continually. I was at the Met for about twenty-two seasons. Then I would go to sing at La Scala, and then I'd be back at the Met. The Met was a kind of home at that particular moment. In other words, every other year someplace else. This way, I kept my hand in. I possibly would have greater notoriety—maybe that's not a good word—but be more famous than I am at this point if I had stuck. Oh my, I forgot: San Francisco Opera, Chicago Lyric Opera. I only sang in Chicago one time, and San Francisco, maybe four or five times in the opera; and I must say I loved working in both places. San Francisco is one of the places I loved very much. I had a particular kind of career, and I have worked with my home, my life, my daughter, and my husband. I must say at this particular time that there are some things that I didn't do that I wish I had done. There are things that I did not do with Von Karajan. After he asked me three times to do the Innsbruck Concert that he gave every year and I couldn't do it. He's actually the person who was responsible for me learning *Trovatore*. He heard me sing and decided that this would be one of the great parts that I would sing. But I was never able to sing with him again. I was supposed to do *Tosca* with him. The ugly head of the allergies came up and I couldn't do it. One of my colleagues stepped in. He asked me another time and I couldn't do it. I think, then, I know he gave up on me. So I was not able to work with him. I'm very, very sorry about this. I'm also sorry at this particular time that I did not go to Bayreuth to do something. That would have been very interesting.

WC: Yes, and also quite historic. So few black singers have performed there.

SV: But we can't do everything in our lives and have a family also. And all of my life, my family has been very important to me. I had to have a family and a career. I couldn't just have a career, because I have seen and read so many biographies of the ones who were left very lonely at the end of a career. You can't really take the applause home with you. I found that out very early on through my teachers; both of my teachers, the one I had in California and the one at Juilliard. I've always gotten along very well in my relationship with the managements. I had kind of a difficult time here in New York City with the Metropolitan, and I always say that I don't put all of the blame on them. I have at least forty percent of the blame, they have sixty! Having said that, my relationships with the singers, my colleagues, and other personnel— I've always gotten along very well with the personnel. I don't think that anyone could really say anything very bad against me in any house that I have been in. I have not been stupid, but I've always been human. I feel that this is very good. I was brought up to be this way— not to feel that I was the only one who had a voice; or that God had seen fit to, you know, favor me. I was brought up in a very religious home, and because of that, my parents always taught me that God giveth and He taketh away also. That if you have a talent you build on that talent, you do not bury it, and so on. . . . All of those wonderful things. To do unto others as you would have them do unto you. They don't always do that, but it doesn't stop me from doing unto them what I would like for them to do unto me. So I would say that at all of the houses in the world that I have sung in, both in opera and also recitals and concerts, I think that I've always had very good relationships with the management. Misunderstandings here and there but nothing that could not be addressed, possibly with the exception of my tenure at the Metropolitan, and for that I am very sorry. I really am very sorry. Sometimes things can't be fixed. I have a great belief that things that are to happen will happen, and if I try too hard to fix them, they can become worse. So I just leave it alone, let it be, because it must be in the great plan that was set out for me.

WC: To what extent does typecasting still exist in opera for the black female, and the black male?

SV: I don't know. When I've gone to the opera, at the Metropolitan, and I've seen black performers performing, I haven't been overly concerned with the existence of typecasting. As I said earlier in our conversation, just as the white singer has to blacken down to do *Otello* I always keep this in my mind, to play that part well; and the Aidas have to blacken down, by the use of makeup, the magic; this is what theater is all about. There will have to be times when we'll be asked to play certain roles, and because maybe the role did call for a black person, we feel put upon. We should not. The role of Aida is a great role. I played, on the other hand, Desdemona. There aren't too many people who would ask me to do Desdemona because she is supposedly blonde, Venetian, and very fair. I played her with makeup, lightened my skin a bit, but dark hair. And I would say that once I opened my mouth, after the first few minutes, people forgot that Shirley Verrett was black and singing Desdemona.

WC: I'm sure of it.

SV: So I think we do ourselves a very great injustice if we continue to think about typecasting, because I don't see it happening, at least when I've been in the audience, and have seen some of my black colleagues perform. They have done all of the roles. It is the females who I'm speaking about. I'm not speaking about the black males. I do remember, however, that George Shirley was given all of the roles that were suited to his voice. The same thing is also true for Robert McFerrin. It is a little-known fact, at least I don't think that too many people know this, Robert McFerrin actually had a Metropolitan contract before Miss Anderson.

WC: Yes. That is indeed a little-known fact.

SV: Miss Anderson sang first because *Ballo* was scheduled to be performed before the date of McFerrin's debut.

WC: That whole thing, the events surrounding and leading up to Miss Anderson's debut were so very well calculated and orchestrated. I was told by Mr. McFerrin that *Ballo* was revived by the Metropolitan to be a vehicle specifically for Miss Anderson. Not that there was any reason to doubt Mr. McFerrin, but the record, particularly the memoirs of Rudolf Bing, certainly make Mr. McFerrin's revelation something that should be believed. *Ballo* had not been done at the Metropolitan in years. There were probably only three people who knew completely what was going on behind the scenes: Rudolf Bing, Sol Hurock, and Dimitri Mitropoulos. Mr. Bing now has Alzheimer's disease, and Mr. Hurock and Mr. Mitropoulos are dead. We'll never know what really went down. The Metropolitan board of directors didn't know what was happening. Miss Anderson was not fully aware of the machinery that was then moving behind the scenes in her life. I've written a paper on all of this that I hope will one day be published. Oh, well. Having said that, let's get back to typecasting.

SV: I think it was *Faust* that McFerrin sang in. He played the brother, which was something unheard of.

WC: Yes, Valentin. Of course he made his debut as Amonasro in Verdi's

Aida within a month after the historic debut of Miss Anderson. He also did the title role in Verdi's *Rigoletto* during his days at the Metropolitan. But it is interesting that you mention Valentin. Mr. McFerrin told me that doing Valentin was his idea, and when this was presented to the powers that be, it was wondered if he could be visually believable in this role. This was after Amonasro who is Ethiopian, and before Rigoletto. The nationality and race of Valentin was discussed. Mr. McFerrin told them that Valentin could be Algerian and went on to remind them that this was why the Metropolitan had a makeup department. His thinking prevailed.

SV: And I've wished all of my life, all of my career that Robert McFerrin could have stayed at the Met. Now, I don't know what happened there and I won't even try to make up anything because I can't. I won't do that. But one day I will ask him what happened. He was there and doing very, very well. George Shirley was there. Whatever happened? George Shirley stayed there a few seasons—a very fine artist. I would love to have seen that particular base grow, and especially under the regime of Jimmy Levine. There was a time for about ten or twenty years, actually into the seventies, that he was putting forth a great effort, like a search for black singers—female and male. And he did bring some into the house. He brought Kathleen Battle into the house. He brought Jessye Norman into the house. He brought some of the young males who I don't know much about into the house. They were not, unfortunately, of the caliber that we're talking about here, of a star or superstar, but they were good. I wish that could have kept up. It now seems, unfortunately, that there are fewer blacks. There are fewer and fewer of us at the Metropolitan Opera, and I would suppose that this is true around the country and the world.

WC: Yes, that does indeed seem to be the situation everywhere. Is there a relationship between support from the black community and opportunities in opera for the African-American artist?

SV: I don't know. What I can say is that I wish that there were more of us singing in the opera houses, because I noticed that when we sang there on a regular basis, more blacks came into the houses for the performances. What we should do is go there for performances anyway. But that's kind of asking for something that probably won't happen. When you go to a Broadway musical or a play and there is a black lead, a James Earl Jones, or if they're doing a Wilson play, the audience is packed with blacks. I would love to have seen this happen in the opera world, and possibly would have, if more of us had made it there. There was that beginning, and I'm sure it's not a thing to do. And I don't knows what comes first the chicken or the egg? I think it could be of great help if the managements saw a great number of black people in the audiences. It's a very good question. What about support from the black community? I feel that it could have a bearing on what happens in the opera house. I feel that those of us who were there, at the Met, the females and the males—Simon Estes, George Shirley, and Mc-Ferrin—we started it—Marian Anderson, Leontyne Price, Gloria Davy, Grace Bumbry . . .

WC: Mattiwilda Dobbs, Martina Arroyo, Seth McCoy.

SV: We did what we had to do. And it would have been really great if at that moment the black community had stepped in and sort of bolstered us up a little bit more. And yes, I do think that if the black community would come out in force to the opera, as we do when there are a lot of blacks on stage, it would be a help. But that's almost asking for the impossible. Because we won't do it unless there are more of us performing, and there won't be more of us performing unless there are more of us in the audience. I don't know. I just know that at this moment we're going through a very, very bad time in seeing black faces on the operatic stage.

WC: Black artists have been singing in opera on both sides of the Atlantic for many decades. What do you see happening in the way of African-American involvement as we end the twentieth cetury and move into the twenty-first century?

SV: I spoke somewhat to this issue when I said that I really do feel the support that the black community gives to plays on Broadway and the musicals like *Sarafina* and *The Piano*. That kind of support is really heartwarming. But to continue . . .

WC: Yes.

SV: I remember in the early years when I saw *Raisin in the Sun* and *The Blacks,* the place was filled with mostly black people. Now, that will not happen in the opera house right now, but it would be really great if black people would make their presence known in the opera house by the twenty-first century, a time that is coming very soon. I think it could help. Overseas—a very, very difficult question to answer. You would need to have a lot of blacks in the different countries. Italy has quite a few blacks now; but whether those blacks, especially the Africans, are interested in the opera world . . . ? I think most of them are interested in making a living at this particular time. I do not know what to say about that. But in America where we have this very sizable black community, it would be helpful if blacks began to go more into opera houses, see the performances. If we want to see us in opera, this will be done. If we don't want to see us in opera anymore, then we won't do it. A lot of blacks have been criticized, those of us who have gone into opera, saying that we were Oreos. I remember that I was called an Oreo on a talk show once because I was not brought up in a Baptist church, where we got a lot of our blues and gospel singers. Great. That's wonderful. But I was brought up in another denomination: Seventh-Day Adventists, where we—now it has changed a lot, but when I was a little girl—sang from anthems, like the Methodists and Episcopalians. I was being called an Oreo because I was reared in a different environment. This is not fair. As blacks we also have to become tolerant of the backgrounds of others, other blacks, and not be judges when we don't really know the whole scene.

WC: Bravo! What were the stimuli that triggered your interest in music, and what are the forces that have sustained and kept you growing through such a distinguished career?

SV: Thank you very much for that. I could not have had greater parents. From the time I was very young, three, four years old, I can remember music in the home. My mother [Elvira Harris Verrett] had one of the most beautiful voices. My father [Leon Solomon Verrett] was a builder. He became a contractor in California when we moved there from New Orleans, the place where I was born. He was a builder in California, but in New Orleans, he did everything: he was a carpenter, painter, wallpaper hanger; he could fix cars; he could upholster furniture; he was quite a fabulous man. My mother was a housewife all of her life, and was actually one of the first persons to get me interested, because of hearing her sing around the house all of the time. She taught me poetry. She started teaching me poetry when she realized that I had a very good memory. She started teaching me poems to recite at church, and the poems became longer, and longer, and longer. So this was a wonderful setup for what I would eventually do. Also, before we went to California when I was a little girl, I was taken to the recitals of Dorothy Maynor and Marian Anderson, or any black singer who came into New Orleans. I was quite young when we moved to California, but even at that early age, I was taken to recitals and concerts. My father was my first voice teacher. He was at the time doing some work with a music group at Dillard University under the directorship of Dr. Frederick Hall. I met Dr. Hall in later years, in New Orleans. So, in a word my parents were the stimuli. I became interested in music because I was surrounded by music. I was surrounded by amateur musicians. As we grew up, we all sang. I, however, was the one who was more interested in really doing something with my voice, not knowing at that time what it was, but my father told me what it would be—that I was going to be another Dorothy Maynor or Marian Anderson, that I was going to be like them, and be a force in the music world. Thank God all of this came true.

WC: I think that I read somewhere that your father was choirmaster at your church in New Orleans.

SV: Hall Johnson was a great force in my life. In Los Angeles I went to study spirituals with him. He gave me a few pointers on the spirituals and then said to me, "You know how to sing them. Some of us don't. Some of us black folk do not know how to sing spirituals, especially the younger generation, because they were not brought up with them, that heritage." We used to sing them at home. Hall Johnson, when I told him that I would be leaving Los Angeles for New York, told me that I would never come back to Los Angeles to live, and that I would have a career. His advice to me is the advice that I give to young people to this day: "Hurry slowly. You'll get there much faster. Like the tortoise and the hare."

WC: And you do Hall Johnson's music so well. I wish that you would record all of his scores. It would be a wonderful legacy.

SV: There was a group in California, it possibly still exists, called the Young Musicians Foundation. The chief officer at that time was Sylvia Kuhen. She was another great force in my life. She was the one who the Godfrey official called asking about talent, and I was suggested and won, along with a pianist: two people. This is how I came to New York, to be on the "Arthur Godfrey Show." I stayed on to go to Juilliard, where I met my teacher, Madam Marion Szekely-Freschi, who was another force in my life. My English diction teacher was another force in my life. My German teacher, my Italian teacher. My German and Italian teachers more than the French teacher who I had at the time. And the school itself, Juilliard itself, I was like a sponge there. I had already been in college for three years when I went to Juilliard. When I went to Juilliard, I was there for business. I started late. I didn't take voice lessons, except for what I did with my dad, until I was in my twenties. Therefore, I had a lot of making up to do. When I went to Juilliard, I went on a scholarship. I auditioned and I got a full scholarship. At that time, I was just getting out of a first marriage. I married while I was still young and still going to college. I was on my own. I didn't want my parents to help me. Therefore, that was how I did it: by auditioning and getting a scholarship. I had great years there. My president was William Schuman. My dean was Mark Schuback. They were really great family. I felt very much loved there. After I married [for the second time], my husband became the great force in my life. He was so helpful in being my voice in business matters at the beginning of my career. He is a white man. My first husband was a black man. It is not because of his being white that I married him. He is who I met in my world, and he was wonderful, and is wonderful after thirty-one years of marriage. And it was very wonderful to have a mate who had such a wonderful head for business. He's an artist. He's a painter. He's a writer. But he had a great mind, he still has a great mind for business. And I think that if he had not been there I would have turned out to be a different kind of singer, possibly much harder in my business dealings. But with him being there, I didn't have to do that; he did it, up to the point that I was signed with Sol Hurock. Then he bowed out of that part of my life, except for giving advice at home.

WC: I must say that I remember your mother being with you at the 1993 National Association of Negro Musicians Convention when you did that wonderful recital, how you sang "Happy Birthday" to her, and how you so lovingly dedicated your group of spirituals to her. I'm sure that her teaching you poetry planted the seed for your love of theater, and your formidable acting skills.

SV: Marian Anderson, Roland Hayes, Dorothy Maynor . . . I remember going to every recital that Marian Anderson gave in Los Angeles. I traveled through a windstorm for the experience of hearing Miss Maynor at Town Hall. It was horrible that night. I was staying with a friend at that time on Fifth Avenue when I first came to New York—at the Wannus Building, 1200 Fifth Avenue. Going through a storm to hear Dorothy Maynor sing. I was not going to be put out of that concert, that recital. I loved her. I loved Miss Anderson. I loved Bill Warfield, who became, and still is, a dear friend and colleague. It was great to be in New York and live at the International House, to develop friendships. They accepted me there. It was while living at the International House that I began to have a great interest in what happened around the world because of all the nationalities that were living there. Learning about Africa from the Africans. Learning about Sweden and France and Ethiopia, you name it. Learning about German, that German didn't have to sound guttural, but could be very beautifully sung and spoken in the right throat. Hearing people read Hindus from the Hindu community. That was wonderful. Meeting a friend who was so great: Jenz Sigar. After dinner we used to go into a rehearsal room and just go through the literature of music. Howard Cook at the International House was my president. I loved it all. I was right where my parents felt that I belonged.

WC: I have asked a lot. You have certainly said a lot. Are there issues and concerns pertaining to opera and the African-American experience that you would particularly like to address?

SV: I feel very, very sad that it looks and it seems as if we are going backward as far as our participation in the opera houses of America, and Europe also. But now I'm speaking as an American. I'm not at all of the performances in Chicago and San Francisco and all of the small opera houses around the country, but judging from what is happening at the Metropolitan, I feel that somehow or other the black community, the African-American community, has to get together in some way to support the ones who are at the Metropolitan and other opera houses in this country, or I think we may disappear.

WC: Thank you very much for that. I very deeply share your concern. I also agree with you. And if we disappear it will be harder for us to reappear, because it's always harder to rebuild than it is to build. And the thought of going back to the way that it was before Todd Duncan and Camilla Williams at the New York City Opera, before Marian Anderson at the Metropolitan, and before some of those who pioneered in Europe—Lillian Evanti, Caterina Jarboro, Florence Cote Talbert, Mattiwilda Dobbs at La Scala, Grace Bumbry at Bayreuth, Simon Estes. And with the way things are going now in most of our homes, churches, and schools, musically, that is, I don't know if it will be possible for us to get back. This is one of the reasons that I am so motivated to do this research into the African-American experience as it relates to opera. I am really afraid that if we don't get some parts of our heritage researched and into the literature now, many things will be lost forever.

SV: There is a lot going on in our lives at this particular time. More of us are on Broadway. I was in my first Broadway show. I'm starting another career, going into the theater world. This is what I would like to eventually end doing. Singing for a bit more, but going to that other love that I've had all the time that I was singing opera. I wanted to do a musical. I finally did a musical, small part, but it was a part for me to get the attention of that community. I was very happy to have been nominated for the Outer Critics Award for the best debut as a newcomer to Broadway. I didn't win, but just to have been nominated was very great, especially for such a small part, as I see it anyway, because I've always been used to lead parts in the opera. It was great to have been nominated and also to have been honored, one of the honorees of the drama league, which means that they are taking me seriously, having done the part of Nettie Fowler in *Carousel*. I'm looking forward now to reading plays and being in plays. If I have to sing a little bit, fine, but I would rather be more talkative at this particular time. So I'm into another part of my life. A part of my life that I knew eventually I would get to. And maybe this is why some of the other things and the little bit of friction that I had with the Metropolitan Opera happened. I'm supposed to be doing this at this time, and what's going to be will be. That sounds fatalistic, and I'm not a fatalistic person. I always believe in the will and what one can do on one's own. But there does come a time—I have had it happen to me—that no matter what you do, it's not going to happen the way you want it to happen. So what you do is to be sensible about it, fall back, and let it be. Let life be! This is what I'm doing at this particular time.

WC: I have never seen or heard you do anything, concert, opera, or recital, that wasn't absolutely fabulous. Thank you for sharing so much of your very rich life with us. And we certainly wish for you the very best in your new career.

New York, New York
1994

William Warfield. *Courtesy of William Warfield.*

9

William Warfield:
Done Made My Vow

William Caesar Warfield has long been recognized throughout the world as one of the great artists of our time. In concert, recital, and theater, Mr. Warfield brings depth of interpretation, total understanding, and intense sensitivity, thusly projecting a complete mastery of the music that has been programmed. William Warfield made his debut as a concert baritone on March 19, 1950, at Town Hall in New York City. Mr. Warfield's artistry has remained for forty-five years a major force in the music world.

I first met William Warfield in the 1960s when I was a music student at Knoxville College where he came to present a recital as part of our lyceum series. By no stretch of the imagination could I have then believed that within the next three decades I would be his conductor in two productions of Handel's *Messiah* at Monumental Baptist Church in Chicago, Illinois!

Born on January 22, 1920, in West Helena, Arkansas, William Warfield grew up in Rochester, New York, where his family moved when he was a child. Mr. Warfield is a graduate of the Eastman School of Music. Private study was done with Otto Hertz, Yves Tinayre, and Rosa Ponselle.

From 1974 through 1990, Warfield was a member of the music faculty at the University of Illinois. Recently he has been guest professor of voice at the University of Texas, San Antonio. Today, along with performing, William Warfield teaches at Northwestern University.

Wallace Cheatham: Would you speak to this paragraph from your autobiography: "It would have been a tragic mistake for me to have followed Leontyne's route into the opera world. Because, to this very day, although the black female virtuosi have been able to reach the extreme heights of opera, black males have never received the same welcome. And in my generation, though I might have helped to make a dent in the prevailing traditions, I would have suffered a stultifying suppression of my talents."

William Warfield: I think that it is a general thing that has to do with just the reluctance to put black men into leading roles. This happens even in Europe, particularly in Wagnerian opera, where they have in their minds that their gods are the blond-haired and blue-eyed, the

epitome of what their males should be; and the idea of—even if they
don't have active racism—the idea of a black man fitting that figure,
it's hard for them to fathom. Here in this country, when George
Shirley was at the Metropolitan, he mentioned that he would come in
many times and take leading roles as a substitute for singers, some of
the European singers who did not appear; but when he wanted to have
the management actually write into his contract certain leading roles,
the Metropolitan was reluctant to do it. This is one of the reasons why
he didn't stay there as long as he might have. He was relegated to just
filling in for some of the big stars from Europe when they would can-
cel, and management would never give him the juicy roles in his contract to do each year. When Simon Estes first went to the Metropolitan, a statement in an interview published in the *New York Times*
stated that if Simon had been a white singer with the reputation that
he had established in Europe, he would have been at the Metropolitan
three or four years prior to his getting there. Simon made such a
tremendous reputation in Europe that it became a foregone conclu-
sion: he had to be invited to sing at the Metropolitan Opera! And so
this attitude, I think, is still there.

WC: It has been said, or so I have heard, that Simon Estes is not singing
at the Metropolitan now because they would not allow him to perform
some of the roles that he has done to great acclaim elsewhere.

WW: We have an organization—Men of Ebos. I, a few years ago, went
to one of their concerts. Black men—tenors, basses, baritones; it was
a magnificent concert. Any one of these men would have been equally
fine at the Metropolitan, on the roster, yet they're not there. You cannot make me believe that all of this has to do with their just not being
the caliber, or not being prepared as well as the white male singers
who are out there. Yes, I find to a certain extent that this general reluctance to put black men in leading roles still exists.

WC: Also: from your autobiography, would you explore this declaration: "If there is to be a career track for the black male in opera there
has to be ample room for the less-than-exceptional, or the striving-to-
be exceptional, as well. There are many such white performers, very
few blacks. The whole idea must be to transcend the exceptional to get
beyond the exceptions, and change the rules themselves."

WW: People who are not playing the main baritone roles, the main bass
roles, the main tenor roles, but the roles that are considered less famous, less important, and whatnot . . .

WC: The comprimario roles.

WW: And one can have a whole career in these roles. Everyone who
sings is not a [Luciano] Pavarotti. Everyone who sings is not a Samuel
Ramey. There are a lot of black youngsters out there who can play minor roles, and unfortunately, there seems to be no place in opera for

them to really make inroads because these roles are always taken by white singers. You have to be the main thing, or the top, if you're black in opera in order to succeed. This is what I was referring to in my book.

WC: It's just another part of the supernigger syndrome!

WW: Now, Opera Ebony and opera companies like that across the country have done things in which some of the blacks who were less exceptional than others had minor roles and played them well and did them well. But for the most part, you will find that only when you're dealing within a university structure. In opera companies at universities like Northwestern, like Illinois, like Indiana, there are blacks doing minor roles, blacks who would not really stand too much of a chance of getting the same kind of a minor role if they were in the grand opera at the Metropolitan, or at La Scala in Milan, Italy. It's all or nothing at all. There seems to be no place in opera where blacks can find a niche for themselves in the less-dramatic or the less-important roles and make a career from it.

WC: This is certainly worth our attention, because there are many white singers who could never do a major role, or in some instances many of the more powerful minor roles, who become mainstays in the major companies performing comprimario roles. But so far no black singer has been able to pull off such a feat.

WW: I don't know if there is a solution to this problem, except that maybe as more of the opera schools that are attached to companies—like the Chicago Lyric Opera Center, the Santa Fe, the Houston Opera School, the Metropolitan Opera School—have black youngsters in them who perform and make great success, those youngsters would then be used to do minor roles in the regular season of those companies. Maybe out of these situations some of the lesser black singers might get a chance to have careers in opera. But at the moment, I do not see too much of this happening.

WC: The advice given to you by Peter Herman Adler when there was contemplation about making an investment in the study of opera performance: "In the first place you're already a star. It is hard to make a beginning as a newcomer when you are already so well known. But more important is the quality of your talent. Your talent is made of many colors, many shades, many intensities. If you make yourself an opera star, you will have to lose those many sounds and create just one sound, their sound. For you, now that would be such a waste." As you now reflect on that advice, do you believe that it was totally based on music and opera, your voice and personality, or do you think there might have been some concern about the lack of opportunity in opera for the black male?

WW: At that point in time I was already pretty well on my way with my career. I had done a movie, Showboat. I had done a concert debut. I had done recitals, oratorios, and things like that. What he referred to was not the many sounds of the voice, but the coloring that I used, shading the voice—in one color for lieder, and then using another kind of a quality for, say, oratorio, and then using yet another quality for opera. In doing that, he pointed out to me that in opera there is a color that one must have. And we see this when we hear opera. We hear a bass. We say, Oh, this is a Verdi bass. We hear someone else. We say this is a Russian bass. We hear somebody else. Oh, this is very much Italian or French. A French sound, and so on and so forth.

WC: When Adler gave that advice, how long would it have taken you to have become schooled in the culture of opera? What would have been involved?

WW: I would have probably had to, depending upon what opera or type of role I was interested in, just take off time, maybe go to Europe, and just work and rework my whole technique toward the color of the sound that would have been expected, say to do a Verdi opera or to do a Russian opera.

WC: Had you pursued a career in European opera, what roles would you like to have done? Why?

WW: Actually the Russian bass baritone roles would probably have fitted me best because my voice had that kind of a timbre. But I would have had to take off time, go back, learn Russian roles, with no assurance really that I would have been able to do any of these things at the Metropolitan or with any of the other companies. So it just seemed an unwise route for me to take, when I was so successful in the things that I was doing. One of the things that I would like to have done is *Boris Godunov.* I did this role once, in concert version, in New York, with James DePriest. It was very successful. There was a tape made of this, which I allowed WILL [a radio station] in Champaign to play one day. The young man, Roger Cooper, who was playing it on his program said that he got many calls asking who is this new Russian bass. And when he told them it was William Warfield singing those arias from *Boris,* they were absolutely astounded. They never knew that kind of a quality in my voice or that it fitted the Russian literature so well. So if I had been really interested, I probably would have gone for things like *Boris Godunov.* I don't know whether I would have been too good with Leporello, or roles like that, comic bass things. But it just seemed that it would have taken too much time and too much diversion to stop what I was doing and go into this just for the sake of saying that now I am an opera star.

WC: You've had a long and distinguished association with Porgy in Gershwin's *Porgy and Bess.* What makes Porgy, the man, the personality, special?

WW: Porgy, to me, was really created in essence as a play. Then it was transferred. I think that Gershwin indeed got the essence of the characterization. Now the plight of Porgy as a beggar and a cripple placed in the environment of Catfish Row was nothing that was particularly unfamiliar to me as a black man. You have a man here that is living in sort of a ghetto. The ghetto has on one side the God-fearing ladies of thus saith the Lord. Sons and daughters of thus saith the Lord who were the Christian people. Then it has the dope peddler: Sporting Life. Porgy is very much a religious man. He believes in religion and a religious way of life. Porgy is also lonely. When Bess is left and nobody will accept her, he takes Bess in. Bess then becomes for him something that he has never had—a true love—and she learns a different kind of love from being associated with him. So the character itself, to me, is out of this kind of context. A man who is God-fearing. He likes to play his craps, but he has a certain capacity for being understanding of somebody else, even though that person may not believe in him. Porgy is also very superstitious. The idea of going to jail! Sporting Life puts the fear of God in him when he tells him about all that they're gonna do. When the man that killed Crown goes into that room, Crown's wounds will begin to bleed, and the white folks will know, that's the one that killed him. He believes in all of that. With a combination of religion, religious beliefs, a basic tendency to do the right thing, and involvement with a woman, this is the kind of mix in the personality of Porgy, and this makes for a man who is really a tremendously interesting character to play! When he comes in the first time, when they tease him about his question, about Bess, and he says: they pass by singing, "they pass by crying, always looking, they look in my door, and they keep on moving. When God made a cripple, he made him to be lonely. Nightime, daytime he got to travel that lonesome road." Then he interrupts immediately and goes back into the crap game. This, to me, provides one of the main insights into what Porgy is as a man.

WC: Your enthusiasm for Porgy is infectious!

WW: I enjoyed doing the characterization of Porgy, and I had a lot of help from people in the cast who had been in the original productions, who knew Gershwin. I even had encouragement from Todd Duncan. As you know, Todd created the role of Porgy. Todd came to see me and was very pleased with what I was doing with the character. Yes, I find the essence of Porgy to be a man of great compassion, a man of great capacity to love, and also a man who has great respect for religion. When Bess is gone, Serena comes, and he prays that God will bring her back to him. This kind of environment was nothing unfamiliar to me. I could identify with him as a man.

WC: A very complex personality indeed. How does this come alive through the music?

WW: This complexity comes forth in the music by the way Gershwin makes transitions. For example, there is very hectic music going on in the crap scene when Porgy first arrives. Then when Porgy begins to sing, the music becomes very quiet and thoughtful—then suddenly it goes back to the crap game hectic agitation. In the scene where Porgy grabs Sporting Life as he is trying to give Bess dope, the music is very dramatic, and shortly thereafter it becomes calm and legato for the duet "Bess You Is My Woman Now." This kind of thing goes on until the very end when Porgy sings in the trio "Bess Oh Where's My Bess" music that is beautiful and plaintive. This is preceded by very dramatic and irritable inquiries.

WC: I understand that during your tenure at the University of Illinois you directed and starred in productions of *Porgy and Bess*. What's involved in directing a production, and how did you prepare?

WW: When we did it at the University of Illinois, that was back in 1976. I actually came to direct it; it just evolved into that. I was asked to be in the production, and also to be the artistic adviser. When I came back to the campus (I went on a tour with the New York Philharmonic, the bicentennial tour with Leonard Bernstein, with whom I did the *Lincoln Portrait* in Europe—did it in English, and in French, and in German), I found that not more than one scene or so had been done; and David Lloyd, who was actually the director, was waiting for me to come back and give advice. Well, at that point there was very little time left. So I just took the bull by the horns and said do this, do that, do the other thing. And all of this came out of my experience from the productions I had done. By that time, I had done the productions in 1952 that Leontyne and I did together with Cab Calloway. I had done productions at the Vienna Volksoper in Vienna. I knew the whole score backwards. I knew what the movement should be, what scenes should be highlighted. And it turned out to be a highly successful production. I was listed as the artistic adviser, but it ended up that I actually directed the show.

WC: You were once married to one of the world's most celebrated opera singers. You were there when Miss Price's career was being developed and built. You watched it soar. As a recitalist and concert artist, you are among the world's most celebrated. Is there a kind of vocal instrument and personality needed for opera that is different from the kind of vocal instrument and personality needed for concert and recital?

WW: The instrument itself has to be so well schooled technically in opera technique. It's not a different basic technique from the use of the voice, but it certainly is more specialized. It's like saying somebody can be an internist as a doctor, but to be a heart specialist, you have to be a cardiologist. And these colors, as I said earlier, having to do with opera, and what part of opera you're going to go into, we call it a "fach". And no one person necessarily has the voice for all of the various different "fachs". Leontyne was Puccini and Verdi. With these composers she made a whole career. She never decided to go into Wagnerian opera, which is a different kind of a color, a different kind of a discipline, a different kind of a technique, a different kind of a sound. You have to know what your voice fits, what your voice is fitted for, and then just immerse yourself in that particular thing until you are so completely good at it that it just rolls out without any kind of an effort. Leontyne was a basic spinto bordering on dramatic. Her voice fitted all of the things that she did. She actually recorded a *Carmen;* but she said that she would never do it in public because the role was too heavy and too low for the kind of voice she had.

WC: She also recorded and performed some Wagner. I have her recording of the "Liebestod" from *Tristan und Isolde,* and I heard her sing "Dich, Theure Halle" from *Taunhauser.* And she set boundaries for herself with Verdi and Puccini. I read somewhere her comments about why, from a vocal perspective, she wouldn't do Abigaille in Verdi's *Nabucco;* and why she didn't do the title role in Puccini's *Turandot.* She said that the character, Turandot, was too icy; yet she recorded her famous aria "In questa reggia." She preferred the other heroine in *Turandot:* Liu. Other arias from Verdi and Puccini operas Miss Price recorded, and probably never even thought of doing the roles. So the evidence confirms that not only did Miss Price know herself vocally, she also knew how to choose roles through which she could most effectively project herself as a personality. Robert McFerrin, when I was working with him, said to me, "Wallace, do you want to know the name of an intelligent singer? Leontyne Price. She doesn't try to sing everything that has been put on paper. Leontyne sings only those things that she knows can be done well." And of course there is a world of difference in singing an aria and singing the role. I also remember reading a writing in which Miss Price stated that she wouldn't do, on stage, Desdemona in Verdi's *Otello* because the libretto, or the score, says that Desdemona is white, but that vocally the role was no problem whatsoever, and that she had recorded it twice.

WW: So this is basically it, I think. When you have an instrument, you must have a good teacher who can tell you that your voice will fit this opera, it will fit that opera, it will fit the other opera. It will not fit this particular opera. Be very careful in the development of your voice. Stick to the things that your voice is made for. If you don't, you will get into a tremendous amount of trouble. We've had people, even the big stars, who have outstretched themselves and done things that they shouldn't have done. Sometimes they've changed from mezzo to soprano, and then figured that this wouldn't work, and come back to mezzo. Things like that. Always because the other "fach" seemed more exciting . . . you know, like the grass on the other side seems a little greener. I can do this, so I ought to be able to do that. It ain't necessarily so! You have a voice that will do certain things, and if you stretch that for something different, it will not work.

WC: In our time it borders on being impossible for a singer to have a major career without an identity with opera. Would you speak to this phenomenon?

WW: This is the situation today. Back when I came along, and that is why I had a career, this did not exist. I was following in the footsteps of Roland Hayes, Marian Anderson, Paul Robeson, Dorothy Maynor. In those days, there was an audience for concerts. The great concert pianists: Rachmaninoff, Paderewski; the violinist, Kreisler; all of these people. It was a great age for concert artists, and you could have a tremendous career in concert, in any of the disciplines, as a pianist, as a singer, or whatever. Because Marian Anderson proved herself as a concert artist, Rudolf Bing decided that she would be the first black singer at the Metropolitan, and she did Ulrica in *Un Ballo in Maschera*. But she was a token. She was already past her prime, had a fabulous career as a concert artist. Nowadays, you're right, it's absolutely right, you can't have a concert career without identifying with opera. Miss Price is not doing opera anymore. She's doing only concerts, and she is able to do this because she established a tremendous reputation as an opera singer. People like Marilyn Horne can do concerts. Pavarotti does concerts to stadiums of people, but only because the reputation itself was created through opera. I'm afraid this situation exists, and I don't see any way that this is going to change soon.

WC: What were the stimuli that triggered your interest in classical music and performance?

WW: If you remember, I am a minister's child. I was brought up in the church. And in the church, anything that smelled of jazz or popular music was taboo. I started studying piano when I was nine years old with the pianist of our church, and therefore I automatically was introduced to classical music. I came along studying anthems, spirituals, classical music in school, singing in the choir. I had no other source. That was it for me, and I was very interested, of course, in doing it. It worked that way. It was not that I ever had a choice of deciding, I'm going to do classical music, or I'm going to do jazz. It was there and I didn't have any idea. Only when I went into the army did I get any kind of an experience having to do with jazz music. And that was because I went to New York and got a boogie-woogie book that Hazel Scott had put out, and I learned to play and then sat in on jazz pianists when I was in the service. But that was only after I left home and felt free to explore this. I could never have done it in my father's house.

WC: You have prepared many songs and concert works. What score, or scores, from each genre did you find the most difficult? Why? The least difficult? Why?

WW: I didn't find any score or scores more difficult or less difficult. I felt more at home in certain genres. I have a really wonderful experience placed with me from Dr. Robert Nathaniel Dett. I was, as a youngster, singing on the radio shows, and I did a little program in which I did a Handel aria, a spiritual, a French song, a German song. Dr. Dett listened to this. That next day I was in his studio, and as we talked, he said, "How do you think you did?" I said, "I think I did very well. I think it went quite well. People have called me and told me that the French was good, and I felt good about that. And that the German diction was fine. And, of course, I'm very used to religious music, so the Handel that I did—I think it was an aria from the Messiah—I felt comfortable with." He said, "How did you feel about your spiritual?" I said, "Oh, well, I was at home when I did that. I mean, well, I've been singing spirituals all of my life." He said, "Ah, ha! Ah, ha, young man. When you get to feel about your German, and about your French, and about your Italian the way you feel about a spiritual, then you will start being an artist." I thought about that. It hit me right between the eyes. And sure enough, as my career progressed, and I became tremendously at ease in German, French, Italian, I found that I was able to bring the same authenticity, the same kind of performance, and the same kind of interpretation that I used when I sang a spiritual and felt totally at home doing so.

WC: Would you speak to your work as a board member of Lyric Opera Center?

WW: This has been a very, very gratifying experience for me. I have been on this board for several years. As you know, we train youngsters and then they get, as I mentioned earlier, some minor roles in different operas that come along in the regular lyric opera season. Being a teacher and being interested in youngsters, I find this particularly gratifying because it puts me in contact with what the youngsters who are ready to step out into a career are doing. There have been several black youngsters who have come through the Lyric Opera School and have done very well, and have done some minor roles in the regular season, and are now out there doing things. There are a lot of young black singers who are doing things out there, and I think we will hear from them. This is one of the most gratifying things that I am doing, along with my teaching, being on that board and being a part of the Lyric Opera Center School.

WC: How has the life of the black classical singer changed through the years?

WW: Just the fact that it is now more or less centered in opera is a big change from when I was a youngster.

WC: Is there a relationship between support from the black community and opportunities for the black classical artist?

WW: I don't find that this is important, although there is much more support now. You can go to operas now and see a great many more blacks. There are even black opera companies. But if you don't have the support of the opera people themselves, the black community's coming forth and giving any added support will make no appreciable difference, I don't think.

WC: What can be expected for involvement of the black classical artist—male and female, in opera, concert, and recital—as we near the twenty-first century?

WW: I think you're going to find a great deal more blacks in classical music and opera. This will also be true for symphonies. We don't have a lot of blacks in orchestras now, but it is on the move up. There are people now in orchestras who head programs that are geared for helping black youngsters to prepare for auditions. I think you're going to find more participation, not only from black artists who are going into classical music, but from the black community that is becoming more interested in this. You will then find that a lot of support will come from the black community. But we've still got a long way to go to create the audience, the black audience, that will come and support these things.

WC: You are past-national president of the National Association of Negro Musicians. What would you like to see NANM become by the time it becomes one hundred years old, something that will happen as the twenty-first century is nearing the end of its second decade.

WW: We just this past August celebrated the seventy-fifth anniversary. It was a tremendous success. We had an all-black orchestra. We had a black composers roundtable.

WC: I was a part of that roundtable.

WW: Compositions of black composers were performed, and we had all kinds of workshops. But as the situation continues to change, having to do with integration of blacks into the mainstream of classical music, I don't know whether this kind of thing will exist as a big need for the organization. I've already discussed the building of black audiences and the things that are happening with the integration of classical music and the appreciation of classical music. I think this will continue, and ideally it will reach a level in which you will not have to do much about it. If the black composer is good, he'll be heard; she'll be heard. If the black singer is good, he'll be heard; she'll be heard. The work of NANM is to perpetuate the tradition of black music. And I think this is something that can be done as an organization straight through, for however long we last. The preservation of the Negro spiritual, and the preservation of those forms of our black music that would have a tendency to get lost—I think this is going to become the job or the main thrust of NANM, the National Association of Negro Musicians, in the future, rather than just providing scholarships. We probably will continue to provide scholarships, but I don't think that we're going to be able to continue limiting those just to black people entirely.

WC: Especially when you have white people supporting the organization.

WW: As a matter of fact, we've had white contestants already in our competitions.

WC: There have also been white judges.

WW: This shows the direction in which these things are going.

WC: I have asked a lot, and you have certainly said a lot. Is there a concern or are there concerns about classical music and the black experience that you would particularly like to address?

WW: I don't have any concerns as such, but I do think that as we progress and get more black audiences, a lot of things will take care of themselves. The black composers like Adolphus Hailstork and Hale Smith aren't writing exactly what you call music for black people; they're writing music for posterity. And it's going to either lie or rest on these themes and these goals, rather than just trying to perpetuate black culture as such. I really don't know in what direction this will go. It's one of the things that we'll just have to watch and see what grows; and be ready to do whatever we can to perpetuate our black history and our black heritage. But at a certain point, I think the whole thing is going to be amalgamated into one musical experience—black, white, gray, whatever you want to call it, in the future.

WC: Thank you, Mr. Warfield, for enriching our world with your tremendous artistry.

Rochester, New York
1995

Selected Bibliography

Alexander, Ray. "Tenor in Whiteface." *Time*, August 13, 1965, p. 54.

Anderson, Marian. *My Lord What a Morning*. New York: Viking Press, 1956.

Bing, Rudolf. *5,000 Nights at the Opera*. New York: Doubleday and Company, 1972.

Cheatham, Wallace. "Black Male Singers at the Metropolitan Opera." *The Black Perspective In Music* 16 (Spring 1988): 3–20.

Dyer, Richard. "Celebrating 50 Years of African Americans in Opera." *Boston Globe,* December 10, 1995, sec. Arts Etc., p. B26.

Dyer, Richard. "Characteristically Verrett." *Opera News* 54 (February 17, 1990): 9–12; 52.

Emery, Lynne Fauley. *Black Dance in the United States from 1619 to 1970*. California: National Press Books, 1972.

Kolodin, Irving. *The Metropolitan Opera: 1883–1966*. New York: Alfred A. Knof, 1966.

Narine, Dalton. "The Maestros." *Ebony,* February 1954, pp. 54–62.

National Opera Association. *Newsletter*. Virginia: National Opera Association, winter 1996.

Shirley, George. "The Black Performer." *Opera News* 35 (January 30, 1971): 6–13.

Smith, Eric Ledell. *Blacks in Opera*. North Carolina: McFarland, 1995.

Southern, Eileen. *Biographical Dictionary of Afro-American and African Musicians*. Connecticut: Greenwood Press, 1962.

Southern, Eileen. *The Music of Black Americans*. 2nd ed. New York: W.W. Norton, 1983.

Story, Rosalyn. "Against the Odds." *Opera News* 59 (April 1, 1995) 24–27.

Story, Rosalyn. *And So I Sing*. New York: Warner Books, 1990.

Verrett, Shirley. "Shirley Verrett." *In Great Singers on Great Singing,* pp. 338–47. Edited by Jerome Hines. New York: Doubleday. 1982.

Warfield, William. *My Music and My Life*. Illinois: Sagamore, 1991.

Index

About the Contributors

Wallace McClain Cheatham is a music specialist at Elm Creative Arts School, and organist at Saint Mark African Methodist Episcopal Church, both located in Milwaukee, Wisconsin. Dr. Cheatham's research has been published in *The Black Perspective In Music* and *Black Music Research Journal*. His compositions have been performed nationally and published by Shawnee, Music 70 and Marvel. In 1992, Dr. Cheatham was choirmaster for the world premier of William Grant Still's *Those Who Wait*.

Throughout the world, to great acclaim, in opera, concert, and recital, **Camilla Williams,** a protégé of Marian Anderson and Geraldine Farrar, has projected and maintained the highest standards of musical performance. Miss Williams broke ground in 1946 when she became the first African-American soprano to become a regular member of the New York City Opera. A member of the company until 1954, her roles were Cio-cio-san in Puccini's *Madama Butterfly,* Mimi in Puccini's *La Boheme,* Nedda in Leoncavallo's *I Pagliacci,* and the title role in Verdi's *Aida.*

Camilla Williams is recognized as a distinguished practitioner of vocal pedagogy. Academic appointments have been held at Bronx College, Brooklyn College, Queens College, and Central Conservatory of Music in Beijing. Since 1977 Miss Williams has been a member of the music faculty at Indiana University. The academic appointments at both the Central Conservatory of Music in Beijing and at Indiana University carried with them for Miss Williams the distinction of being the first African-American professor of voice at these schools.

In addition to being an internationally acclaimed concert singer, past president of the National Association of Negro Musicians (the oldest black arts organization in the world), and associate dean at the University of Michigan School of Music, **Willis Patterson** made a major contribution to the song literature when he compiled *Anthology of Art Songs by Black Composers* (Edward B. Marks Music Corporation, 1978). Additionally, Mr. Patterson spearheaded at the University of Michigan the preparation and recording of *Art Songs by Black Composers* (1978, SMDO15), which contains most of the songs in the *Anthology.* The recording showcases an array of outstanding singers including Mr. Patterson, Hilda Harris, George Shirley, and Laura English Robinson. The 1990 CAMI video, *Spirituals in Concert,* that was produced for television in association with Deutsche Grammophon, made use of Dr. Patterson's knowledge as one of two music consultants. *Spirituals in Concert* featured Kathleen Battle and Jessye Norman.